**NATIONAL
GEOGRAPHIC**

T R A V E L E R

naples &
southern italy

TRAVELER

naples &
southern italy

by Tim Jepson
photography by Tino Soriano

National Geographic
Washington, D.C.

CONTENTS

Pages 2–3: The Renaissance splendor of the Castel Nuovo, Naples
Opposite: Marina Piccola, Sorrento, along the Amalfi Coast

TRAVELING WITH EYES OPEN

Alert travelers go with a purpose and leave with a benefit. If you travel responsibly, you can help support wildlife conservation, historic preservation, and cultural enrichment in the places you visit. You can enrich your own travel experience as well.

To be a geo-savvy traveler:

- Recognize that your presence has an impact on the places you visit.

- Spend your time and money in ways that sustain local character. (Besides, it's more interesting that way.)

- Value the destination's natural and cultural heritage.

- Respect the local customs and traditions.

- Express appreciation to local people about things you find interesting and unique to the place: its nature and scenery, music and food, historic villages and buildings.

- Vote with your wallet: Support the people who support the place, patronizing businesses that make an effort to celebrate and protect what's special there. Seek out shops, local restaurants, inns, and tour operators who love their home—who love taking care of it and showing it off. Avoid businesses that detract from the character of the place.

- Enrich yourself, taking home memories and stories to tell, knowing that you have contributed to the preservation and enhancement of the destination.

That is the type of travel now called geotourism, defined as "tourism that sustains or enhances the geographical character of a place—its environment, culture, aesthetics, heritage, and the well-being of its residents." To learn more, visit National Geographic's Center for Sustainable Destinations at *www .nationalgeographic.com/travel/sustainable.*

naples &
southern italy

ABOUT THE AUTHOR & PHOTOGRAPHER

Author **Tim Jepson** has been a lifelong devotee of Italy. Since graduating from Oxford, he has spent long periods of time living and traveling in the country and five years as a writer and journalist in Rome. Over the years he has written 15 books on the country, as well as articles for the *Daily Telegraph, Vogue, Condé Nast Traveller (U.K.),* and other publications. He wrote the *National Geographic Traveler: Italy, National Geographic Traveler: Florence & Tuscany, National Geographic Traveler: Sicily,* and *National Geographic Traveler: Piedmont & Northwest Italy.*

Now based in London with the *Daily Telegraph,* Jepson continues to visit Italy regularly, and, as a keen hiker and outdoor enthusiast, he takes a particular interest in the rural areas. He also revels in Italy's more sedentary pleasures—the food, wine, art, and culture. Jepson has also worked on Italian programs for the BBC and commercial television, and his career has included spells in a slaughterhouse, on building sites, and as a musician playing piano and guitar in streets and bars across Europe.

Born and raised in Barcelona, Spain, **Tino Soriano** divides his work between photojournalism and travel photography. He has received a First Prize from the World Press Photo Foundation as well as awards from UNESCO, Fujifilm, and Fotopres. In addition to Portugal, since 1988 Soriano has photographed in Spain (Catalonia, Andalucia, Galicia), France, Italy, Sicily, Scotland, and South Africa on assignments for National Geographic. His work has also appeared in *Geo, Merian, Der Spiegel, Paris Match, La Vanguardia,* and *El Pais* as well as many other major magazines around the world. Soriano has also written *El Futuro Existe* (a story about children with cancer), *Travel Photography* and *Beats from a Hospital* (both in Spanish), and *Dalí, 1904–2004.* He also regularly lectures and teaches workshops at the University of Barcelona. He photographed *National Geographic Traveler: Portugal, National Geographic Traveler: Sicily,* and *National Geographic Traveler: Madrid.*

Charting Your Trip

Southern Italy offers all the pleasures of Italy as a whole, but with a decidedly more Latin twist. While the rest of the country has often looked north to Europe, the cities and regions of the South—Naples, Palermo, Sicily, Campania, Puglia, Calabria—are Mediterranean creatures whose outlook and heritage have been shaped by centuries of Arab, Greek, and Spanish domination.

Climate and geography, too, are different at these more southerly latitudes—hotter, drier, and harsher—resulting in a more varied medley of landscapes than the pastoral hills, broad plains and high Alps of the North.

Any visit to the South should start with **Naples,** long the region's capital, a vibrant, sometimes overwhelming city ruled by the classic Italian passions of family, food, fashion, soccer, religion, and more. Among many other things, it boasts a wealth of historic churches, palaces, and museums, as well as some superb places to eat, not least its traditional pizzerias.

If You Have One Week

Two to three days will allow you to see Naples's highlights—the **Museo Archeologico,** one of Europe's foremost archaeological museums; the art collections of the **San Martino** and **Capodimonte** galleries; and **Spaccanapoli,** the old center, teeming with ancient palazzi, tiny streets, and ornate churches. Better to spend a week here, though, partly to let the city get under your skin—it can take a day or two to get used to Naples's assault on the senses—and partly because the city is ideal as a base for excursions.

Chief of these are trips to two of the world's most famous archaeological sites: **Pompeii** and **Herculaneum,** Roman towns buried by the eruption of **Vesuvius,** the dormant volcano that looms over Naples. Herculaneum is just 5 miles (8 km), Pompeii 15 miles (24 km) southeast of the city. A long day would allow you to see both: an even longer one might include a trip up Vesuvius itself.

Also within easy reach of Naples is the **Amalfi Coast,** which runs for about 30 miles (48 km) along the southern flank of the Sorrentine Peninsula. Equally accessible is the island of **Capri,** just off this peninsula's western tip. Both are celebrated for their mountain and maritime scenery,

A statue of San Nicola, or St. Nicholas. The saint is entombed in Bari.

and for the Amalfi Coast's necklace of little towns—
Positano, Praiano, Amalfi, Ravello. However, a day
trip from Naples will do justice to neither, and you
should allow at least two to three days here. Hiking,
diving, boat trips, and other outdoor activities are
all possible.

Heading South

If you have more time, then the best target
farther afield is **Puglia,** the "heel" of the Italian
"boot." This increasingly well-known region is
celebrated for the city of **Lecce,** a baroque jewel
257 miles (413 km) from Naples, as well as for
the evocative fortress at **Castel del Monte;** the
strange *trulli* houses around **Alberobello;** a wealth
of Romanesque churches; and the landscapes of
the **Gargano Peninsula.**

Puglia is a particularly appealing if you have
an interest in food. The area is one of Europe's key
producers of wine and olive oil, and its restaurants are some of the best in the South.
Local and foreign tour operators increasingly offer residential cookery courses and wine
and gastronomic vacations in the region (see sidebar p. 147). Distances here, though, are
greater than around Naples—from Lecce to the Gargano, for example, is 150 miles (240
km), and it makes sense to devote at least four or five days to the area.

Neighboring **Basilicata** is a wilder, less explored region, best known for the
cave dwellings, or *sassi,* at **Matera** (111 miles/179 km from Lecce), and the mountain
landscapes of the **Pollino national park.** A third region, **Calabria,** also has its majestic
mountain parks—the **Sila** and **Aspromonte**—as well as an intermittently pretty coastline,
exemplified by the appealing little resort of **Tropea.** Although still lacking the many
marked trails of the Alps and elsewhere in northern Italy, both the **Pollino** and **Sila**
parks offer good hiking opportunities (see pp. 166–169).

On southern Italy's fringe—on Europe's fringe—is the island of **Sicily,** a world
apart, and a crossroads of Mediterranean cultures and conquerors over three millennia.

NOT TO BE MISSED:

Eating a pizza in a traditional
pizzeria **70–71**

The archaeological site at
Pompeii **86–92**

The alluring Ravello **104–107**

Boating or driving along the
Amalfi Coast **110–113**

The enchanting island of
Capri **114–121**

Matera and its *sassi* **158–161**

A drive or hike up Mount
Etna **187, 190**

Agrigento's temples **193–195**

Visitor Information

Naples has three central visitor centers:
Via Santa Lucia 107 *(tel 081 240 0914,
closed 2–2:30 p.m. & Sun. p.m.),* Via San
Carlo 9 *(tel 081 402 394, closed 2–2:30 p.m.
& Sun. p.m.),* and Piazza del Gesù 7
(tel 081 551 2701). There is also a fourth
information point in the Stazione
Centrale *(tel 081 268 779),* the city's main
railroad station. The city's official visitor

information website is *www.inaples.it.*

Outside Naples, most towns have
a visitor center *(ufficio informazioni* or
azienda di turismo). Smaller towns and
villages may have a smaller office known
as a Pro Loco, with shorter opening hours
and more limited information. You should
also consult official regional visitor information websites (see p. 204).

When to Go

The general rule is to avoid July and August, the hottest, most expensive, and busiest months, especially on Capri, Sardinia, the Amalfi Coast, and all seaside resorts. Spring (late April–May) is delightful, especially in the countryside, and the weather is often still excellent across the region as late as October. (See p. 204 for more detailed information on when to visit.)

(See p. 204 for more detailed information on when to visit.)

Here the attractions are many, from the crumbling baroque grandeur of the island's capital, **Palermo,** to the Greek temples at **Agrigento, Selinunte,** and **Segesta;** and from the historical riches of towns like **Taormina, Siracusa,** and **Cefalù** to the majesty of **Mount Etna,** Europe's highest active volcano, and the sublime Roman mosaics near **Piazza Armerina.** The wealth of sights, and the distances involved, means you'll need a week even to scratch Sicily's rich surface.

Sardinia requires still greater commitment, because you'll need to fly or take a 16-hour ferry journey to get here. Many mainland Italians happily make the trip, at least in summer, for the island's many fine beaches and beautiful seas.

Cars, Trains, Planes, & Ferries

From a practical point of view, Naples is the obvious place from which to begin a tour. It is easy to reach from abroad, with direct flights from most European capitals and, in summer, from North America. It is also easy to reach from elsewhere in Italy, thanks to the main rail line (www.trenitalia.it) and autostrada, or freeway (www.autostrade.it), to Rome 142 miles (228 km) to the north. From Florence, farther north, it takes three hours by high-speed Frecciarossa train. From Venice or Milan consider an internal flight.

Moving around the South itself is less easy. With a few notable exceptions, the transport system is less developed than in northern Italy. Good road and rail links run along the east and west coasts, but in the often mountainous interior, highways and railroads are slower, less prevalent, and the services less frequent. Trains will get you to all key centers—notably from Naples to Palermo (fastest journey time 9 hrs. 20 mins.), Bari (3 hrs. 38 mins.), Lecce (5 hrs.), and points in between. Off the beaten track, though, you will need patience.

A car is necessary if you wish to explore the mountain areas of Calabria and Basilicata; the trulli, churches, and castles of Puglia; the landscapes around Matera; and the interior of Sicily and Sardinia. Roads are slow in these areas, so allow plenty of time for journeys. A car is not necessary in Naples—in fact, the very heavy traffic makes a car a

Safety

Naples needs more care than many European cities. Street crime is common. You are safe in the city center, but always beware of pickpockets or thieves (sometimes on motorcycles) who might snatch bags and cameras in crowded areas. Be especially careful boarding buses or ferries, or entering museums, and do not leave coats, bags, or cameras where they can easily be snatched when you're sitting at sidewalk cafés. Avoid the port, parks, railroad station, and any peripheral or quiet areas after dark. Only take licensed cabs. Do not carry wallets in your back pocket; do not pull out large numbers of bills when paying; deposit valuables in the hotel safe; and never leave possessions in parked cars.

Strollers and diners enjoy a seaside promenade in Diamante, Calabria.

liability—nor for making excursions from the city or to visit and explore the Amalfi Coast.

Buses, trains—or, for a price, a cab—will take you to Herculaneum, Pompeii, and Vesuvius, and organized tours are offered by many operators in the city; a train also runs from Naples to Sorrento for onward bus or cab access to the Amalfi Coast. Numerous ferry and hydrofoils from Naples (see p. 206) also serve this coast (and link its towns), as well as Sorrento and the islands of Capri, Ischia, and Procida. Naples also has twice-daily ferries to Palermo (10 hrs.) and two to three services weekly to Cagliari (16 hrs.): internal flights may be a better option if you are short of time.

The road along the Amalfi Coast offers one of Italy's most famous drives, but you could equally well make the journey by bus, or see the coast from the sea on a boat trip (see p. 109). If you do want to drive, bear in mind that parking can be difficult, rental rates will be high, and that the road is often narrow, has many twists and turns, and experiences heavy traffic in summer. ■

Etiquette

Southern Italy is generally more conservative socially, culturally, and politically than the North. Always dress appropriately in churches (no shorts, bare shoulders, or short skirts) and do not enter churches during services. Be ready for a "me-first" approach from many locals when it comes to driving, boarding public transit, or approaching a store counter. Be polite but firm when waiting in line: Hang back and you will never be served. (See p. 207 for more on etiquette and local customs.)

History & Culture

Painted tiles depict the Amalfi Coast near Praiano.
Opposite: A classical Greek temple in Agrigento, Italy

Naples &
Southern Italy Today

Southern Italy is its own country—a world apart that is generally poorer, more Latin, and more rooted in tradition than its northern counterpart. Yet it is also a region of incomparable art, beauty, and culture. In the land south of Naples, its peerless capital, you will find Pompeii, Capri, Sicily, the beaches of Sardinia, and the unmatched scenery of the Amalfi Coast.

Southern Italy is a region, in short, with some of the finest sights in Europe, never mind Italy—sights made all the more rewarding if you relish the unknown. This is

The lights of Naples illuminate the city's port under the profile of Mount Vesuvius.

partly because the landscapes are often empty and quiet, and partly because you will often have the region's lonely villages and time-locked towns to yourself. It is also because the South, the so-called Mezzogiorno, or land of the midday sun, comes closest to resembling that fabled phenomenon, the "real Italy." At least it represents the real Italy that many outsiders, ignorant of the country's modern élan—north and south—would like to imagine.

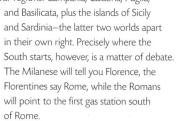

The . . . Mezzogiorno, or land of the midday sun, comes closest to resembling that fabled phenomenon, the "real Italy."

Southern Italy is changing, make no mistake, but classic vignettes still prevail in some of its rural and urban back-waters—the black-clad peasant woman, the washing hung across streets—as do the time-honored passions of food, family, soccer, love, and religion. Poverty and other social ills may occasionally be amplified, but so, too, by and large, are the Old World ideals of honor and hospitality.

At its most basic, the area consists of four regions: Campania, Calabria, Puglia, and Basilicata, plus the islands of Sicily and Sardinia—the latter two worlds apart in their own right. Precisely where the South starts, however, is a matter of debate. The Milanese will tell you Florence, the Florentines say Rome, while the Romans will point to the first gas station south of Rome.

Wherever the border, the region's unique character has been variously molded. Geographically, it is forever isolated, far from the prospect of industrial salvation. Climatically, it bakes under an almost African sun, a blight to agricultural initiative. Geologically, its soils are mostly poor, its mountains devoid of raw materials. Socially, its countryside, although magnificent to the outsider, has been depleted by emigration. Historically, it has been endlessly conquered—by Phoeni-cians, Carthaginians, Greeks, Romans, Arabs, Normans, Swabians, Angevins, Aragonese, and Bourbons. And for centuries much of it remained in thrall to feudal tradition and the deadening hand of Spanish rule, twin afflic tions that led to the social, economic, and agricultural stagnation that lingers in places to this day.

But if a crowded and tumultuous history has bequeathed a vaguely troubled present, it has also delivered an incomparably rich array of art and architecture. More to the point, it has worked with the region's geography to create a land of extraordinary variety. Northern Italy has its distinctive cities and landscapes, but in many ways it is also an increasingly homogenized entity, not something you could ever say of the South.

No one, for example, could confuse the heady, sensual drama of cities such as Naples and Palermo with the restrained, northern veneer of Milan or Turin. Or fail to see the exotic, almost Arabic flavor of parts of Sicily or the Greek look of the azure seas, sun-drilled plains, and whitewashed villages of Puglia. Or refuse to revel in the contrast between Capri and Ischia, balmy, hedonistic islands of dulcet beauty, and the uncompromising wilderness of Calabria's Aspromonte. Or ignore the charms of Lecce, a jewel of baroque architecture, and the eerie lure of nearby Matera, an otherworldly town of rock churches and ancient cave dwellings. Some visitors will opt for the pastoral perfection of the Gargano, the spur of the Italian "boot"; others will prefer the fabled coasts and cliff-hung villages of Amalfi and Calabria. Some will relish the fabulous Greek temples of Sicily, while others will be happy simply to luxuriate in the fine hotels and on the warm beaches of Sardinia's Costa Smeralda.

EXPERIENCE: Learn Italian

It's a commonplace claim, but a true one: If you want to learn a language quickly and properly, there is no substitute for immersing yourself in the culture in question. Naples has one of the most distinctive—and impenetrable—dialects of any city in Italy, but at a language school you'll only learn mainstream Italian, with the chance, if you wish, to practice and pick up snippets of Neapolitan dialect in shops and restaurants.

Centro Italiano di Napoli (tel 081 552 4331, www.centroitaliano.it) offers Italian language courses at its school at Vico Santa Maria dell'Aiuto 17 in the historic heart of the city. Chose between intensive, short-term courses (10 individual 1-hour sessions over a week) or longer one-, two-, three-, and four-week courses.

Language courses can also be combined with lessons in Neapolitan cooking, pizza-making, and Italian culture and design. The company can also organize courses for visitors staying farther afield in Sorrento or on Capri or Ischia.

Wherever else you go in the area, however, you should be sure to leave time for Naples, southern Italy's long-standing capital. Chaotic, noisy, and ebullient, this is one of the most Italian and yet most individual of cities, a microcosm of all that is good and bad in the South. For every filthy street, there is a sumptuous baroque church; for every tenement, a glorious palazzo; and for every crazed driver, a gesture of old-fashioned good manners. In Capodimonte and the Museo Archeologico the city has two of Europe's greatest museums. Nearby Pompeii and Herculaneum, Roman settlements preserved by the eruption of Mount Vesuvius, contain two of its foremost archaeological sites. An old Neapolitan proverb—and there are many—claims that if you spend a day in Naples you'll hate it, a week and you'll love it, a year and you'll never want to leave.

Naples will never lose its unique appeal, nor ever fully solve its many problems, but it has begun to leave the worst of its past behind—the squalor, dirt, corruption, graft, political inertia, grinding poverty, and more. Among other things, much has been done in the last ten years to improve the city's fabric. Streets have been closed to traffic, garbage is

La Martorana in Palermo, Sicily, combines Arab and Norman architecture.

actually collected, museums are open longer, hotels have improved, and the metro is being extended.

In these changes, as well as in their limitations, Naples reflects southern Italy as a whole. Money has poured into the region since World War II, only to be squandered on doomed industrial enterprises or, just as commonly, lost in a mire of criminal and political corruption.

Now, though, some of the improvements seem to be sticking, and agriculture and other initiatives are beginning to bloom. Change, however belated and precarious, is in the air. No one, therefore, should come to southern Italy expecting find the moribund backwater of 50 years ago. Nor should they come expecting to find an entirely decorous and straightforward region. Southern Italy can be entrancing and infuriating by turns. But like many of the more demanding things in life, once encountered and understood, it can also prove the most rewarding and endlessly beguiling of experiences.

Be sure to leave time for Naples. . . . Chaotic, noisy, and ebullient, this is one of the most Italian and yet most individual of cities.

The Land

Geographically, much of southern Italy is a continuation of the features of the peninsula to the north. The country's main mountain range, the Apennines, forms the peninsula's spine, making a southerly march through Campania, Basilicata, and Calabria and into the mountain ranges of northern Sicily. Vast massifs distinguish the range's great central uplands: the brooding wastes of the Pollino in Basilicata, the forested and more sprawling slopes of the Sila in Calabria, and the utter wilderness of the Aspromonte, the almost impenetrable mountainous toe of the Italian "boot."

Useful Words and Phrases

Excuse me (in a crowd or asking for permission) *Permeso*
Excuse me (asking for attention) *Mi scusi*
Hello (before lunch) *Buon giorno*, (after lunch) *Buona sera*
Hi or **Bye** *Ciao*
Please *Per favore*
Thank you *Grazie*
You're welcome *Prego*
Have a good day! *Buona giornata!*
OK *Va bene*
Goodbye *Arrivederci*

Good night *Buona notte*
Sorry *Mi scusi* or *Mi dispiace*
Here *qui*
There *li*
Do you speak English? *Parla inglese?*
I'm American (man) *Sono americano*, (woman) *Sono americana*
I don't understand *Non capisco*
Where is...? *Dov' e?*
My name is... *Mi chiamo...*
I'd like... *Vorrei*
How much is it? *Quanto costa?*

The long heel of the boot, by contrast, consists of the vast plains of Puglia, the second largest expanse of flatland in Italy after the Po Valley in the North. Puglia also has areas of low, sun-drenched hills, rich in olives and vines. This landscape of dry, limestone uplands extends into parts of neighboring Basilicata, a region with striking badlands scenery of bare, harsh plateaus and deep canyons. Other parts of Basilicata are more pastoral, such as the wine-growing region around Monte Vulture. In Puglia the Gargano, the spur of the Italian boot, is a forested and cliff-edged upland at odds with the otherwise largely flat margins of the region's Adriatic coast.

> **Much of the Calabrian and Campanian shore consists of spectacular cliffs edged by the Tyrrhenian Sea.**

Calabria is the most mountainous area, with barely a plain worthy of the name, save on its eastern coast. There the shore, like the long coast of eastern Basilicata, is washed by the limpid waters of the Ionian Sea. On southern Italy's west coast, by contrast, much of the Calabrian and Campanian shore consists of spectacular cliffs edged by the Tyrrhenian Sea, a landscape that reaches its zenith at the majestic Amalfi Coast south of Naples.

Sicily and Sardinia are virtually separate entities, the largest and second largest islands in the Mediterranean respectively. While Sicily's terrain is immensely varied, all of its natural features pale beside 10,900-foot (3,323 m) Mount Etna, the highest point in southern Italy and Europe's most active volcano. Its presence is due to southern Italy's position astride major faults in the Earth's crust, the same faults that account for the presence of Mount Vesuvius, another of the South's many anomalous landforms.

Sardinia's landscapes, by contrast, are more uniform and—a sublime coastline aside—less spectacular, dominated by the sprawling granite uplands of the 6,017-foot (1,834 m) Monti Gennargentu.

Economy

Southern Italy's economy is a puzzle. Statistics confirm that the area is poorer than the North: About 23 percent of adults are officially unemployed (rising to 58 percent among the young in Naples and other areas). It is no wonder, for conventional industries and employment prospects have long been blighted by distance from markets, lack of raw materials, poor infrastructure, and a history that favored feudal subsistence over industrialization. Yet signs of obvious poverty are few. Why? The South's enormous "black" or submerged economy, for one thing, accounts for 27 percent of the area's actual economy, according to the World Bank. Thus many young southerners work for their parents, or in bars, or on piecework projects. Naples is one of Europe's major producers of shoes, for example, a business where most stages of production are contracted out.

On a more positive note, areas of enterprise have begun to flourish in parts of the South, especially in the field of tourism. Sicilian, Calabrian, and especially Puglian cities are attracting new visitors, many brought by way of the innovative routes introduced by Europe's burgeoning no-frills airlines. Intense agriculture, notably on the Calabrian coast, is also a success, as are the so-called *poli creativi* (literally, "creative poles"). These are small pockets of specialist enterprise such as the *polo divani,* a sort of "Sofa Valley" around Altamura and Matera, the focus of a flourishing modern furniture industry. And around Naples, companies specializing in fiber optics are proving successful, while Sardinia has spawned the Tiscali company, one of Europe's telecom and digital giants. ■

Neapolitan children enjoy an alfresco snack. Much of life in southern Italy takes place on the street.

Food & Drink

Some of Italy's finest culinary staples—pasta, pizza, mozzarella, olive oil, and tomato sauce—have their origins in southern Italy. A place overflowing with the bounty of land and sea, the South is also a region with a culinary tradition that combines dishes from as far back as the ancient Greeks, Arabs, and Normans, and from as far afield as Spain, North Africa, and the Middle East.

Scholars dispute the precise origins of pasta and pizza, but whatever the truth, Naples seems to have a strong claim to both—certainly to pasta classics such as spaghetti and macaroni and pizzas such as the *marinara* or *margherita*. That pizza

A pasta shop on Via Benedetto Croce in Naples purveys one of the region's mainstays.

should hail from the South is no accident, for in the simple genius of the marinara, with its topping of tomato, garlic, and basil, is encapsulated much of the area's approach to all things culinary. First, it is a dish that is straightforward to make and uses only the simplest ingredients. Second, it is inexpensive, a vital consideration in a region whose history has long made poverty the culinary mother of invention. Thus the South's cuisine always makes inspired use of the ingredients at hand, including the fish and seafood of every coast and island (clams, squid, octopus, tuna, and swordfish are ubiquitous); wonderful fruit, notably the lemons of Amalfi and oranges of Sicily; countless vegetables, in particular eggplants and zucchini; a panoply of beans and nuts; a wide assortment of game; countless hams and salamis; and numerous cheeses such as pecorino and ricotta.

The South's cuisine always makes inspired use of the ingredients at hand, including the fish and seafood of every coast and island.

The classic mozzarella dish is *insalata caprese,* a salad from Capri made from tomatoes, olive oil, basil, and mozzarella.

Dishes such as *caprese* salad will be familiar to many visitors, thanks to the fact that the vast majority of Italian immigrants to the United States and elsewhere were southerners, and they took their recipes with them. Other dishes you may recognize include *spaghetti alle vongole* (spaghetti with clams) and *melanzane alla parmigiana* (eggplants and melted parmesan), both Campanian dishes. From Sicily come *pasta alla Norma* (tomatoes, salted ricotta, and eggplant) and *cassata* (sweetened ricotta, sponge cake, candied fruit, and almond paste). Many Sicilian dishes owe their origins to the culinary novelties (rice, marzipan, citrus fruits, couscous, cane sugar, cinnamon, saffron, ice cream) introduced to the island by the Arabs.

Other dishes, of course, will be new to you, for every area of the South has its specialties. The trick is to try them. In Naples these might include *sartù* and *timballo* (rich pies), dumpling-like *gattò*, *scialatielli* (eggless noodles), or *zucchine a scapece* (zucchini with mint and vinegar). In Basilicata you might find the robust *gnumariddi* (lamb offal with sweetbreads cooked with garlic and cheese), while in Puglia—a wonderfully diverse gastronomic region—dishes include *mitili* (excellent Taranto mussels), *fasulare* and *piedi di porco* (both unusual shellfish), *orecchiette* or "little ears" (a local pasta), and *maritata* (a soup of chicory, fennel, and celery).

In Sicily, the South's most gastronomically varied region, be sure to try *pasta con le sarde* (with sardines, wild fennel, raisins, saffron, and pine nuts), a dish introduced by the Arabs, or the sweet-and-sour *caponata* (slow-cooked vegetables, olives, raisins, and pine nuts), a dish that probably goes back to the ancient Greeks.

Wine

Where wine is concerned, southern Italy has a long but, until recently, rather undistinguished history. Archaeologists suggest wine has been made in Sicily since at least 1400 B.C., while elsewhere in the region wine has probably been enjoyed since at least 750 B.C., the time of the first Greek settlers.

The South's climate and terrain are good—almost too good—for making wine, and the intense sun, long summers, and high and dependable yields mean that until lately the region produced quantity rather than quality where wine was concerned. Many wines, especially in Puglia, used to be (and still are) strong *vini da taglio*, literally "wines of cut": They were produced in bulk and sent to make vermouth or to "cut" the weaker wines of France and northern Italy, boosting their color and alcoholic content. Only 5 percent of southern Italy's wine was bottled in the region.

Recently, however, there has been a dramatic change in the region's winemaking. Modern techniques of viticulture and viniculture have been introduced, especially in Sicily, and the island is now one of Europe's most exciting wine destinations. The reasons for the South's improved wines are the same as elsewhere in Italy: Namely, the land's natural advantages for wine-producing have finally been recognized by innovative winemakers prepared to use modern techniques and to blend or adapt native and foreign varietals.

In Campania, the finest new red wines are being made from the traditional Aglianico grape, notably Taurasi, a 100 percent Aglianico; The best producers are Caggiano, Mastroberadino, and Feudi di San Gregorio. Also good are Aglianico di Taburno (Ocone, La Rivolta, and Cantina del Taburno); the Amalfi Coast's Costa d'Amalfi Furore Rosso blend (Gran Furor-Marisa Cuomo); and the highly rated Vigna Camarato (Villa Matilde).

Mozzarella

Mozzarella cheese is one of Campania's finest foodstuffs. It is made from the milk of a rare, indigenous buffalo *(bufala)*, though a poor substitute, *fior di latte*, is made from cow's milk. The smoked version is known as *provola*, the small balls *bocconcini* (small bites), and the braids *treccie*.

Mozzarella takes its name from the verb *mozzare*, to cut, after the manner in which the large mass of cheese is cut in the early stages of production. The best comes from around Caserta, Battipaglia, and the plains between Salerno and Paestum. When buying, look for the labels "Mozzarella DOC" or "Mozzarella DOP" (visit www.mozzarelladop.it for more information). Buy directly from farms or from a delicatessen *(salumeria)* in Naples such as Antiche Delizie *(Via Pasquale Scura 14, tel 081 551 3088, closed Thurs. p.m. & a period in Aug.)*.

Farm stays or visits are possible across the region, allowing you to see mozzarella production first-hand: Try La Tenuta Seliano *(tel 082 872 4544, www.agriturismo seliano.it, closed Nov.–March, $)*, near Paestum, which has a lovely setting.

Southern Italy's wines are not traditionally notable, but that is changing.

Among the whites, the traditional Falanghina grape has emulated Aglianico's renaissance, with similar results. Its name means "little stick," this having been one of the first vines to be trained over a support, rather than up a tree (wines thus trained are labeled *vigneti ad alberata*). Falanghina is one of Campania's most popular whites, with Mustilli, Molo, Villa Matilde, and Feudi di San Gregorio all making good versions.

Basilicata has little in the way of wine, the exception being Aglianico del Vulture, a spicy and powerful red grown in the volcanic soils of Monte Vulture. Paternoster is the best producer. Calabria is similarly restricted, with plenty of moderate wines and just one or two notables such as Cirò, introduced by the Greeks and claimed by Calabrians to be Italy's oldest wine. Librandi and San Francesco are good versions.

In Puglia, Cerignola from Foggia is a standout red, along with San Severo (Alfonso di Sorda is the producer of choice) and the powerful Primitivo of Manduria. The best of the new breed of producers is Rivera, founded in 1950, whose prize wine is Il Falcone, a complex red.

Sicily has plenty of producers in the Rivera mold, all blending fabulous old varieties (Grillo, Inzolia, Nero d'Avola) with Chardonnay, Cabernet, Syrah, and other mainstream grapes. Good whites include Vigna di Gabbri and the more basic Donnafugata from producer Tenuta di Donnafugata; Colomba Platino and Bianco di Valguarnera from Corvo; and Cometa and Chardonnay from top winery Planeta. Good reds include Planeta's Santa Cecelia, Burdesse, and La Segreta Rossa; Fazio's Torre dei Venti; and Spadafora's Don Pietro. Don't overlook the sweet Marsala (stick to producers such as Florio and Pellegrino) or the sublime dessert wines of Pantelleria and the Aeolian Islands. ■

History of Naples & Southern Italy

The history of southern Italy is a tortuous affair, largely distinct from that of northern Italy and dominated by invaders and foreign rulers. Some, such as the Greeks, Arabs, and Normans, were good, while others were predominantly bad, including the French, Spanish, and—until recently—the Italian state.

The first peoples inhabited southern Italy at least 100,000 years ago, though the earliest substantial evidence of human habitation comes from cave paintings in Sicily (dated around 8700 B.C.) and the Neolithic dolmens (stone memorials) of Puglia, which date from around 4000 B.C.

By around 3000 B.C., tribes of Indo-European extraction had descended on the peninsula, and over the course of 2,000 years they evolved in southern Italy into several distinct peoples with related languages. The Opici and Oscans (or Ausones) held sway around the Bay of Naples, while the Samnites (or Samnians) occupied much of Campania, the central Apennines, and the deep south. The Daunii prevailed in northern Puglia, the Messapians in southern Puglia, and the Bruttians and Lucanians in Calabria and Basilicata. Sicily was the preserve of the Elymians, Sicani, and Siculi.

Southern Italy's proximity to Greece meant that these peoples, and probably cultures before them, had strong links with the Greeks. In time, Greece's growing population, together with the Greeks' need to secure westerly trading routes, meant that the Greeks began to place colonies in Sicily and along the southern Italian coast.

> **A band of Greeks created a trading post on an island they called Pithekoussai, present-day Ischia, in the Bay of Naples.**

One of the earliest settlements was established around 775 B.C., when a band of Greeks created a trading post on an island they called Pithekoussai, present-day Ischia, in the Bay of Naples. Discouraged by the island's rumbling volcanic activity, some of the settlers crossed the bay to Cumae (Cuma), where they established a more permanent and influential colony just west of present-day Naples.

In time, major Greek colonies sprang up across southern Italy. Some—such as Sybaris, Kroton, Metapontum—are now little more than ruins; others, such as Rhegium (Reggio di Calabria), Tara (Taranto), and Siracusa (Syracuse), are still important towns. One, Parthenope, was created on the slopes of Pizzofalcone, the hill that divides part of modern-day Naples.

The new colonies of Magna Graecia (Greater Greece) prospered—Syracuse would become the largest city in Europe—but also fought among themselves. Two of the main antagonists were Cumae and nearby Parthenope. By about 470 B.C., Cumae had triumphed and created a new colony close to the vanquished (and possibly destroyed) Parthenope. This community it called Neapolis, the New City, a settlement whose

A resident of the colony of Pompeii is preserved by the ash that caused his death.

Battle of Cannae

Ancient Rome's battles in southern Italy were not confined to the Greeks. A more powerful foe, the Carthaginians from North Africa, engaged the Romans over many years in the so-called Punic Wars. The Carthaginians' finest commander was Hannibal, one of history's greatest generals. By 216 B.C., he had already inflicted a stunning defeat on the Romans at the Battle of Lake Trasimeno (217 B.C.) in central Italy. On August 2 of that year he met a vastly superior Roman force near Cannae, on the Puglian plains. Precise figures are hard to establish, but around 85,000 Romans faced 40,000 Carthaginian troops.

During the battle, brute force met cunning: The Romans marched headlong into the heart of Hannibal's infantry, which deliberately retreated, drawing the Romans on as parts of Hannibal's infantry and cavalry peeled away to encircle the oncoming Romans. Surrounded, the Romans were easy prey. Some accounts say 60,000 to 80,000 Romans died, compared to 8,000 of Hannibal's men. In terms of men lost, it was the Roman's second heaviest defeat in history.

ancient grid can still be seen in the central streets of its bustling modern-day descendant, Naples.

Even as the Greeks prospered, so they were challenged, first around the sixth century B.C. by the Etruscans, a highly developed people from Tuscany and other parts of central Italy; then by the Samnites, a warrior-pastoral tribe from the Abruzzi Mountains to the north; and lastly—in Sicily at least—by the Carthaginians, a rising Mediterranean force whose power base was Carthage in North Africa.

The Rise of Rome

Although the colonies held off all comers, neither they nor their erstwhile challengers proved a match for Italy's ultimate rising power: Rome.

After defeating the Samnites by about 358 B.C. and taking Neapolis around 330 B.C., the Romans turned their attention in 280 B.C. to the cities of Magna Graecia. On Sicily, the last surviving Greek colony, Syracuse, fell in 212 B.C., cementing a Roman hold on southern Italy that would endure for some 600 years. Sardinia fell in 176 B.C.

Rome then availed itself of the South's considerable riches, building the first major consular road, the Via Appia, to Cumae (and later to Brindisi) to facilitate the flow of trade and wealth between the capital and its new territories. Land was often divided into vast feudal estates, or *latifundia,* whose aristocracy of baronial or absentee landlords would be the curse of the South until the land reforms of the 1950s.

As attention moved to Rome and the North, so the old southern Greek cities became increasingly marginalized. Meanwhile, poverty was rife in a countryside being bled dry—another thread that would run through the region's subsequent history. Unrest in the South led to two celebrated but ineffectual rebellions: the so-called Social War of 91 B.C., in which allied cities fought for equality with Rome, and the uprising in 73 B.C. of Spartacus, a former gladiator from Capua, near Naples.

These events aside, the greater dramas of the empire largely passed southern Italy by. Naples and its surroundings often provided little more than a bucolic retreat for poets such as Virgil, Ovid, and Horace, and for wealthy Romans such as the first-century emperors Augustus and Tiberius, both of whom had villas on the island of Capri. Posterity might have overlooked the period almost entirely but for one cataclysmic event: the eruption of Vesuvius and the entombment of the small Roman towns of Pompeii and Herculaneum in A.D. 79.

Rome's eventual decline saw the South fall prey to the invading Goths and Vandals, the reputed barbarians. The empire's symbolic end (long after its actual loss of power) was marked by the exile in A.D. 476 of the last emperor, Romulus Augustulus, by the Goth king, Odoacer.

The Byzantines

The arrival of the Goths and Vandals marked the start of 500 years of fragmentation and confusion across the region, exacerbated by the defeat of the Goths in 563 by Belisarius and Narses, generals of the Byzantine emperor, Justinian.

The Byzantines ruled Constantinople, the capital of an eastern empire (Byzantium) formed when the Roman empire was divided in two in A.D. 286. Their power outlived that of Rome by over 500 years, during which time they recaptured parts of the old western empire, including Puglia, Naples, and much of the South.

The picture was complicated by the arrival in 573 of the Lombards, an aggressive power from northern Europe who absorbed much of northern Italy, and then by the advent of the Arabs of Egypt and North Africa, who captured much of Sicily and parts of Puglia in the eighth century. Thereafter, southern Italy became an administrative patchwork, with areas of Byzantine, Arab, and Lombard control.

As time went by, however, and the central authority of the respective rulers waned, powerful barons, cities, and regions began to assert a de facto independence. Naples's nominally Byzantine dukes, for example, declared independence in 763, and in the tenth century, Amalfi emerged as one of Europe's leading maritime powers.

Amalfi aside, the South's only other coherent power of the time was Sicily, thanks to the almost entirely benign influence of its Arab rulers. Their 200-year reign would be a golden age, the incomers promulgating new ideas in science, philosophy, the arts, and agriculture. They introduced irrigation, along with crops and goods such as dates, citrus fruits, cotton, silk, sugar, flax, rice, nuts, and henna. Trade blossomed, and with it Palermo, whose wealth and dazzling court made it the Mediterranean's leading cultural and mercantile center.

> [Palermo's] wealth and dazzling court made it the Mediterranean's leading cultural and mercantile center.

By the 11th century, however, unrest in North Africa, along with the fact that the Arabs never established a workable central authority in Sicily, left the island vulnerable to attack. Much the same was true of southern Italy, its fragmented state an invitation to any determined foreign power.

Power from the North

A strong foreign power duly arrived in the shape of the Normans, who originated in Scandinavia and settled in northern France in 911. Renowned fighters, they found work as papal and other mercenaries across Europe, but especially in the strife-torn lands of southern Italy. Here, the outstanding Norman fighters were a group of brothers by the name of de Hauteville. One of them, Roger (1031–1101), captured Palermo in 1072. Another, Robert (ca 1015–1085), took Capua (in 1062), Amalfi (1073), and Salerno (1077).

Between them, the Normans soon controlled, or commanded allegiance from, all of southern Italy. Roger became king of Sicily and the South as Roger I in 1091 and was succeeded by his son, Roger II (1095–1154), who ruled from 1101. Naples took a back seat to Palermo, home to the Norman court, but the South in general prospered, bolstered by Roger's toleration of the region's ethnically mixed population and his fusing of the best of Arab, Byzantine, Lombard, and Norman traditions.

The Norman system of rule, however, was a feudal one and relied on a peasantry and the kings' supporters being rewarded with grants of lands and titles. This compounded the effects of the Romans' earlier latifundia, exacerbated the effects of peasant poverty, and created numerous semi-independent barons. Roger's less able son, William I (1120–1166), would face several baronial rebellions, though it was the inability

The fleet of the Norman Roger de Hauteville, 11th-century ruler of Sicily and the South

of William's son William II (1153–1189) to produce an heir that would have the most profound consequences.

In the absence of a natural successor, William II nominated his father's sister Constance (Constanza) as his heir. She was married to Henry of Hohenstaufen (1165–1197), the son of the great Holy Roman (German) Emperor Frederick I, better known as Barbarossa. Thus southern Italy's destiny became linked to that of Europe's northern imperial powers. Henry soon became Emperor Henry VI (and king of Sicily) but died after his coronation, leaving Constance as the regent for their three-year-old son, the future Emperor Frederick II (1194–1250).

A man of prodigious talents, the adult Frederick was a consummate statesman, commander, scholar, and legislator, known to contemporaries as Stupor Mundi, or the Wonder of the World. Under him, southern Italy would know one of only two or three periods of good government in its 2,500 years of recorded history. Among other things, he kept Palermo as his capital and created a university that made Naples a prime intellectual center.

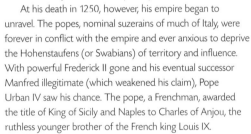

Southern Italy's destiny became linked to that of Europe's northern imperial powers.

At his death in 1250, however, his empire began to unravel. The popes, nominal suzerains of much of Italy, were forever in conflict with the empire and ever anxious to deprive the Hohenstaufens (or Swabians) of territory and influence. With powerful Frederick II gone and his eventual successor Manfred illegitimate (which weakened his claim), Pope Urban IV saw his chance. The pope, a Frenchman, awarded the title of King of Sicily and Naples to Charles of Anjou, the ruthless younger brother of the French king Louis IX.

The Anjou, or Angevins, had an army to back up their new claims. They defeated Manfred and the imperial Hohenstaufen forces in southern Italy in 1266. Manfred was killed and his nephew and heir, 14-year-old Conradin, captured and beheaded by Charles in Naples in 1268. The unpopularity this caused, especially in Sicily, was compounded by heavy new taxes and a vicious campaign of revenge against former Hohenstaufen supporters. In desperation, Sicilian nobles began to plot against Charles with an antipapal faction in Aragon, part of present-day Spain, whose ruler, Peter III of Aragon (1239–1285), was married to Manfred's daughter, Constanza. This, in his eyes and those of most Sicilians, gave him a claim to Sicily and the rest of the Hohenstaufens' original domain.

Spanish Rule

As Charles's oppression continued, 1282 saw a popular revolt against the Angevins that precipitated the eventual arrival of the Aragonese in Sicily. The Sicilian Vespers, as the revolt became known, was allegedly sparked on Easter Monday when a French (Angevin) soldier insulted a woman as the bell of Palermo's Santo Spirito church was calling her to vespers. The congregation reacted with fury, provoking a riot that quickly spread, eventually consuming Sicily in a frenzy of chaos and killing.

Philip of Aragon landed at Trapani in western Sicily five months later. Within days he had been acclaimed king of Sicily, though the so-called War of the Vespers, waged mostly in Spain and at sea between Aragonese and Angevin forces based in Naples, would last another 21 years. The outcome was the rule of the Aragonese in Sicily, with the Spaniards securing a presence on the island for the next 578 years. After 1410, Spain ruled through a long succession of viceroys. In Naples, meanwhile, Charles's descendants, the Angevins, ruled a separate kingdom that embraced much of mainland southern Italy.

Certain Angevin rulers were successful, notably the third monarch, Robert "the Wise" (r. 1309–1343), a patron of leading cultural lights from the North such as the painter Giotto and writers Petrarch and Boccaccio. For the most part, however, the 14th and 15th centuries were times of bickering between Angevin factions, and thus of weak government. This weakness, compounded by the feudal heritage of the Normans and Swabians, led in turn to civil strife, depopulation, unchecked disease (malaria especially), and catastrophic economic decline in the countryside. Thus were sown some of the seeds—contempt for rule of law, lack of civic responsibility, corruption, poverty—that have born bitter historic fruit until virtually the present day.

By the 15th century, Italy was increasingly a pawn in the games of greater European powers, notably Spain, which had been united after the marriage in 1469 of Isabella of Castile and the Aragonese king, Ferdinand II. By 1503, Spain's military and diplomatic muscle had secured the Neapolitan crown and added it to the Sicilian domain already under Spanish control.

Spain was powerful and resolutely administered, the more so after Ferdinand and Isabella's heir, Charles V, was also crowned Holy Roman emperor, linking the Spanish and imperial Habsburg (Austro-German) thrones. But with one or two exceptions—such as the rebuilding of the Neapolitan district now known as the Quartieri Spagnoli (Spanish Quarters)—the 200 years of Spanish rule in Naples and the South would ultimately bequeath death, chaos, corruption, and revolution.

As in Sicily, day-to-day control in Naples was entrusted to viceroys, who levied crippling taxes to help fund Spain's wider imperial ambitions. The Spanish king, Philip IV, observed that "Naples is a gold mine which furnished armies for our wars and treasure for their protection." At the same time, southern Italy was ignored as Spain looked west to its colonies in the New World. In later centuries, as Spain

A Scandal at Court

Amy, or Emy, Lyon was born in 1761, the daughter of an English blacksmith. By the age of 20, she had become a celebrated beauty and a model for such leading British artists as Sir Joshua Reynolds. She was also the mistress of one Charles Greville, who, wishing to be free of her to marry, encouraged her to travel to Naples as a diversion for his uncle, Sir William Hamilton (1730–1803), the British envoy to the Neapolitan court. Far from being a brief distraction, Emy became the second Lady Hamilton, scandalizing the Neapolitan court. When Lord Horatio Nelson came to Naples in 1798, Emy—now Emma—began an affair with the British naval hero, a connection that would endure (she bore him a daughter named Horatia). The three established an open relationship that titillated first the Neapolitan, then the London court, for a decade.

fell into decadence, southern Italy became even poorer. The countryside stagnated (one viceroy alone condemned 18,000 men to death for banditry), sending peasants flocking to Naples in search of a moderately better life. By the beginning of the 17th century, the Neapolitan capital was Europe's largest city, with a population of more than 300,000.

Forces on the wider European stage came into play once more in 1700, when it became clear that the last of the Spanish Aragonese rulers, Charles II (Charles V of Naples; r.1665–1700), would die without an heir. Given Spain's stature, this had huge geopolitical ramifications and led to the Wars of the Spanish Succession.

The Bourbon Monarchy

In Naples the wars led to the installation of an independent Bourbon monarch in 1734, the Bourbons being the new line of Spanish kings. The first of these kings was the wealthy and ambitious Charles III of Bourbon (1716–1788), who, among other things, introduced much needed reforms, extended the Palazzo Reale, and built the San Carlo opera house, archaeological museum, and the palaces of Caserta and Capodimonte.

Charles's relatively enlightened reign was an anomaly, however, and subsequent Bourbon rulers muddled through virtually another century of decline. A brief respite came in 1799, when Napoleon conquered Italy in the wars that followed the French Revolution. Only Sicily escaped the French general's clutches, providing a bolthole for the vapid Bourbon monarch of the time, Ferdinand IV, who fled to the island aided by the British Navy and Admiral Horatio

Bourbon monarch Ferdinand IV ruled southern Italy between 1759 and 1825.

Nelson. Naples and the South were briefly ruled by Napoleon's brother, Joseph, and then by his brother-in-law, Joachim Murat. Following Napoleon's defeat at Waterloo, however, and the subsequent Congress of Vienna (1815), Europe was carved up anew. Ferdinand IV was allowed to return to Naples, taking the confusing title of Ferdinand I of the Kingdom of the Two Sicilies (technically Sicily and the South had previously been separate realms). With him and his successors came a cycle of autocracy, repression, complacency, exploitation, and occasional rebellion that continued until 1860, when the Risorgimento, or campaign to unify Italy, reached its climax.

The Risorgimento

Italy at the time of the Risorgimento was divided among the House of Savoy, which ruled much of the northwest; Austria, which controlled the north and east; the French-backed papacy, whose domain extended across much of central Italy; and the Bourbons, who controlled Sicily and southern Italy. Skillful diplomacy on the part of the Savoys, who spearheaded the unification campaign, won them the backing of Britain and France and the help of the French Army, which duly dislodged the Austrians in 1859. A year later, the charismatic soldier Giuseppe Garibaldi (1807–1882), frustrated by what he saw as the Savoys' slowness, raised a band of troops—the Mille, or Thousand—and decided to force the issue.

On May 11, 1860, Garibaldi landed at Marsala on Sicily's west coast. Four days later his small band defeated a Bourbon force of 15,000. By the end of July, Messina had been taken, and on September 7 Garibaldi entered Naples. Sicily was free of Spanish rule for the first time since 1282. As Garibaldi moved up from the south, revolts and events elsewhere saw the new Kingdom of Italy proclaimed on March 14, 1861.

The distant, northern-based government soon proved as unable to address the South's ills as any Spanish administration. Naples suffered from its loss of status as a capital—Florence then Rome became the focus of the new kingdom—and taxes and tariffs designed to favor the burgeoning northern industries further depressed the South. Nascent southern industries nurtured by the well-intentioned if heavy-handed Ferdinand withered. Discontent soon reemerged. During the 1860s some 100,000 new Italian troops were employed trying to deal with "bandits" in the South.

Unrest was quelled not only by repressive government action, but by gangs employed by landowners or their shadowy middlemen. This was a contributory factor, along with centuries of lawlessness, to the growth of the Mafia in Sicily, as well as the similar Camorra in Naples and 'Ndrangheta in Calabria—all three still extant today. So desperate was the lot of most southerners that many emigrated, and an estimated 2.5 million left for the Americas, Australia, and elsewhere between 1880 and 1914.

Benito Mussolini and Fascism enjoyed little success outside Naples and the major cities, but local politicians and dignitaries throughout the conservative and right-leaning South, with a long tradition of paying lip service to the rulers of the day while furthering their own interests, duly adopted the uniforms, slogans, and other trappings of the new regime in the 1920s. Agriculture again suffered as perfectly good pasture, olive groves, and orchards were replaced by fields of grain, part of Mussolini's "Battle for Wheat."

In Sicily and Puglia . . . tourism and revitalized agriculture . . . have started to have a transformative effect.

World War II

During World War II, Sicily's strategic position saw it chosen by the Allies as the obvious bridgehead for an attack on Europe's "soft underbelly." During Operation Husky in the summer of 1943, U.S. and British troops landed on the island's southeast coast, liberating Sicily after 38 days of heavy fighting. Many towns and cities were bombed during this and other campaigns, including Naples, which suffered far more grievously than is generally known (more than 20,000 people died). The bombing of the port and major industries, not to mention the utter poverty suffered by Neapolitans and other southerners during the war, would greatly hamper postwar recovery.

After the war, the new republican government started with good intentions, acknowledging the problems of the South with the introduction of the Cassa per il Mezzogiorno, a colossal undertaking designed to channel funds toward reconstruction and rejuvenation of the region. Well-meaning administrators, however, had reckoned without the reactionary propensities, not to mention downright corruption, of many local politicians. Nor had they taken in the colossal scale of the poverty and the concomitant ills of high crime,

Residents of Palermo, Sicily, greet U.S. soldiers after the liberation of the city in 1943.

unemployment, poor education, and decaying infrastructure. Funds for reconstruction "disappeared" on a vast scale, were used to buy political or other favors, or were misspent on industrial initiatives doomed almost from the start. Planning laws were flouted on a massive scale, resulting in the vast numbers of badly built eyesores that scar the environs of Naples (where 80,000 new buildings appeared in the 10 years after 1950) and many other southern towns.

Even as the North boomed, enjoying the *dolce vita* years of the 1960s, much of the South entered a new Dark Age, failing to benefit from the events that transformed the rest of Italy from a peasant economy to one of the world's leading industrialized nations. In 1973, a cholera outbreak in Naples provided a literal and grimly symbolic illustration of the region's problems. A terrible earthquake in 1980 near Salerno, which claimed 3,000 lives, only compounded the misery.

Until as late as 1993, the prevailing right-wing Christian Democratic political party, often in shadowy cahoots with organized crime, controlled virtually every corner of southern Italian life. Only with the collapse of the equally dubious postwar "consensus" that had kept the right in effective power across the country for decades—a situation seen by the West during the Cold War as an essential bulwark against a potentially Communist Italy—did matters improve.

In 1993, the left-wing Antonio Bassolino was elected mayor of Naples. He embarked on a massive cleanup, restoration, and anti-crime campaign. This was given impetus by the G7 meeting in the city a year later between the heads of leading industrialized nations. Improvements continue to this day. Matters, too, may be improving in Sicily and Puglia, where tourism and revitalized agriculture, among other things, have started to have a transformative effect. In Basilicata, too, interest in the cave dwellings of Matera and the addition of the Pollino and other national parks may represent a turning of the tide. But the history of the South is too troubled for anyone to cry victory just yet. ■

The Arts

The immense cultural patrimony of southern Italy owes much to four periods of artistic transcendence, namely, the Greek, Roman, Norman, and baroque eras. It has also benefited from the literary, musical, and cinematic traditions forged by artists, writers, and directors from across Italy.

Architecture & Painting

The South's earliest architectural works are the Nuraghic structures of Sardinia, while the earliest examples of art are prehistoric incised and painted figures in the Grotta Genovese, a cave on the Sicilian island of Levanzo. Sicily is also home to other early art, namely, the incised pottery of the Stentinello, a Neolithic culture whose use of decorative motifs suggests the influence of traders and settlers from as far afield as Cyprus, Syria, Anatolia, the Aegean, Egypt, and North Africa.

Greek & Roman Art: Later came the Greeks, who exerted a powerful artistic influence across much of coastal southern Italy. Their most striking legacies are the well-preserved amphitheater at Taormina and the sixth-century B.C. temples at Paestum (in Campania) and Agrigento, Segesta, and Selinunte (in Sicily).

Early Byzantine churches survive at Stilo in Calabria; there are Byzantine paintings in the cave churches at Matera (Basilicata).

In Naples, little survives except for a few fragments of walls and shops and the street plan of the Greeks' old city. Most monuments have also vanished from the many Greek sites elsewhere in the South, though the archaeological museums of Naples, Taranto, Reggio di Calabria, and elsewhere are filled with artifacts removed from these sites.

The same museums contain an even greater array of art from the Roman period, much of it heavily influenced by the Greeks. Some of the best is in Naples's Museo Archeologico, most removed from excavations at Pompeii and Herculaneum, home to Italy's best-preserved Roman domestic buildings. Elsewhere, relatively little survives of Roman vintage, save for villas on Capri and a few other spots, an arch at Benevento (Campania), and the amphitheater at Cumae. One great exception is the Villa Imperiale and its superlative mosaics at Piazza Armerina in Sicily.

Early Christian Art & the Dark Ages: Early Christian art is largely confined to the catacombs of Syracuse (Sicily) and San Gennaro (Naples) and the fifth- or sixth-century mosaics in the baptistery of Naples's Duomo. Early Byzantine churches survive at Stilo in Calabria; there are Byzantine paintings in the cave churches at Matera (Basilicata) and a wonderful fifth-century bronze statue of a Byzantine emperor at Barletta (Puglia).

Much has also been lost from the so-called Dark Ages, the 500 years that followed the fall of Rome, though the cultural influence of the two dominant cultures of the

The majestic interior of the Cappella Sansevero, Naples

DᐧOᐧMᐧDᐧFRANCISCOᐧDEᐧPAVLAᐧFERDINANDVSᐧIᐧ

The neoclassical church of San Francesco di Paola in Naples was modeled on the Pantheon.

period, the Byzantines and Lombards, survived in the work of subsequent artists. The influence of the former is best seen in the 20 or more 11th-century bronze doors across the South, many cast and crafted in Constantinople, the Byzantine capital.

In the 10th and 11th centuries, these Lombard and Byzantine influences were combined with those of the Arabs, who ruled Sicily for 200 years. They were also entwined with those of the Normans, who dominated much of the South after 1070. The new French invaders brought with them the Romanesque architectural style and the patronage and political and economic stability that allowed the arts to flourish. The chief legacies of this exotic and multistranded flowering were the Romanesque churches of Puglia—among the South's greatest architectural glories—the Cappella Palatina in Palermo, and the nearby cathedral at Monreale (Sicily).

The firm rule of Frederick II in the 13th century resulted in the building of many castles, including the Castel del Monte (1240, Puglia), one of Italy's most striking buildings. The French Angevin kings, who ruled much of the South from 1268 to 1442, introduced the Gothic style to the region, and especially to Naples, where it can be seen in the Castel Nuovo (begun 1279), the cathedral, and the churches of San Domenico, San Lorenzo Maggiore, and others.

Pre-Renaissance: The presence of the Angevin court also served to draw south some of the great pre-Renaissance artists emerging in the North. These included the Roman painter and mosaicist Pietro Cavallini (active 1273–1309), who decorated San Domenico's Cappella Brancaccio (1308–1309); the Sienese artist Simone

Martini (1284–1344), who painted the sumptuous St. Louis altarpiece (1317) in the Capodimonte gallery; the Sienese sculptor Tino di Camaino (1285–1337), whose tomb monuments around Naples's churches are his masterpieces; and finally Giotto, the Florentine genius who frescoed the Cappella Palatina (1330) of the Castel Nuovo (though all but a few fragments of his work are now lost).

The Renaissance: As in the pre-Renaissance, so in the Renaissance itself, when the South, with one or two exceptions, relied on central and northern Italian artists to introduce the innovations of the 15th century's great artistic resurgence. In Sicily, stifled by its conservative Spanish rulers, only Antonello da Messina (1430–1479) joined the first rank of Renaissance painters. The Florentines were the ones who made their mark, including Donatello and Michelozzo, who created the great Brancaccio tomb (1428) for the church of Sant'Angelo a Nilo in Naples. In 1475, another Tuscan, Antonio Rossellino, crafted the altar of the Nativity for Naples's Monteoliveto.

Raphael, Masaccio, Titian, Michelangelo, and other great northern names also grace the walls of Naples's superlative Capodimonte gallery, along with some of the more minor artists produced by Naples and other southern towns. These include painters such as Niccolò Antonio Colantonio (active 1440–1470), Andrea da Salerno (1480–1530), and Polidoro da Caravaggio (1500–1543). Among the sculptors are Giovanni da Nola (1488–1558) and Giovanni Santacroce (1502–1537).

Despite the number of artists working in Naples and Sicily, southern Italy never produced the art or artists of the caliber spawned by central and northern Italy. Some of this was due to the apathy of its mostly Spanish rulers, reluctant, as Spain itself declined, to lavish their dwindling resources on art. Artistic change, when it did come, was often the result of individual genius, as in the case of the Spaniard Giuseppe Ribera (1588–1652), whose bold religious paintings inspired a school of followers. More influential still was Caravaggio (1571–1610), a fugitive from Rome whose 1606 sojourn in the city

Caravaggio

The artist Michelangelo Merisi da Caravaggio (1571–1610) spent just four years in Naples—interrupted by sojourns to Malta and Sicily—but his dark, iconoclastic, and technically brilliant work would influence countless of the city's painters. A maverick, he appeared in Naples in 1606 after fleeing Rome, where he had killed a man—possibly accidentally—following a bet on a game of tennis. Naples was home to the Colonna family, powerful patrons, and with their support Caravaggio won a string of important commissions, including his last major work, "The Martyrdom of Saint Ursula," one of only three paintings by the artist still in the city; it hangs in the gallery of the Banco Intesa Sanpaolo (Via Toledo 185, www.palazzozevallos.com.). The other two are the "Opere della Misericordia," or Seven Acts of Mercy, in the Pio Monte della Misericordia (see p. 53) and the "Flagellation," in the Palazzo Reale di Capodimonte (see p. 74). Tantalizingly, a fourth work, a "Resurrection," was displayed in the church of Sant'Anna dei Lombardi until 1792. Some say it perished in the earthquake of that year, others that it was removed for safekeeping. In any event, it has never been found.

and theatrical paintings would inspire countless Neapolitan and other artists.

Among the most accomplished of Caravaggio's followers were Salvatore Rosa (1615–1673), best known for his landscapes and battle scenes; Giovanni Lanfranco (1582–1647), a leading fresco painter who found fame in Naples after working in Rome; and Luca Giordano (1634–1705), the prolific master of the frivolous and colorful works that would come to dominate late Neapolitan painting. The last was also the teacher of Francesco Solimena (1657–1747), the finest Neapolitan painter of the 18th century. Also worthy of note is Artemisia Gentileschi (1593–1652/3), whose dramatic "Judith and Holofernes" (now in the Capodimonte Gallery), among other works, influenced many of her Neapolitan contemporaries.

Patron & Alchemist

Don Raimundo di Sangro (born 1710) was a remarkable figure, a leading light of Neapolitan society, grand master of the Freemasons, a soldier, prince, scientist, man of letters, and—say some— an alchemist and dabbler in the occult. Also a patron of the arts, he commissioned some of the era's leading artists to decorate the Capella Sansevero, including Francesco Maria Russo, who created the joyous ceiling fresco of the "Glory of Paradise" (1749).

Baroque Art: Later, the normally conservative Catholic Church provided the engine of artistic change, stimulated by the Counter-Reformation, the 16th- and 17th-century drive to wrest back the initiative from Protestantism. Part of this drive involved the building of extravagantly decorated churches designed to remind congregations of the majesty and authority of the Church.

As a result, ornate baroque art proliferated, especially in Sicily, partly because it suited the Sicilians' love for the decorative, a passion that dated back to the Arab period, and partly because of the Sicilians' flair for color, gilding, and other embellishments. The island's greatest baroque architects were Filippo Juvarra (1676/8–1736), who would find fame as far afield as Rome, Turin, and Madrid, and Rosario Gagliardi (ca 1700–1770), who was largely responsible for rebuilding Noto and other Sicilian towns destroyed by the earthquake of 1669.

The baroque also flowered in glorious isolation in Lecce (Puglia), thanks to the city's fine local stone, a period of mercantile prosperity, and, as elsewhere, the commissioning zeal of new or rejuvenated religious orders such as the Jesuits. The style also triumphed in Naples, where the leading light was Cosimo Fanzago (1591–1678), a tortured but multitalented sculptor, artist, and architect who was responsible for the cloister at the Certosa di San Martino, among other works. Giuseppe Sanmartino (1720–1793) was the most notable baroque sculptor, remembered above all for his extraordinary "Veiled Christ" (1753) in Naples's Cappella Sansevero.

Neoclassical Revival: The arrival of the Bourbon monarchs after 1734 brought a fresh impetus to Neapolitan affairs as the new kings sought to create buildings that matched their grand dynastic ambitions. The two leading figures of 18th-century Italian architecture both played their part: Ferdinando Fuga (1699–1781), who was summoned from Rome to build the Albergo dei Poveri (begun 1752), a vast poorhouse, and Luigi Vanvitelli (1700–1773), who was given the task of creating the colossal 1,200-room palace and gardens at Caserta (1751–1754).

The Bourbons also built Naples's San Carlo opera house in 1737 (theater-building would be a feature of the age) and promoted the excavations of Pompeii and Herculaneum, though more to enrich their collections of classical artifacts than out of any finer archaeological feeling. The discovery of Pompeii's mosaics, wall paintings, and other treasures led to a resurgence of interest in the classical world. Part of this neoclassical revival included the design of buildings such as Pietro Banchi's San Francesco di Paola (1817), a distinctive Neapolitan church that copies the ancient Pantheon in Rome.

Modern Times: As elsewhere in Italy, art and architecture in the South during the 19th and 20th centuries never recaptured the heights achieved earlier. Countless foreign artists visited the region, however, among them the Frenchman Jean-Baptiste Corot (1796–1875) and the British J.M.W. Turner (1775–1851). Small local schools also emerged in Naples, including the Scuola di Posillipo (Ercole Gigante, Salvatore Fergola, Consalvo Savelli) and the later Scuola di Resina (Federico Rossano, Giuseppe de Nittis), founded in 1864, both of which were devoted to landscape painting. More recently, the Sicilian artist Renato Guttuso (1912–1987) and sculptor Emilio Greco (1913–1995) found fame in Italy and beyond.

In the South, the disastrous effects of World War II bombing and the ravages of 50 years of rampant and often illegal building are slowly being addressed, exemplified by regeneration projects in Palermo and the willingness of towns such as Salerno to employ cutting-edge architects to revitalize urban spaces.

Literature

The South's earliest literary glory was borrowed or reflected. Many of the events in Homer's epic *The Odyssey*, for example, take place in Sicily, and the island was the setting envisaged by the Greek philosopher Plato (ca 427–347 B.C.) for the utopian state in his *Republic*. In time, patrons in the island's Greek colonies lured other Greek writers, notably poets such as Pindar (522–443 B.C.) and the playwright Aeschylus (525–456 B.C.), both of whom worked in Syracuse.

Later, Roman writers were drawn to Naples, using many of the region's evocative locations in their writings. One of the greatest, Virgil (70–19 B.C.), wrote most of his *Georgics* and much of the *Aeniad* here. Other celebrated Roman literary figures who wrote of or in Naples include Horace (65–8 B.C.), the poet and satirist who spoke of "restful Naples," and Ovid (43 B.C.– A.D. 17), who described how the city was "born in idleness." Horace was also drawn to nearby

An open-handed statue and other Baroque detailing grace a structure in Lecce, Puglia.

Baia, along with Martial (A.D. 40–102) and Petronius (A.D. 27–66), the last satirizing the town's famously licentious habits in his *Satyricon*.

Medieval Naples contributed innovative literary idioms, notably the *commedia dell'arte*, a 17th-century theatrical form involving such stock characters as Harlequin, Pantaleone, and Pulcinella. The masked, white-robed figure of Pulcinella, vacillating between comedy and tragedy, is often seen as a symbol for Naples itself.

Much later, the city would also give birth to the much loved Eduardo de Filippo (1900–1984), one of Italy's finest playwrights. In dramas such as *Napoli Milionaria* (1945) and the black comedy *Filumena Marturano* (1946), he painted portraits of Naples that are unflinching in their depictions of poverty and despair. Several of his plays, including *Filumena Marturano,* were turned into films (see p. 42).

Uncompromising realism also formed the cornerstone of the writings of Giovanni Verga (1830–1922), the first major Sicilian writer to make a lasting impact on the international stage. In novels such as *I Malavoglia* (1881), Verga explored what he saw as the real Sicily, portraying the lives of ordinary Sicilians in a characteristically somber prose style.

Realism also influenced the early work of Sicily's best known writer, Luigi Pirandello (1867–1946), whose plays and experiments with form and content won him the Nobel Prize for Literature in 1934. His play *Six Characters in Search of an Author* (1921) explored the theme of isolation and the role of individuals in alien situations.

Pirandello's body of work was in contrast to the single, lyrical masterpiece of Giuseppe Tomasi di Lampedusa (1896–1957), an aristocrat whose posthumously published novel *Il Gattopardo (The Leopard)* is a magnificent exploration of the profound social changes in Sicily in the mid-19th century.

Tomasi di Lampedusa is widely translated, as is Leonardo Sciascia (1921–1989), who in novels such as *The Day of the Owl* (1961) used the conventions of crime fiction to explore the complexities of the Mafia and Sicilian life. Social issues were also the concern of poet Salvatore Quasimodo (1901–1968), awarded the Nobel Prize for Literature in 1959.

The principal traits of Sicilian literature continue to flourish in the work of Andrea Camilleri (born 1925), whose crime novels are not only highly realistic but make powerful use of Sicilian expressions and dialect.

> **Lyrical and often melancholy songs such as "O Sole Mio" and "Torna a Surriento" are major features of the city's popular image.**

Music

Even if you've never been to Naples, you probably know a Neapolitan song. The mandolin-playing musician and lyrical and often melancholy songs such as "O Sole Mio" and "Torna a Surriento" are major features of the city's popular image at home and abroad. Most of the songs are from the 19th century, but they have influenced latter-day musicians such as the Naples-born Pino Daniele (born 1955), whose hugely popular songs mix Neapolitan dialect, the blues, and the rhythms of the tarantella, a fevered folk dance with southern Italian roots.

In classical music, the South boasts Alessandro Scarlatti (1660–1725), a seminal figure in the development of Naples's *opera seria* (opera inspired by myth and historical themes) and the lyrical strains of *bel canto*. The city also gave birth to *opera buffa,* lighter comedies that evolved in response to the gravity of *opera seria*. The style's main exponent

Pino Daniele (center) in concert

was the Neapolitan Domenico Cimarosa (1749–1801). Opera in Naples was boosted by the presence of the San Carlo opera house (1737), second only to Milan's La Scala, as well as the advent of vocal stars such as Enrico Caruso (1873–1921). But a Sicilian, Vincenzo Bellini (1810–1835), proved the most influential of southern Italy's opera composers in operas such as *Norma* (1831). More recently, Sicily has produced modern composer Giovanni Sollima (born 1962), whose combination of classical and contemporary styles echoes the work of Philip Glass.

Cinema

Southern Italy is a filmmaker's dream: The region's complex and often contradictory nature makes it ripe for interpretation and cinematic exploration; the ravishing countryside and historic towns provide locations galore.

Many of the region's best early films were based on the great literary works of Sicily. The Italian director Luchino Visconti, for example, used Giovanni Verga's masterpiece, I Malavoglia, as the inspiration for his 1948 movie La Terra Trema (The Ground Trembles), the tale of a fishing community near Catania. In Naples, the plays of Eduardo de Filippo provided a similar inspiration, notably Filumena Marturano, filmed by Vittorio De Sica as Matrimonio all'Italiana (1964) and starring Marcello Mastroianni and Sophia Loren. The latter, an icon of international cinema, was born in Pozzuoli, close to Naples.

Landscape and more serious themes were the inspiration for Roberto Rossellini in Stromboli: Terra di Dio (Stromboli: Land of God). The 1950 movie stars Ingrid Bergman as a refugee involved in an affair with a fisherman amid the harsh volcanic landscapes of Stromboli, one of Sicily's Aeolian islands. The same islands are settings in the Taviani brothers' visually stunning Kaos (1984), based on bittersweet stories by Luigi Pirandello.

A more poetic view of the Aeolians appears in Michael Radford's touching 1994 movie Il Postino (The Postman), set on Salina in the 1950s, starring the Naples-born comic and actor Massimo Troisi (1953–1994). Il Postino garnered several Oscar nominations and was hugely popular abroad, echoing the success of Giuseppe Tornatore's Nuova Cinema Paradiso (1988), a nostalgic look at the arrival of the talkies in Sicily.

Southern Italy's extraordinary landscapes have also provided locations for other filmmakers, including Francis Ford Coppola, whose Godfather trilogy (1972–1990) was partly set in Sicily. The Talented Mr. Ripley (1999) with Jude Law, Matt Damon, and Gwynneth Paltrow was based in Ischia. Elsewhere, the Reggia in Caserta served as Queen Amidala's palace in two Star Wars installments, and Matera doubled as the Holy Land in Mel Gibson's The Passion of the Christ (2004).

More recently, Neapolitan cinema has returned to the gritty realism of the postwar years with Matteo Garrone's Gomorra (2008), based on the best-selling book by Roberto Saviano. Gomorra deals with Naples's brutal and seedy underworld, a far cry from the sunny narratives of De Sica. ∎

EXPERIENCE: A Night at the Opera

Opera fans should visit Naples's **Teatro San Carlo** (Via San Carlo 98/F, tel 081 797 2331 or 081 797 2412, www.teatrosancarlo .it, guided tour $$), which dates from 1737, making it the oldest continuously used opera house in Europe. The performance quality is considered second only to that of Milan's La Scala. The season runs almost year-round, with a break in late July and August; tickets sell quickly, but can be obtained online—aim for central seats as sightlines can be poor. You can also experience the drama, and special passion that go with seeing opera in Italy in Palermo, at the **Teatro Massimo** opera house (tel 091 605 3521, www .teatromassimo.it). Or, for a less formal experience, often outdoors, arts festivals such as those held in **Ravello** (see pp. 104–107) or at the **Villa San Michele** on Capri (see p. 119) often include operas, or arias and overtures.

The capital of southern Italy, a complex and passionate city whose long history has left it with a gloriously rich artistic heritage

Naples

Ready for the busy Neapolitan night

Naples

Naples (Napoli) has rarely wanted for praise. Set on a peerless bay and backed by Vesuvius's brooding volcanic profile, the city has been celebrated by poets and painters since classical times. Among its myriad attractions are world-class museums, sublime architecture, the lure of its exuberant streets, delicious food—the pizza was born here— and the proximity of historic and scenic jewels such as Pompeii and the Amalfi Coast.

But not everyone falls for Naples. Peter Nichols, the famous Italian correspondent for the *Times* of London in the 1970s, wrote that "Naples is one of the great tests. Some people hate it and some people love it." But those who do not love it, he added, "I think are afraid of something."

Reasons to be wary are obvious, at least to people who have not visited the city, or have not visited recently. Naples has long been a byword for urban degradation, crime, poverty, pollution, and traffic chaos. Certainly the miles of dispiriting suburbs and car-wracked streets can jar. But in which major city is this not the case? More to the point, the last ten or so years have seen a dramatic change in Naples,

a literal and metaphorical cleanup instigated by Antonio Bassolino, the city's robust mayor between 1993 and 2000.

More remains to be done, of course, but if Naples does still have an edge and a character, then these are to the good, for they are some of the city's most distinctive features. This is a place so Italian as to be almost a cliché—a city of pizza, opera, busy markets, family, petty crime, organized crime, soccer, religion, raised voices, singing waiters, Sophia Loren (born nearby), and the sort of washing-hung streets used as a visual shorthand for Italy in countless movies.

Few places bring you quite so close to the teeming realities and visceral charms of life in the Italian South, and few people on Earth are quite as exuberant, sharp, fatalistic, and fiercely individual as the Neapolitans. There are certainly areas of Naples, as in any city, where you would not travel after dark, or even by day, but in the city center simply be aware, not wary.

NOT TO BE MISSED:

VIA A. SCARLA
VIA DOMENIC
Stazione Cimarosa
VILLA FLORIDIANA
Museo Nazionale della Ceramica
CORSO VITTORIO EMANUELE
VIA FRANCESCO CRISPIO
RIVIE
PIAZZA DELLA REPUBBLICA
VIA FRANCESC
PIAZZA SANNAZZARO CARACCIOLO
Porticciolo di Mergellina
VIA FRANCESCO CARACCIOLO
Mergellina

After a stop at one of the city's visitor centers (see p. 9), you might start exploring with the Duomo. The cathedral is close to the heart of the ancient city, whose Greek and Roman plan is still followed by the streets of the *centro storico* (historic center) to the west. Here you will find some of the city's finest churches, notably San Lorenzo and San Domenico. Detour north to see the Museo Archeologico Nazionale, Italy's greatest archaeological museum, and then visit two more marvelous

churches, Santa Chiara and the Gesù Nuovo, before following Via Toledo, Naples's compelling main street, toward the port and the palaces and grand squares of royal Naples. Next, devote a day each to the city's other great museums, the Certosa di San Martino and Capodimonte.

Finally, remember that Naples is a city devoted to life. Much is colorful, direct, and immediate. Only the city's charm is slow, subtle, and insidious. ∎

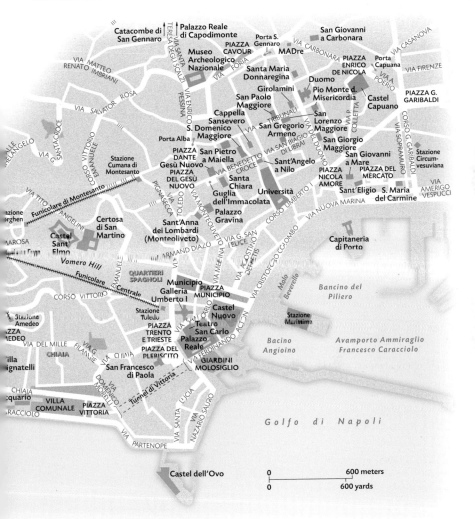

Duomo

Situated at the eastern edge of historic Naples, and close to the vast Piazza Giuseppe Garibaldi—many visitors' unprepossessing introduction to the old quarter—the Duomo (cathedral) is the ideal place to embark on a tour of the city center. Not only is it a good spot from which to get your bearings, but it stands close to the city's religious, cultural, and ancient heart.

The Duomo's lavish baroque interior was built in the shape of a Latin cross.

The Duomo probably dates from A.D. 324, when Constantine, the first Christian Roman emperor, built a basilica here known as Santa Restituta. Some of it still forms part of the present church. In the fifth century, a new church, Santa Stefania, was built at right angles to the basilica. Then in 1272, the new Angevin king, Charles I, ordered the creation of another cathedral in French Gothic style.

Charles's cathedral was completed in 1313, but at great cost to Santa Restituta and Santa Stefania, much of which was destroyed. The facade, too, has suffered, the original replaced in 1407 after an earthquake. Today, only the portals from 1407 survive, incorporated into a bland Gothic exterior from 1905.

Little on the exterior prepares you for the overwhelming baroque interior. More than 110 ancient columns of African and Oriental granite divide the naves, supporting a glorious painted ceiling and flanked by portraits of 46 saints by Luca Giordano and his pupils. Other major artworks include the 14th-century frescoes, mosaic floor, and tomb of Cardinal Arrigo Minutolo in the **Cappella Minutolo** (the second chapel to the right of the high altar). Most people, however, make straight for the **Cappella di San Gennaro**

EXPERIENCE: Attend the Festa di San Gennaro

Little is known of San Gennaro, or St. Januarius, other than that he was probably born in Benevento, in southern Italy, and martyred during the persecutions of Emperor Diocletian at the end of the third century. His relics came to Naples's cathedral in 1497, where they became the source of numerous miracles.

You will need to book hotels early if you want to attend one of the three occasions on which the vials of the saint's blood are displayed (see below), especially on September 19, when the city is extremely busy. It is difficult to get into the Duomo itself for the ceremony, but events are usually broadcast on screens outside. Even if you are not inside, the whole city has a febrile atmosphere that makes these days in September, December, and May great times to visit.

(1608–1637), or Tesoro, the large chapel midway down the church's right (south) aisle.

Naples's much revered patron saint, Gennaro (Januarius) was the bishop of the nearby town of Pozzuoli. He was martyred in the town in A.D. 305. Shortly after his death, so the story goes, his nurse collected his blood, some of which found its way into two vials now kept in the cathedral (along with a reliquary containing the saint's skull). His other remains are in an urn in the magnificent marble *confessio*, or **Cappella Carafa** (1497–1508), below the high altar. The work of Malvito da Como, the chapel is one of the city's loveliest Renaissance creations.

Around the two vials has grown the most important of Naples's many festivals—the "miraculous" liquefaction of the saint's blood three times a year. The most important of these dates is the saint's feast day on September 19; the others are the Saturday before the first Sunday in May and December 16. The first liquefaction reputedly occurred a century after Gennaro's death, but records date only to 1389.

A fervent crowd watches the ceremonies, which take place in the cathedral. It can take between two minutes and an hour for liquefaction to occur; the longer it takes, the more ominous the portents for Naples in the coming year. No scientist has been allowed to test the blood, but suffice it to say that on two occasions when liquefaction failed, there followed the last major eruption of Vesuvius (in 1944) and the Irpinia earthquake that killed more than 4,000 people (in 1980). The treasury has 45 silver busts of other saintly protectors who have been marshalled when Gennaro has been considered dilatory in his guardianship of the city.

Opposite the saint's chapel is the entrance to the remains of the basilica of **Santa Restituta** (or Archaeological Zone). Inside, among more recent 17th-century adornments, are the side chapels with fine bas-reliefs and 14th-century mosaics, remains of 4th-century mosaics, and the 5th-century **San Giovanni in Fonte,** Europe's oldest baptistery (the font probably comes from an ancient temple to Dionysus). ∎

Duomo

🅐 Map p. 45

✉ Via del Duomo 147

☎ 081 449 097

🕐 Church: closed Mon.–Sat. 12:30–4:30 p.m. & Sun. 1:30–5 p.m. Archeological Zone: closed Mon.–Sat. noon–4:30 & Sun. p.m.

💲 Church free, Archaeological Zone & baptistery $$

www.duomodinapoli .com

Museo Archeologico Nazionale

The Museo Archeologico Nazionale (National Museum of Archaeology) is one of the world's great museums. It is home to sculptures that rival the collections of Rome and has a wealth of mosaics, wall paintings, and beautiful artifacts removed from Pompeii, Herculaneum, and other major southern Italian sites.

Among the fine mosaics at the Museo Archeologico is this depiction of the Battle of Issus.

In 1777, King Ferdinand I chose the 17th-century palace holding the museum to be a home for the vast collection of paintings and sculptures he had inherited from his mother, Elisabetta Farnese. To this were added artifacts from Pompeii and Herculaneum (towns buried by Vesuvius in A.D. 79; see pp. 86–93 & 80–83). The collection was divided after coming to the Italian state, the paintings going to Capodimonte (see pp. 72–75) and the sculptures and most other artifacts remaining in the Museo Archeologico.

As with many great museums, there is almost too much to see. The countless rooms, spread over four floors, are also rather confusing, with distinct itineraries difficult to plot. Labeling, too, is not what it might be. If time is short, confine yourself to the best of the Farnese bequest and other

Greek and Roman sculpture, most of which is on the ground floor. Then make for the topmost floor (from Room 66 onward), which is home to some of the loveliest wall paintings removed from Pompeii and Herculaneum. The basement level features ancient Egyptian artifacts—fun if you are traveling with children, but otherwise for enthusiasts only—while the mezzanine level (between the first and second floors) is devoted largely to mosaics.

Excellent audio guides with English commentaries are available for the museum. Note, though, that some of the many rooms may be closed and that exhibits are often moved or reordered.

Visiting the Museum

The classical sculptures on the **ground floor** come mainly from the 300-year-old Farnese collection, many of them accumulated in Rome by Alessandro Farnese during his reign as Pope Paul III (1534–1549). Some are original Roman works, most of them excavated from Rome's Terme di Caracalla (a bath complex near the Colosseum). Other exhibits are Roman copies of Greek originals, graphically illustrating the degree to which Roman culture borrowed from that of the Greeks, who were present in Naples and parts of southern Italy for hundreds of years.

The first major exhibit in the opening room, the **Galleria dei Tirannicidi,** is one such copy, a sculpture portraying the mythical characters Harmodius and Aristogeitou. This is a second-century A.D. copy of a bronze work made by Kritius, one of ancient Greece's most celebrated sculptors, for the Agora (marketplace) in Athens in 477 B.C. Close by is another Roman copy, the "Doryphorus," or "Spear Bearer," a facsimile of a 440 B.C. sculpture by the Greek master Polylitus. For centuries the figure was considered the archetype of the perfectly proportioned male form.

Rooms 8–16 contain some of the highlights of the collection, many of them remarkable for their sheer size. The vast spaces of the gallery provide a perfect setting for even the most colossal sculptures. The most imposing

INSIDER TIP:

After the Museo Archeologico Nazionale, stroll down Via Santa Maria di Costantinopoli. At Piazza Bellini, enjoy a drink at Caffè Intra Moenia.

—MAGGIE TURQMAN
National Geographic senior research librarian

of all is the third-century "Toro Farnese" ("Farnese Bull") in **Room 8,** one of the largest classical sculptures in existence (it is a copy of a second-century B.C. Greek original). Standing over 13 feet (4 m) high, it depicts the punishment Zethus and Amphion meted out to Dirce, Queen of

Museo Archeologico Nazionale

🅰 Map p. 45
✉ Piazza Museo Nazionale 19
☎ 081 442 2149
🕐 Closed Tues.
💲 Museum $$$, Gabinetto Segreto guided tours (every 30 mins.) $

www.archeona.arti .beniculturali.it

Caffè Intra Moenia

✉ Piazza Bellini 70
☎ 081 290 988
www.intramoenia.it

Secret Cabinet

The Gabinetto Segreto (Secret Cabinet), a repository of erotic art from Pompeii and Herculaneum, has long been renowned, but for many years it was kept under lock and key. The Romans, though, were far from offended by explicit images; on the contrary, they relished erotic art and made no moral judgments about sexual behavior. The steam rooms of public bathhouses would contain graphic murals or mosaics of sex, and Mars, Jupiter, and other gods were often portrayed in rampant sexual congress.

Images of phalluses—with wings, hats, bells, and more—were everywhere, considered talismans to ward off the evil eye or as symbols of fertility, virility, or good luck. Even a baker's shop might sport a phallus, simply to suggest the wealth of fresh bread inside. The Gabinetto is not for the prudish, however, as some of the images are genuinely shocking—the statue of the god Pan, for example, caught in flagrante with a nanny goat, was doubtless taboo even in Roman times.

Thebes, for the attempted murder of their mother: She was tied to a bull and trampled to death.

Between **Rooms 11** and **12** is the almost equally gargantuan "Ercole Farnese" ("Farnese Hercules"), showing a massively muscled Hercules leaning on his club. The statue also hailed from the Terme di Caracalla. After its excavation it greatly influenced the Renaissance sculptors of the day. Collections here also include the **Gemme della Collezione Farnese** in Rooms 9 and **10,** about 2,000 smaller precious objects from the Farnese hoard. The most celebrated is the "Tazza Farnese," a large cameo carved from sardonyx stone, famous for its translucence. It was probably made in Alexandria, Egypt, in the second century B.C.

Mosaics

The 15 or so rooms of the **mezzanine level** are devoted mainly to mosaics, many of them removed from Pompeii and Herculaneum. The east wing of

the floor, though, has exhibits displaying some 200,000 ancient and medieval coins and medals. This floor also contains the most infamous of the gallery's exhibits, the **Gabinetto Segreto** (Secret Cabinet), filled with erotic or pornographic art and artifacts from Pompeii. Always controversial, it was opened to public view again in 2000 (see sidebar above). It can be seen as part of a reserved tour but is out of bounds to children under 11.

The mosaics, though, are the mezzanine's undoubted highlights, this being the greatest such collection of its type in the world. Many of the detached panels show delightful everyday scenes. Others are dramatic set pieces, as with the museum's finest mosaic— Alexander the Great defeating the Persian fleet under Darius at the Battle of Issus in 333 B.C. **(Room 61).** This colossal work was found in the Casa del Fauno in Pompeii.

The **first floor** (American second) has a multitude of rooms and is the most difficult floor to navigate. It is also subject to reorganization. Centered on the massive Salone dell'Atlante, or Sala Meridiana, it generally divides between rooms devoted to wall paintings and other artifacts from Pompeii and (in the west wing) displays illustrating the prehistory of Naples and its hinterland.

As ever in the museum, there is something of interest in virtually every room, but if time is tight, make immediately for **Room 66,** the first in a series of salons that are devoted to the wall paintings of Pompeii and other sites in Campania.

Entire rooms have been reconstructed from villas at these sites but, as elsewhere, it is often the domestic details that are most fascinating. Thus **Room 77** has images from everyday life in Pompeii—a baker selling his loaves, a brawl in the town's amphitheater, a portrait of a loved one, and so on. **Rooms 80–84,** by contrast, contain the entire set of murals removed from the Temple of Isis at Pompeii.

Artifacts

Rooms 85–89 present beautiful objets d'art retrieved from Pompeii, notably silverware, glassware, and terra-cottas, as well as a collection of Roman arms and armor, including some striking gladiator helmets.

In the opposite wing, to the right as you enter the Sala Meridiana, **Rooms 114–117** are devoted to finds from the Villa dei Papiri at Herculaneum. Such were the number and quality of these artifacts—50 marble sculptures, 21

bronzes, and thousands of papyrus manuscripts—that it is believed the villa once belonged to a highly eminent citizen, possibly Lucio Pisone, Julius Caesar's father-in-law. **Rooms 130–140** feature ceramics and miscellaneous artifacts that were removed from Paestum and other Campanian sites. ■

The "Toro Farnese" marble sculpture is one of the highlights of the museum's ground floor.

A Walk through Old Naples

A walk through Naples's *centro storico* (historic center) yields a tight-packed quarter filled with churches, shops, palaces, piazzas, people, and tenements whose arrangement has remained unchanged for more than 2,500 years.

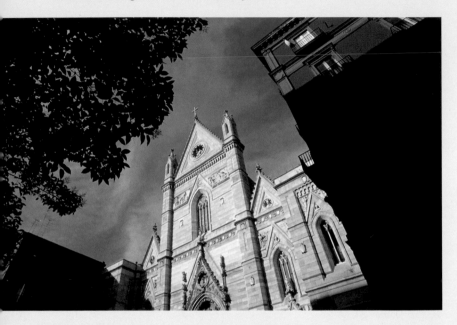

Naples's Duomo, built in the late 13th century, is dedicated to San Gennaro.

Exploring the city's ancient heart is straight-forward, though you will need to weave from street to street, occasionally doubling back if you are to see all the many churches, galleries, and hidden corners of this busy district.

The area is centered around two of the *decumani* (main streets) of the Greek and Roman city, whose arrow-straight east-to-west course remains unaltered to this day. The most important is the most southerly of the pair, which goes by the generic name of "Spaccanapoli," literally "Split Naples," because that is what it does. Along its course the street has several different names—notably Via Vicaria Vecchia, Via San Biagio dei Librai, and Via Benedetto Croce. It concludes in Piazza del Gesù Nuovo. A block north of Spaccanapoli is the

NOT TO BE MISSED:

Duomo • San Lorenzo
Maggiore • San Paolo della
Maggiore • Cappella Sansevero

second of the decumani, the even busier Via dei Tribunali. Almost all of what you want to see is on or just off the streets, though it should be stressed that the bustle on these extraordinary thoroughfares is an attraction in itself.

For the sake of orientation, start at the **Duomo ❶** (see pp. 46–47), and then walk a few steps north on Via del Duomo to **Santa Maria Donnaregina ❷** (*Vico Donnaregina 26,* *tel 081 299 101)*. The church has irregular hours, but if you are lucky you will be able to enter the small 18th-century cloister (found off an alley to the right) with a door on the left that leads to the older of the site's two churches. This more venerable building was commissioned in 1293 by Mary, the queen of Charles II of Anjou, after an earthquake destroyed an earlier eighth-century chapel on the site.

At the end of the austere interior is the queen's tomb (1323–1326), a magnificent work by the Tuscan master Tino da Camaino. In the choir (the rectangular gallery) are celebrated frescoes (begun 1308) by Pietro Cavallini (ca 1250–1330), a Roman painter whose importance is increasingly being recognized.

Retrace your steps past the Duomo and turn left on Via dei Tribunali. A few paces down on the right is **Pio Monte della Misericordia** ❸ *(Via dei Tribunali 253, tel 081 446 944 or 081 446 973, www.piomontedellamisericordia.it, church & gallery closed p.m. daily & Wed., $$)*, a charitable organization that has been active since 1601. The high altar of its octagonal church here (1658–1678) contains one of Italy's finest 17th-century paintings, Caravaggio's "Opere della Misericordia" (1607). A vast composition, it illustrates the seven acts of charity, with a virtuoso use of chiaroscuro (light and shadow).

Outside the church, across the road in Piazza Riario Sforza, is the **Guglia di San Gennaro,** one of many similarly ornate

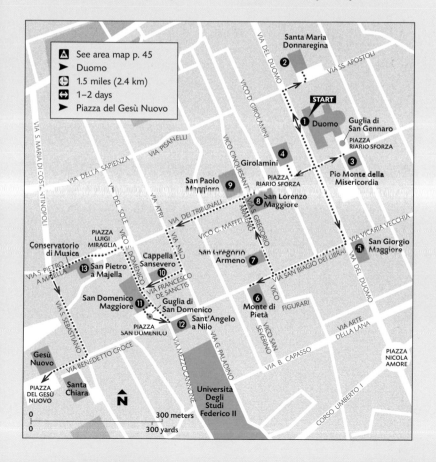

columns dotted around the city. This one was raised in 1660 by locals who believed that San Gennaro, the city's patron saint, had saved Naples from an eruption of Vesuvius in 1631.

Retrace your steps briefly and walk west on Via dei Tribunali. Just past the intersection of Via del Duomo you come to another

---

MADre

MADre stands for Museo d'Arte Contemporanea Donna Regina, Napoli's leading publicly funded modern art gallery (Via Settembrini 79, tel 081 1931 3016, www.museomadre .it, closed Tues., $$). Reopened in 2005, the gallery's palazzo home, just north of the Duomo, was remodeled by Portuguese architect Alvaro Siza. The first main floor features permanent installations by Anish Kapoor, Richard Serra, Jeff Koons, and others, and upper floors are devoted to temporary exhibitions.

---

church-and-gallery combination on the right, the little-visited **Girolamini** ❹ (Via dei Tribunali, tel 081 292 316), also known as San Filippo Neri (1592–1619), and the Quadreria or **Pinacoteca Girolamini** (entered at Via del Duomo 142, tel 081 294 4980, www.girolamini.it, closed p.m. daily e Sun.). Fine paintings in the church include a fresco by Luca Giordano on the west wall; "St. Alessandro Moribondo" by Pietro da Cortona (first chapel on the right, or south wall); and an altarpiece in the sacristy of St. John the Baptist by Guido Reni.

En route to the gallery, which forms part of the church's conventual buildings, visit the lovely cloister with its lemon and medlar trees and (if open) the glorious library, especially the latter's beautifully decorated Sala Grande. The charming little gallery has first-rate works by heavy hitters such as Sermoneta, Guido Reni, Luca Giordano, Battista Caracciolo, and Giuseppe Ribera, among others.

A one-block stroll south at this point on Via del Duomo takes you to **San Giorgio Maggiore** ❺ (Via del Duomo 237/A, tel 081 287 932, closed 12:30–5 p.m. daily e Sun. p.m.), founded in the fourth century by St. Severus (364–410). Most of the ancient church was damaged by fire and replaced in the 17th century, but fragments from the older building survive, namely Severus's relics (behind the altar), his marble throne (to the right), and some architectural remnants of the fourth-century basilica.

From San Giorgio, walk west on Via San Biagio dei Librai for your first taste of Spaccanapoli. Just beyond Vico Figurari (fourth on the left) is the little-known **Monte di Pietà** ❻ (Via San Biagio dei Librai 114, tel 081 580 7111, Sat. 9 a.m.–7 p.m. e Sun. 9 a.m.–2 p.m.), a palace whose courtyard conceals a gem of a chapel with fine baroque paintings and a beautiful sacristy.

San Gregorio Armeno

Opposite Vico Figurari take Via San Gregorio north (right off Via dei Tribunali) to visit the church and Benedictine convent of **San Gregorio Armeno** ❼ (Via San Gregorio Armeno 1, tel 081 552 0186, closed p.m. daily), a few steps up on the left. Via San Gregorio is famous across Naples for its many workshops devoted to the year-round manufacture of the presepi (Christmas crèches) for which the city has long been renowned.

The church owes its fame to holy relics brought by nuns fleeing the religious uncertainty of Constantinople in 726. These include the bones of Santa Patrizia, a native of Constantinople, relics that created a large cult following among Neapolitans. Like Gennaro, Patrizia has vials of her blood in church hands, but unlike Gennaro's thrice-yearly liquefactions, Patrizia's blood is said to liquefy weekly, every Tuesday.

The conventual church is richly decorated. Its gilt ceiling (1582) is wonderful, with 16 paintings depicting martyred saints. Also look for the damaged frescoes by Luca Giordano in the cupola and west wall. Patrizia's relics are kept in the chapel alongside the high altar.

Outside the church, pass under the arch across the street and turn left into Via G. Maffei, where you'll find the entrance to the **convent** (climb the long staircase and press the bell). Note the bronze drums here, used to pass provisions to the nuns, who were forbidden contact with the outside world until 1922. If the nuns are not at prayer, you should be admitted to the cloister, a lovely and peaceful retreat heavy with the scent of orange trees.

San Lorenzo Maggiore

Return to Via San Gregorio and turn left to meet Via dei Tribunali. Turn right; a few steps bring you to the church of **San Lorenzo Maggiore** ❽ *(Via dei Tribunali 316, tel 081 454 948 or 081 211 0860, church closed 1–5 p.m., excavations closed Sun. p.m., church free, excavations $$)*. A fascinating sight, San Lorenzo offers two attractions: the church itself and the excavations in the archaeological zone beneath the church.

The large Franciscan church, one of the most important Gothic buildings in the southern Italy, was begun by Charles I of Anjou on the site of a sixth-century chapel. The facade dates from 1742 (save for the fine doorway, from 1325), but the church's interior has been largely restored to the Gothic purity of the 13th-century original. In the ambulatory (the walkway around the altar) are a series of exquisite tombs.

To the left of the bell tower (1507), a door leads to the chapterhouse and cloister, below which is the enthralling **archaeological zone.** Here you can literally stand at the heart of the old Greek, Roman, and medieval city, where ongoing excavations have uncovered 2,000-year-old streets and buildings.

Turn west once again down Via dei Tribunali and, just beyond Via San Gregorio, set back across the street, stands the lofty church of **San Paolo Maggiore** ❾ *(Via dei Tribunali, Piazza San Gaetano, tel 081 454 048, closed Sun.)*. Inside, the highlights are frescoes in the sacristy by Francesco Solimena (among Naples's greatest 18th-century painters), the statue of the Guardian Angel on the left of the central nave (by Domenico Antonio Vaccaro), and the Cappella Firrao (left of the presbytery), one of Naples's most beguiling baroque chapels. The piazza also

The Cappella Sansevero is celebrated for the 18th-century sculpture of the "Veiled Christ."

has an entrance to the old Greek and Roman aqueduct, which can be seen on guided tours.

Cappella Sansevero

Continue west along Via dei Tribunali and then turn left down Via Nilo. Take the second right (Via Francesco de Sanctis) and on the right is the beautiful and mysterious **Cappella Sansevero** ⑩ *(Via Francesco de Sanctis 19, tel 081 551 8470, closed Tues. & Sun p.m., $$).* Created in 1590 as the private mausoleum of the local di Sangro family (whose palaces are found around the neighborhood), the chapel took on its present appearance between 1749 and 1766 under the hand of Don Raimundo di Sangro (see sidebar p. 38).

In addition to fine paintings, the chapel has remarkable sculptures, many involving veils or nets. The most famous is the "Veiled Christ" (1753) by Giuseppe Sammartino (1720–1793) in the center of the chapel, a work of extraordinary realism. In the crypt are two macabre figures with reconstructed arteries and organs. These apparently belonged to servants of the mysterious Raimundo, whom he part-

INSIDER TIP:

Sansevero Chapel's "Veiled Christ" is a virtuoso accomplishment of stone with softness and transparency.

—ILARIA CAPUTI
National Geographic contributor

preserved during his experiments into the circulatory system. Both were injected with embalming fluids, local lore claiming that the servants were not necessarily dead at the time.

Continue west to the end of Via Francesco de Sanctis and you emerge in **Piazza San Domenico,** one of the city's prettiest squares, where you will see several former di Sangro palaces at Nos. 3, 12, and 17. Also here are tempting cafés (try the Gran Caffè Aragonese at No. 5/8 or Scaturchio at No. 19) and the church of **San Domenico Maggiore** ⑪ *(Piazza San Domenico 8/A, tel 081 459 298, closed noon–5 p.m.),* entered either on the square from the rear by a sweeping marble staircase or through a fine 13th-century portico at Vico San Domenico 18.

The church was much favored by the city's Aragonese nobility and its chief attractions are the various frescoes and tomb monuments they commissioned. The best are the **Cappella Saluzzo** (south aisle, left of the entrance), whose arches and tomb of Galeotto Carafa (1507–1515) are the work of the Tuscan sculptor Antonio da Settignano; frescoes by Pietro Cavallini; and the tomb of Archbishop Brancaccio (died 1341), possibly by Tino da Camaino, in the Cappella Brancaccio (second right).

In the piazza's southeast corner, past the Guglia di San Domenico column celebrating the city's deliverance from plague in 1658, and across Via Benedetto Croce, is **Sant'Angelo a Nilo** ⑫ *(Piazzetta Nilo 23, tel 081 211 0860, closed p.m. daily).* Built in 1385 for the Brancaccio family, it is known for the exceptional tomb monument (1426–1427) of the church's founder, Cardinal Rinaldo Brancaccio. Situated to the right of the altar, it was sculpted by the great Tuscan artists Donatello and Michelozzo in Pisa and then shipped to Naples.

Cross the road and walk past the right flank of San Domenico, pausing to glance into the church of **San Pietro a Majella** ⑬ *(Piazza Luigi Miraglia 393, tel 081 459 008, closed Sun. p.m)* on the left at the intersection with Via dei Tribunali: It preserves a mixture of original 14th-century Gothic and later baroque features. Next door is the **Conservatorio di San Pietro a Majella,** a prestigious music academy that accounts for the music shops in Via San Pietro a Maiella to the west (the continuation of Via dei Tribunali) and Via San Sebastiano (the first left turn). The latter street takes you to Via Benedetto Croce and **Piazza del Gesù Nuovo** (see p. 58).

Via Toledo & Around

Via Toledo is Naples's main street, linking the city's ancient heart and Spaccanapoli to the waterfront and the castles of Royal Naples. A vibrant bustle of life and people, it also divides the city's business district in the east from the Quartieri Spagnoli to the west, an area whose warren of alleys and tenements offers many of the classic vignettes of "old" Naples.

Strolling down Via Toledo, one of Naples's busiest shopping streets

Most cities have an obvious center: a square, a park, or a landmark that over the centuries emerges as a meeting place or symbolic heart. Not Naples. Piazza Garibaldi in the east is large, but peripheral, while Piazza del Plebiscito in the south, though a stage for mass public gatherings, lacks the soul and human touch (bars, restaurants, intimacy) required of an actual or symbolic center of city life.

Which leaves Via Toledo, a mostly pedestrian-only thoroughfare of stores and banks. It is a long river of humanity day and night, but especially in the evening, when the *passeggiata*, or *struscio*—the slow-walking promenade of well-dressed Neapolitans, young and old—makes its stately but exuberant progress up and down the busy street's southern margins.

The street takes its name from the Spanish viceroy Don Pedro de Toledo (r.1532–1553), who built it as part of the most far-reaching program of urban redevelopment

Via Toledo
Map p. 45

Santa Chiara

- Map p. 45
- ✉ Church: Via Santa Chiara 49 Cloister: Via Benedetto Croce 16
- ☎ Church: 081 552 6280 Cloister: 081 552 1597
- 🕑 Church closed 12:30–4:30 p.m., cloister closed Sun. p.m.
- 💲 Church free, cloister $$

www.santachiara .info

www.oltreilchiostro .org

in the city's history. Whole quarters were razed and streets created, an exercise that more than doubled the city's habitable space.

The street was renamed Via Roma in 1860 in honor of Italian unification, but it eventually reverted to its old name. You may still hear both used. It has recently started to enjoy something of an architectural revival, some city funds having been directed toward the street's many venerable facades and palaces.

The street and its people-watching options are attractions in themselves, but the thoroughfare also provides the framework for sightseeing as you move south from the *centro storico.* Start your exploration either in Piazza Dante (recently spruced up to elegant effect) or at **Piazza del Gesù Nuovo** at the western end of Via Benedetto Croce.

This latter square is home to two splendid churches, Santa Chiara and Gesù Nuovo (also known as Trinità Maggiore), but the first thing that catches the eye is the **Guglia dell'Immacolata** (1747–1750), or Column of the Virgin Mary, a capricious (some might say grotesque) baroque spire that is typically Neapolitan in its ostentation. All frills and fancy, it is based on the devotional objects—part float, part sculpture—that have been made for religious celebrations in the city for centuries.

Gesù Nuovo

The spire was raised by the Jesuit order (many of the saints it depicts are Jesuit favorites), as was the nearby church of **Gesù**

Nuovo (*Piazza del Gesù Nuovo 2, tel 081 557 8151, closed 12:30–4 p.m. & Sun. p.m.*). The church was built between 1584 and 1601, but much of the facade is earlier, dating from a palace on the site built in 1470.

Inside, the church is a dazzlingly overwrought array of baroque stucco, frescoes, and marble, with an astounding ceiling and paintings by Luca Giordano, Solimena, Giuseppe Ribera, and other leading Neapolitan artists. The large bronze statue and the room on the right of the church relate to Giuseppe Moscati (died 1927), a much loved local doctor who was canonized in 1987 following a wave of public support. Moscati abandoned a promising academic career to treat the poor of Naples for free, often secretly leaving money under their pillows. Rooms in the church are filled with hundreds of touching ex-votos (devotional objects) representing cures effected by the doctor or his saintly intervention.

The splendor of the Gesù Nuovo is in stark contrast to the austerity of the nearby church and convent of **Santa Chiara.**

It was not always thus. Santa Chiara represents one of the most tantalizing losses of artistic riches in the city. Built between 1310 and 1328 by Sancia, wife of the Angevin (Anjou) king Robert I, the church was intended as the sepulcher of Naples's Angevin dynasty. Kings and royal scions were buried here, along with leading aristocrats, most of them in tombs created by the foremost Tuscan and other sculptors of their day. Between 1742 and 1757, the interior was remodeled with a splendor that was apparently remarkable even by Naples's extravagant standards.

On the night of August 4, 1943, however, Allied incendiary bombs rained down on the church and its surroundings, starting a fire that destroyed most of the church's interior and damaged or obliterated its large monuments. Restoration ensued in 1953, recreating the purity of the original 14th-century Gothic church and salvaging or copying some tombs.

The finest of these is that of Robert I (died 1343) behind the high altar (note how the king is represented no fewer than four times), the work of the Florentine brothers Giovanni and Pacio Bertini. Also striking is the tomb of Robert's son, Charles, Duke of Calabria (to the right), by the Tuscan sculptor Tino da Camaino. The church's sacristy has a beautiful 14th-century portal and tantalizing 13th-century fragments of fresco by Giotto, the greatest of Italy's early medieval artistic innovators.

Behind the church to the right is the lovely **Chiostro delle Clarisse** (Cloister of the Poor Clares),

a large, peaceful retreat strikingly decorated with majolica tiles and terra-cottas. It is one of the loveliest places in Naples.

A short walk to the southwest (bypassing the nearby Piazza Matteotti and its ugly Fascist-era post office) takes you past the appealing Renaissance **Palazzo Gravina** (1513–1549) to another fine church, **Sant'Anna dei Lombardi,** also known as Monteoliveto or Santa Maria di Monteoliveto *(Piazza Monteoliveto 44, tel 081 551 3333, closed 12:30–4:30 p.m. & Sun.).* Begun in 1411, this was to the Aragonese kings what Santa Chiara was to the Angevin monarchs.

Frescoes and other works of art adorn the Chiostro delle Clarisse in the church of Santa Chiara.

Don Pedro of Aragon, for example, commissioned the Fontana di Monteoliveto (1699) in the piazza outside, one of Naples's prettiest baroque fountains; several of his Aragonese compatriots are buried inside. Tuscan sculptors were again responsible for most of the tombs.

Highlights include the monument to Maria d'Aragona (died 1470), daughter of Ferdinand I, by Benedetto da Maiano and Antonio Rossellino, two of Tuscany's finest 15th-century sculptors. It can be found in the Cappella Piccolomini, to the left of the entrance. Benedetto also left an "Annunciation" (1489) and other works in the Cappella Mastrogiudice (first chapel on the right, or south, side). Virtually every chapel in the church has something

EXPERIENCE:
Food at Christmas

Naples always offers a memorable eating experience, but visit almost any restaurant in the city in the build-up to Christmas and you'll be able to sample little-known specialties that you won't find at other times of the year, or anywhere else in Italy. Dinner on Christmas Eve, the *cena della Vigilia,* is meatless, and traditionally consists of *spaghetti alle vongole* (spaghetti with clams), *capitone e baccalà fritta* (fried eel and salt cod), *insalata di rinforzo* (marinated vegetables), and *rococcò,* an almond pastry, for dessert. Lunch the next day starts with the classic Neapolitan Christmas Day dish, *minestra maritata* (chicken broth with vegetables), followed by pasta and then the chicken from which the broth was made. Dessert is *struffoli,* a colorful pastry, usually accompanied by a glass of liqueur such as limoncello (see p. 102).

of interest. Be sure to take the passage by the fifth chapel on the right to see Guido Mazzoni's terra-cotta "Pietà" (1492). A great favorite with Neapolitans, the eight life-size figures around Christ are supposed to be portraits of the royal court and other contemporaries of the artist.

Quartieri Spagnoli

Walk the short distance down Via Morgantini to Via Toledo, and virtually across the street is Via Pignasecca, which leads to one of the city's most colorful street markets. This provides a hint of the picturesque and occasionally squalid vignettes provided by the streets of the Quartieri Spagnoli immediately to the south.

This dense labyrinth on the west side of Via Toledo was part of Viceroy Toledo's 16th-century urban redevelopment program, its buildings intended to house the Spanish garrison and its horses. Very quickly, however, its tiny rooms and stables became homes for Naples's poorest inhabitants, the so-called *bassi* dwellings, slums of the worst sort. Today, this area has one of the world's highest population densities and some of Europe's worst levels of unemployment, illiteracy, and infant mortality.

It would be wrong to romanticize this area (though improvements are being made), but there is no doubt that this is where you will encounter many of the iconic images of Naples—kids' soccer games, women in black, and colorful laundry across the streets. ∎

Underground Naples

Below a city in which every street has its history lies an underground world in which almost everything is mysterious. No one knows exactly how many caverns, quarries, shafts, and other cavities riddle the Naples underworld, though more than 700 have been cataloged. Nor do records show the length of the Greek, Roman, and other tunnels in the city's soft foundations—about 270 miles (450 km) have so far been explored.

Stone, history, and geological circumstance account for most of this subterranean world. Stone, because the rock beneath Naples is barely rock at all; it's a soft, easily excavated volcanic deposit known as tuff. The volcanic activity that created the tuff also caused earthquakes and other geological disturbances that opened up underground fissures. In time some of these became underground streams, many of them later adapted to provide water for Naples's early Greek and Roman inhabitants. You can take a 90-minute guided tour along about half a mile (1 km) of one of these aqueducts, with access from Piazza San Gaetano 68 *(tel 081 296 944 or 081 368 3.54, www.napolisotteranea.org).*

Naples also has two early Christian catacombs that are open to the public, plus a third at San Severo that can be seen by appointment *(tel 081 544 1305).* The most eerily atmospheric are the **Catacombe di San Gennaro** *(Via Tondo di Capodimonte 13, tel 081 741 1071; guided tours on the hour Mon.–Sat. 10 a.m.–5 p.m., Sun. 10 a.m.– 1 p.m., $$$ combined ticket with San Gaudioso),* known for the length of time they were used— from at least the second to the tenth centuries— and the range of their faded frescoes from the same period.

Southern Italy's most important catacombs, the San Gennaro burial grounds probably began as the private cemetery of an early Christian family, but became more popular after the burial here of Sant'Agrippino. The tomb and adjacent basilica of this third-century bishop of Naples became a place of pilgrimage. More important, the bones of San Gennaro, Naples's patron saint, were kept here from the fifth to the ninth century, when they were moved to

Skulls in Naples's Fontanelle cemetery

the Duomo. The area is arranged on two levels: The burial places of Gennaro and Agrippino are on the lower level, while the upper level features fine "arcosolium" tombs, frescoed niches that would once have held sarcophagi.

The city's second catacombs, the **Catacombe di San Gaudioso** *(Piazza Sanità 14, tel 081 544 1305, www.catacombedinopoli.it; guided tours on the hour 10 a.m.–1 p.m., $$$ combined ticket with San Gennaro),* were once Roman cisterns. Their use as a cemetery probably began after the burial here of San Gaudioso in 452. The caves preserve a few frescoes and evidence of the burial rite used here in the mid-17th century. Then, corpses were buried standing, with only their heads encased. Once the body had partially rotted, the corpse was removed (the thankless task performed by convicts) and the skull placed above a portrait of the deceased. The skulls remained here until the cholera outbreak of 1974, when they were moved to Fontanelle cemetery.

Royal Naples

Royal Naples gathers around the vast Piazza del Plebiscito. It embraces the palaces, churches, fortresses, and other buildings built by the great Angevin, Aragonese, and Bourbon dynasties that controlled the city's destiny for the best part of 800 years.

The imposing spectacle of Castel Nuovo by night

Palazzo Reale

- Map p. 45
- Piazza del Plebiscito 1 (Biblioteca entered from Via Vittorio Emanuele III)
- 081 580 8111
- Palace closed Wed., Biblioteca closed Sat. p.m. & Sun.
- Palace $$, courtyard & gardens free

The monumental buildings and wide-open spaces of Royal Naples are at odds with most other areas of the city. At the same time, the program of local renovation, not to mention the disruption caused by the extension of the Naples subway, is typical of recent improvements to the city's fabric.

Piazza del Plebiscito is the area's obvious focus, a majestic square returned recently to its former glory by the removal of a parking lot and the banning of traffic. Its graceful colonnade of Doric columns was begun in 1809 under the city's French ruler, Joaquin Murat, while the distinctive church of **San Francesco di**

Paola (Piazza del Plebiscito, tel 081 764 5133, closed 12:30–4:30 p.m.)—a neoclassical copy of Rome's Pantheon—was created between 1817 and 1846 by the Bourbon kings to celebrate the removal of the French and their own return to power. The equestrian statues of the Bourbon monarchs Charles III and Ferdinand I are largely the work of the 19th-century sculptor Antonio Canova.

On the opposite (western) side of the square is the **Palazzo Reale**, begun in 1600 by the Spanish viceroy of the day in anticipation of a visit from Spanish king Philip II that never materialized. Much enlarged thereafter, it subsequently welcomed Bourbon and later Italian Savoy kings. One of the latter, Umberto I, commissioned the eight statues in the first-floor niches, each representing a ruler from one of the eight royal houses that prevailed in Naples over the years.

Thirty state rooms are open to the public, most of them (splendid ceilings aside) uninteresting except for the monumental staircase, the charming Teatrino di Corte (an ornate private theater from 1768), and the lovely reading rooms of the palace's Biblioteca Nazionale (National Library).

Immediately north of Piazza del Plebiscito is the smaller **Piazza Trento e Trieste,** home to the **Caffè Gambrinus** (*Via Chiaia 1–2, tel 081 417 582*), the city's most historic café, and (behind a plain facade on the east of the square) the celebrated **San Carlo opera house** (see sidebar p. 42). One of Europe's largest opera houses, San Carlo opened in 1737 but has been altered greatly over the years. Its opulent 3,000 seat, in it velvet and gilt interior can be seen (rehearsals allowing) on regular 20-minute guided tours.

Just off the square's west side is Via Chiaia, Naples's premier shopping street. A few steps north off Via Toledo is **Galleria Umberto I,** a steel-and-glass shopping arcade (1890), less salubrious now than in its early 20th-century heyday, when it was the meeting place for the city's intelligentsia.

From the gallery and Via San Carlo walk east to **Piazza Municipio,** another huge square dominated on its eastern flank

by the **Castel Nuovo** or Maschio Angioino (Angevin Fortress). Looking like a castle should, with massive walls and five circular towers, the fortress was begun in 1279 by Charles I, the first Angevin king. It quickly became the seat of the royal court, attracting writers such as Boccaccio and Petrarch and painters like Giotto, who in 1330 frescoed the castle's main hall and chapel. Only a few fragments of the frescoes remain.

While Giotto's masterpiece is lost, the castle retains one of southern Italy's architectural highlights, the glorious Renaissance facade (1454–1467), an incongruous white marble triumphal arch squeezed between the dark stone of two of the castle's towers.

Walk the Line

In Piazza del Plebiscito it is a Neapolitan tradition to attempt to walk between the two bronze equestrian statues with your eyes closed. Start with your back to the Palazzo Reale and aim to bisect the horses. You'll find it's harder than it looks, a result of the piazza's barely discernible slope.

Inside, the paintings and other artifacts of the **Museo Civico** (Civic Museum) are not distinguished, but the museum and castle interior (now City Hall) are worth visiting for the chapels (especially the Cappella Palatina), Sala dei Baroni (Hall of the Barons), and state apartments. ∎

San Carlo Opera House
- Map p. 45
- ✉ Via San Carlo 98/F
- ☎ 081 797 2331 or 081 797 2412 or 081 797 2312
- 💲 Guided tour $$

www.teatrosancarlo.it

Castel Nuovo & Museo Civico
- Map p. 45
- ✉ Piazza Municipio
- ☎ 081 420 1241 or 081 420 1342
- 🕐 Closed Sun.
- 💲 $$

Chiaia

Chiaia is the name given to the western district between the Vomero hill and the sea, a generally quieter and more refined quarter of the city than the historic center. Home in parts to chic
hotels and designer stores, this is an area to come to less for churches and museums than for
peaceful strolls in pretty parks and along seafront promenades.

Colorful houses edge a beach in the Mergellina area, in the newer part of Naples.

Chiaia
 Map pp. 44–45

In the 19th century, Naples, like
many European cities, developed
a taste for broad thoroughfares,
parks, and airy promenades,
converting the old mule tracks
that ran along the seafront
to Posillipo and Mergellina to
the west. Wealthy Neapolitans
began to build villas and art
deco (or Liberty) homes in the
area at the beginning of the
20th century, taking advantage
of what was then—and partly
remains to this day—an area
with green spaces far from the
cramped *centro storico*.

Today, you can still follow these
converted tracks and sample the

parks, starting from Piazza Vittoria
at the eastern fringe of the Chiaia
district. From here you can enter
the **Villa Comunale,** a popular
public park inaugurated in 1781
after the demolition of numerous
old buildings on the site. Then
it was open only one day a year;
now it is open daily. Come here
on a Sunday afternoon, in particular, to sample a slice of Neapolitan
life, for this is when local families,
the important business of a large
lunch completed, come to stroll
and watch their children run riot.

At the heart of the park
is the **Acquario,** or Stazione
Zoologica Anton Dohrn *(tel 081*

583 3111, closed Sun. p.m., Mon., & Nov.–March, $), Europe's oldest aquarium. Founded by a German naturalist in 1872, the two-story building preserves its original tanks, which are filled with 200 species of marine creatures found in the Bay of Naples.

North of the Villa Comunale, across the Riviera di Chiaia, is another park and villa, the **Villa Pignatelli** (Riviera di Chiaia 200, tel 081 410 7066 or 081 761 2356, closed p.m. daily & Tues., $). The house was built in 1826 and bought by the Rothschild dynasty in 1841, passing to the state in 1952. Today its interior is worth a brief visit for its beautifully appointed rooms and museum of decorative arts.

You could return to Via Caracciolo and continue walking west as far as **Mergellina,** in its day a small fishing village and still home to a fishing fleet and busy fish market. Here, too, is the large **Piazza Sannazzaro,** full of cheap restaurants and one of the city's more popular nightspots.

Alternatively, walk north from the Villa Pignatelli toward Piazza Amedeo, passing through narrow streets at odds with the wide open spaces to the south. Just east of

Piazza Amedeo is the base station of the Chiaia funicular railway (see sidebar below), which will take you up the hill to Via Domenico Cimarosa and a point on the northwest tip of another large park, the **Villa Floridiana** (Via Domenico Cimarosa 77, tel 081 578 1776 or 081 407 881). You can also approach the park from the city center on the Funicolare Centrale, close to Piazzetta Augusteo in the Quartieri Spagnoli (see p. 60). King Ferdinand gave the park and villa to his wife in 1815. It passed to the Italian state in the 1920s.

This is a favorite spot for walkers and joggers, as well as for casual visitors who come to enjoy the superb views from the terrace at the park's southerly margins. The park's villa houses the **Museo Nazionale della Ceramica** (tel 081 229 2110, closed p.m. daily & Tues., $), whose 6,000 exhibits make up one of the world's finest collections of its type. As well as numerous European ceramics, including superlative pieces from Capodimonte (see pp. 72–75), the museum has medieval, Japanese, and Chinese exhibits, including artifacts from the Ming (1368–1644) and Tang (618–906) dynasties. ■

Funiculars of Naples

The four funiculars (cable railroads) of Naples are picturesque and practical, providing an efficient means of negotiating the city's hills. The Centrale (from Piazza Fuga to Piazzetta Duca' d'Aosta), which opened in 1928, is one of the world's longest funiculars (4,167 ft/1,270 m long, with a height gain of 558 ft/170 m). It's also one of the busiest, carrying over ten million passengers a year. The Chiaia cable railroad (Rione Amedeo to Piazza Vanvitelli) dates from 1889, making it the world's third oldest funicular after Giessbachan in Switzerland and San Francisco's Telegraph Hill. Discussions are underway to build two new funiculars as part of the city's evolving transit system.

Certosa di San Martino

Dominating the skyline high above the old city, the Certosa di San Martino is an enormous monastery whose magnificent church holds a host of artistic treasures and whose beautifully restored convent contains a superb museum devoted to the city's long history. Next to it is the wonderfully renovated Castel Sant'Elmo, a formidable fortress now converted into one of Naples's foremost exhibition spaces.

The Certosa, now a museum, began life as an abbey for the Carthusian order of monks.

Both the Certosa and Castel Sant'Elmo rise above the waterfront and *centro storico* on the **Vomero** hill, once a pastoral retreat from the city but now mostly covered with modern buildings. At its heart is **Piazza Vanvitelli,** a vast space that buzzes with life and people on summer evenings. The best approach to the square and the Certosa is on the Montesanto funicular railway from Piazza Montesanto to Via Alessandro Scarlatti just north of the castle and monastery (three of the city's four funiculars climb the Vomero hill; see sidebar p. 65).

The monastery was founded in 1325 by the Carthusian order, whose religious houses are known as Charterhouses in English, or *certose* in Italian. It was greatly altered in the 16th and 17th centuries, but it fell into disrepair until shortly after World War II. The last 50 years have seen a long period of renovation for the monastery that has only recently restored the building to its considerable former glory.

Today, the monastery complex is beautiful in its own right, especially its church and cloisters, but is made doubly alluring by the wonderfully varied exhibits in the 90 rooms of the **Museo Nazionale di San Martino.** Note that the ticket to this museum will also grant you access to the church and Castel Sant'Elmo, though additional charges may apply at the latter during major exhibitions.

The Church

Off the monastery's stunning **Cortile Monumentale,** or Great Cloister, is the Certosa's main church, whose 17th-century facade, with its few fragments of an earlier Gothic frontage, conceals a glorious baroque interior filled with paintings and sculptures from some of Naples's finest 17th- and 18th-century artists. Most of these works were commissioned over the centuries by the Certosa's wealthy priors or their benefactors.

Inside the church, the remarkable "Ascension of Christ" (1637–1640), a painting by Giovanni Lanfranco, dominates the magnificent vaulted ceiling. Behind you, the church's entrance wall holds the "Deposition" (1638), a masterpiece by artist Massimo Stanzione. To either side are portraits of Moses and Elias by Giuseppe Ribera, who was also responsible for the paintings of the prophets (1638–1643) above the church's chapels.

These chapels and other side rooms contain other Neapolitan masterpieces, including statues by Giuseppe Sammartino (1720–1793) in the fourth chapel on the right. In the chapel across the nave (fourth on the left) are three canvases by Francesco de Mura (1696–1782) and frescoes (1623–1626) on the life of the Virgin by Battista Caracciolo. The choir and wall behind the high altar have a Nativity (1642) by Guido Reni, the "Communion of the Apostles" (1651) by Ribera, and Caracciolo's "Washing of Feet" (1622).

INSIDER TIP:

Naples's western hills are the perfect vantage point from which to photograph Vesuvius looming over the bay.

—PATRICIA DANIELS
National Geographic Books editor

The sacristy has some lovely *intarsia* (inlaid wood), including 56 walnut panels depicting biblical scenes, while beyond the sacristy's antechamber the **Cappella del Tesoro** (treasury) contains Ribera's "Deposition" above the high altar and a ceiling fresco of "The Triumph of Judith" (1704), the last work of Luca Giordano. Also be sure to see Caracciolo's paintings in the chapter room and *parlatorio,* where the monks talked with visitors—from the verb *parlare,* hence the English word "parlor."

Certosa di San Martino

- **A** Map p. 45
- ✉ Largo San Martino 5
- ☎ 081 229 4589
- 🕐 Closed Wed.
- 💲 $$

The Art of the Cameo

Cameos are tiny bas-reliefs, usually made of two layered materials, one light, one dark. The lighter layer is carved to reveal the cameo's figure—often a portrait in profile—atop the darker layer. Cameos were popular in Roman times, and it was the discovery of Roman cameos at Pompeii that reawakened interest in the art across Europe in the 19th century.

They have long been a Neapolitan tradition, thanks to the abundance of local coral and lava, both of which are beautifully colored and easily carved. Many shops in Naples, and in the region, sell cameos, but most are of poor quality. A notable exception is De Paolo (Via Annibale Caccavello 67, tel 081 578 2910) in the Vomero district.

The Museum

The Certosa's museum occupies numerous rooms and salons around the Chiostro Grande and smaller Chiostro dei Procuratori. Start with the *pinacoteca,* or picture gallery, which is mostly laid out on two floors in the rooms of the former Quarto del Priore (Prior's Apartments).

The paintings here reflect the vast patronage available to the monastery over several centuries, with works of art by most of Naples's leading 17th- and 18th-century artists. Look in particular for pictures of Sts. Sebastian and Jerome by Ribera, Lanfranco's "Our Lady of the Rosary," and Stanzione's "Baptism of Christ." Also note Spadaro's ceiling frescoes in **Rooms 14** and **15.** Their central landscape depicts the still empty San Martino hill on which the Certosa would later be built.

Subsequent rooms in the museum's north and east wings hold many more fascinating images, maps, and paintings of old Naples, including the delightful Tavola Strozzi in **Room 32,** an anonymous work portraying the return of the Aragonese fleet

and with a depiction of Naples as it appeared in the 15th century. Equally captivating is Didier Barra's "Bird's-Eye View of Naples," painted in 1647.

Many other rooms are devoted to the decorative arts, their exhibits the fruits of numerous private bequests to the monastery over the years. Among the varied pieces are ceramics, medals, coins, arms, armor, corals, ivories, precious stones, and some exquisite porcelain and glassware, the last displayed in the monastery's former pharmacy. Other rooms delve into Naples's musical and theatrical past, with displays, among other things, devoted to the San Carlo opera house.

Most people, however—certainly most Neapolitans—are drawn to the famous collection of *presepi* (Christmas crèches), and in particular the Cuciniello crèche, a charming work that features the figures of 180 shepherds, 10 horses, 8 dogs, and 309 miscellaneous objects. The large, eye-catching painting in the refectory near the collection of presepi is "The Wedding at Cana" (1724) by Nicola Malinconico.

Some areas of the museum may be closed, notably the **Museo dell'Opera,** which contains displays related to the construction of and alterations to the Certosa over the centuries. Usually open, however, and an essential part of any visit, are the monastery's well-tended gardens, ranged on three tiers. One is devoted to the monks' vineyards (the grapes are still harvested), the second to the priors' vegetable garden, and the last to a garden for medicinal plants. Over and above the contents, however, is the majestic view the gardens offer of the city below.

Castel Sant'Elmo

The vast bulk of the Castel Sant'Elmo looms over western Naples, a deliberately intimidating expression of the power cultivated by the city's various rulers for more than 700 years. For much of the 19th century the castle was used as a prison, its dour associations and historical connotations making it a place avoided by most Neapolitans until recently.

Built between 1329 and 1343 for the Angevin monarchs, the castle was converted into its present six-pointed star (using stone excavated from the moat) by Naples's Spanish viceroys in the 16th century. Its function was to discourage popular revolt among Naples's habitually discontented population. It probably takes its name from the tenth-century church of St. Erasmus that once stood on the site, Erasmus having been corrupted over the centuries

to Elmo. An earlier Norman watchtower was also incorporated into the 14th-century fortress.

Today, the well-restored castle is one of Naples's leading cultural spaces and hosts many major exhibitions. Whether you come to see one of these shows or merely to admire the castle, be sure take the elevator to the top floor, the **Piazza d'Armi:** The glorious 360-degree view is one of the best in the city. ■

Castel Sant'Elmo
- Map p. 45
- Via Tito Angelini 20
- 081 578 4030
- Closed Wed.
- $ (separate fee for exhibitions)

The Castel Sant'Elmo fortress has dominated the Neapolitan skyline for almost 700 years.

Pizzas & Pizzerias

Let's not argue about whether Naples invented the pizza. Let's just say it's true, and that some time after the arrival of the tomato from the New World, Neapolitan street stalls were selling baked and leavened dough covered with garlic, oil, tomato, and cheese and that the cult—for it is a cult—of the pizza was born.

Loading pizza into a wood-burning oven

A quarter of all restaurants in Italy, they say, are pizzerias, making an estimated seven million pizzas a day. And some of the best, of course, are in Naples. The first may have been the Antica Pizzeria Port'Alba, which opened in 1830. Before that, pizzas had been made at street stands, where they were bought by itinerant salesmen who then hawked slices around the streets in small metal boxes or on *tavolini* (wooden boards).

This custom persisted until recently. There are still *pizza a taglio* (cut pizza) outlets in Naples and across Italy. Indeed, the idea of a pizzeria as a place to sit down and eat is relatively recent.

Many Neapolitans order pizzas to go, folded *a fazzoletto* (like a handkerchief).

The earliest pizzas were simple, this being the food of the poor—just dough with a little oil and garlic. Others were lumps of bread studded with off-cuts of meat or other leftovers and then fried (fried pizza is still occasionally available in Neapolitan pizzerias).

The arrival of the tomato brought with it the first of Naples's two classic pizzas, the *marinara* (tomato, oregano, oil, and garlic). The second, the *margherita*, came in 1889, when master *pizzaiolo* (pizzamaker) Raffaele Esposito was called to make a pizza for the visit to Naples of the

Italian king Umberto I and his queen, Margherita. Of the three pizzas offered for royal delectation, the queen chose the most patriotic—the one with the colors of the Italian flag: red (tomato), white (mozzarella), and green (basil).

Esposito hailed from the Pietro Il Pizzaiolo pizzeria, still in existence, but today known as **Pizzeria Brandi** *(Salita Sant'Anna di Palazzo 1, tel 081 416 928, www.brandi.it)*. It is a little touristy now, certainly, but still a touchstone for classic Neapolitan pizza.

Other landmark pizzerias include **Da Michele** *(Via Sersale 1/3, tel 081 553 9204, closed Sun. Oct.–Aug.)*, which sells only the marinara and margherita and has been in business since 1870. President Bill Clinton stopped at **Di Matteo** *(Via dei Tribunali 94, tel 081 455 262, closed Sun.)* for two "American" pizzas (onion, hot sausage, and French fries) during the 1994 G7 summit.

Trianon da Ciro *(Via Pietro Colletta 46, tel 081 553 9426)* has been going since 1935, while **Cafasso** *(Via Giulio Cesare 156, tel 081 239 5281, closed Sun.)* is the purists' favorite. **Borgo Orefici** *(Via Luigi Palmieri 13, tel 081 552 0996, closed Sun.)* is another authentic spot, as is **Pellone al Vasto** *(Via Nazionale 93, tel 081 553 8614, closed Sun., no credit cards)*, near the main railroad station, with long lines in the evenings.

And the secrets of a classic pizza? The best ingredients (it goes without saying); a natural

The classic pizza margherita

yeast starter, known as *o'criscito* or the "mother"; dough that has been allowed to rise and ferment for between 8 and 36 hours; a wood-fired oven; and extremely high baking temperatures (around 750°F/400°C), so that the pizza is cooked quickly (any longer than 90 seconds and the dough starts to harden).

And the confirmation you're eating the real thing, beyond a soft, airy crust (lightly crisp at the edge) and a hint of wheat, yeast, and wood ash? Irregular air bubbles in the crust. If there aren't any, or the dough has a uniform, cakelike texture, then either an industrial or incorrect yeast has been used, the dough has not had ample time to rise, or the pizza has been rolled, not tossed—an abomination in Neapolitan eyes.

EXPERIENCE: Street Food

Street and traditional food is a vital part of the Naples eating experience. Some of the best old-style takeout food, including pizza, can be obtained from **Timpani e Tempura** *(Vico della Quercia 17, tel 081 551 2280, www.timpanietempura.it, closed Sun. D)*, **Giuliano** *(Calata Trinità Maggiore 33, tel 081 551 0986, closed Sun.)*, **Friggitoria Vomero** *(Via Domenico Cimarosa 44, tel 081 578 3130, closed Sun. & Aug.)*, and **Fiorenzano** *(Via Ninna 1–3/*

Piazza Montesanto 6, tel 081 551 2788, closed Sun.). The last two are especially known for their fried, roasted, and other snacks.

Other good traditional pizzerias include **Antonio e Antonio** *(Via Partenope 24)*, **Capasso** *(Porta San Gennaro 2, closed Tues.)*, **Da Esterna** *(Via dei Tribunali 35, closed Sun.)*, and **Lombardi a Santa Chiara** *(Via Benedetto Croce 59, closed Mon.)*.

Palazzo Reale di Capodimonte

The Palazzo Reale (Royal Palace) is Naples's most dazzling palace, a sumptuous retreat built for the Bourbon kings on the northern outskirts of the old city. Inside, spread over more than a hundred beautifully decorated rooms, is one of Italy's most important collections of paintings, sculptures, and decorative arts.

Capodimonte began life in 1738 as a hunting lodge.

When Bourbon king Charles III began work on Capodimonte in 1738, the plan was for no more than the most splendid hunting lodge in Europe. Yet it would be 20 years before the first rooms were ready and exactly a century before the project was completely finished. By this time the hunting lodge had become one of the most lavish palaces in Europe, a vast royal residence set amid sweeping grounds that rivaled even Versailles, the great palace of the French kings outside Paris.

One reason for the palace's expansion over a century was Charles's acquisition of the so-called Farnese collection, a mouthwatering array of paintings and sculptures he inherited from his mother, Elisabetta Farnese. One of Italy's grandest dynasties, the Farnese family had accumulated the collection over three centuries.

Most of the bequest, which included works from virtually all the leading European medieval and Renaissance painters and sculptors, was installed in the palace by 1759. In the years that followed, it was complemented by acquisitions made by later Bourbon monarchs, as well as by collections of arms, armor, porcelain, and other decorative arts. The collection eventually passed to the state and was opened to the public as the **Museo Nazionale di Capodimonte** in 1957.

The museum is one of Italy's finest—even better since recent restoration—and on a par with the Uffizi in Florence and the Accademia in Venice. It is also very large and, as such, properly requires a couple of days to do it justice. A morning or so will suffice, however, if you wish only to see the principal paintings and sculptures, most of which have commentaries in English.

You should also leave time to visit the lovely grounds, which can be entered for free and seen separately from the museum. The palace lies to the north of the old city, too far to walk comfortably, so take a cab or one of the many buses that run here from Piazza Dante and elsewhere. Note that it is convenient to combine a trip to the palace with a visit to the nearby Catacombe di San Gennaro (see p. 61).

Farnese Collection

Over several centuries the Farnese dynasty numbered popes and countless wealthy and powerful individuals, many of whom proved intelligent and avaricious collectors and became

patrons of some of Italy's finest painters and sculptors. By the time hereditary chance brought the collection to Naples, it amounted to approximately 200 works by the greatest names in the European canon—Raphael, Botticelli, Titian, Bellini, El Greco, Brueghel, and many more.

The museum displays much of the collection intact in 30 rooms on the first of the palace's two upper floors. It starts with **Room 2,** devoted to the Farnese themselves, including portraits of Cardinal Alessandro Farnese, the future Pope Paul III, attributed to Raphael (painted 1506–1511) and Titian (1545–1546). Alessandro became a cardinal at 14. Also here are Titian's celebrated portraits of Alessandro as Paul III and in the company of his nephews, Ottavio and Alessandro.

INSIDER TIP:

Take in the large, peaceful park around the palace; Neapolitans enjoy it particularly on weekends in good weather.

—TINO SORIANO
National Geographic photographer

Room 3 has a Crucifixion by Masaccio, one of the great innovators of the Florentine Renaissance, part of a polyptych (1426) later dismembered. **Room 4** features a cartoon by Michelangelo of a group of soldiers (1546), a preparatory sketch for a work now

Palazzo Reale di Capodimonte

- ⚠ Map p. 45
- ✉ Via Miano 2
- ☎ 081 749 9111 or 081 749 9109
- 🕒 Museum closed Wed.
- 💲 Museum $$$, park free

www.museocapodimonte.it

Neapolitan Painting

The 44 rooms on the palace's second floor (American third) contain paintings of which any world capital would be proud, but which in the context of the Farnese collection are often overlooked. United by a single theme, the paintings reflect the art of Neapolitan painters and artists drawn to Naples to work from the 13th to 19th centuries. Many were brought here after Napoleon suppressed the city's monasteries. Others were bought, donated, or brought here for conservation or security reasons from Naples's churches and palaces.

The earliest is a Byzantine-style Madonna (1290) by an unknown Campanian artist in Room 63. The most celebrated is "St. Louis of Toulouse Crowning Robert of Anjou" (1317), a painting created for the church of San Lorenzo Maggiore by the Tuscan artist Simone Martini (Room 66). Equally prized are Caravaggio's great "Flagellation" (1607) in Room 78 and Artemisia Gentileschi's "Judith and Holofernes" (1612–1613) in Room 87. Also represented are Giotto, Sodoma, Titian, and Vasari.

Other areas of the museum have galleries of contemporary art and photography associated with the city, including Andy Warhol's "Vesuvius" (1985).

in the Vatican in Rome. Also here is a similar preparatory cartoon by Raphael of "Moses before the Burning Bush" (1514), again for a work now in the Vatican.

Room 5 has two panels by Masolino (1428), commissioned by Pope Martin V. **Room 6** continues the connection with Tuscan and Umbrian Renaissance painters, containing works by leading lights such as Botticelli, Perugino, Luca Signorelli, and Filippino Lippi.

Artists of the Venetian Renaissance make their appearance in **Room 8.** They include Giovanni Bellini and his "Transfiguration" (1478–1479), one of the masterpieces of this most sublime of painters. Almost as lovely is Andrea Mantegna's early 15th-century portrait of Francesco Gonzaga, alongside works by other leading painters from Venice and the Veneto region.

Room 9 introduces paintings from Rome (notably by Giulio Romano and Sebastiano del Piombo) and **Room 10** displays canvases by leading Tuscan mannerist painters, such as Iacopo Pontormo's "Scene of Sacrifice" (1540) and Rosso Fiorentino's "Young Man" (1527).

Room 11 contains one of the great Italian masterpieces, Titian's ambiguous and seductive "Danaë" (1544–1546), painted for the private chambers of Cardinal Alessandro Farnese. The princess in the painting is probably a portrait of Alessandro's young mistress. The same young lover may be portrayed in Titian's portrait of a young lady (1545–1546) nearby, though other critics maintain the model was the painter's daughter, Lavinia.

The Farnese family had its roots in Lombardy and Emilia-Romagna (notably Parma and Ferrara), which explains the disproportionately large number of paintings by artists from these two northern Italian regions. Thus **Room 12** has several works by one of the area's leading 16th-century lights, Coreggio, and **Rooms 19, 20, 21,** and **22** are devoted to the art of the Bolognese painters Annibale and Agostino Carracci and their followers and contemporaries.

Subsequent rooms introduce miscellaneous precious objets d'art and works by Flemish masters such as Van Dyck, Pieter Paul Rubens, and Pieter Bruegel the Younger.

Royal Apartments

The floor with the Farnese collection also contains many of the palace's royal apartments, another 30 or so rooms showcasing an outstanding range of European decorative arts. Paintings, furniture, and other treasures come in a cascade, with porcelain a highlight, the result of Charles III's obsession with this and other ceramics.

Within a year of starting Capodimonte, the king had created the Reale Fabbrica della Porcellane (Royal Porcelain Factory) on the palace grounds; it is still there as a craft school. The Capodimonte ware made there and elsewhere became renowned across Europe. Some of the finest items are displayed in **Rooms 35–36**, notably the Servizio dell'Oca, a 300-piece dinner service commissioned by Ferdinand IV in 1793. There are also examples of porcelain and other ceramics from Meissen, Vienna, and Sèvres.

Other highlights among the many extravagantly appointed rooms are the Sala da Pranzo, or dining room **(Room 37)**; Salone delle Feste, or ballroom **(Room 42)**; the armory **(Rooms 46–51)**; and the queen's chamber, or Salottino di Porcellana **(Room 52)**, lined with 3,000 pieces of Capodimonte porcelain. ■

Rooms in the royal apartments are filled with a rich collection of paintings and valuable antiques.

More Places to Visit in Naples

Castel Dell'Ovo

The third of Naples's castles, after the Castel Nuovo and Castel Sant'Elmo, the Castel dell'Ovo (1154) dates from the city's period of Norman domination, though its prominent island also held a Roman (and probably a Greek) outpost. The Roman writer Virgil is said to have stayed on the island and buried an egg (*ovo* or *uova*) here, the legend being that should the egg break, then disaster would ensue. In fact, the castle's name probably derives from its egg shape or from *lowe,* German for lion—after the emblem of the 13th-century Swabian (German) Frederick II, whose troops were garrisoned here. You can cross the bridge and wander up to and around the ramparts, but much of the interior is made up of offices or is undergoing restoration.

⛰ Map p. 45 ✉ Via Partenope
☎ 081 240 0055

San Giovanni a Carbonara

A church begun in 1343 atop a spectacular flight of steps, San Giovanni was partly intended as a mausoleum for the city's Angevin rulers. Were it not slightly outlying, it would be more visited, for it contains some of the city's finest tombs. The best is that of King Ladislas (1428) behind the high altar, 63 feet (19 m) high and the work of Marco and Andrea da Firenze. The latter also worked on the unfinished tomb of Sergianni Caracciolo in the round Cappella Caracciolo del Sole (1427) behind the altar.

⛰ Map p. 45 ✉ Via Carbonara 5
☎ 081 295 873 🕐 Closed p.m. daily & Sun.

The Waterfront

Naples's often ugly waterfront east of the Castell dell'Ovo has barely recovered from being bombed in 1943. A visit should be paid, however, to the wonderful street market *(closed p.m. daily & Sun.)* that fills Vico Sopramuro (which runs south off Piazza G. Garibaldi) and to the church of **Santa Maria del Carmine** at its southern end *(Piazza del Carmine 2, tel 081 201 196, closed Sun. p.m.).* With an ancient foundation, rebuilt in the 13th century, the latter is gaudily baroque in the perfect Neapolitan manner. It's also the focus of popular devotion, thanks to the hanging crucifix and the image of the Madonna della Bruna behind the main altar, both associated with miraculous events. Also see the nearby 13th-century church of **Sant'Eligio** *(Via Sant'Eligio)* and little **San Giovanni a Mare** *(Via San Giovanni Maggiore 8)* a few steps farther west. The latter is Naples's only surviving Norman church.

⛰ Map p. 45

EXPERIENCE: Attend a Soccer Game

Soccer is a passion across Italy, and Naples is no exception. The city's main team, SSC Napoli, has had mixed fortunes over the years. Its heyday came in the 1980s, when the arrival of the Argentine maestro, Diego Maradona, led to the team winning first place in Italy's major soccer league, Serie A, in the 1986–1987 and 1989–1990 seasons. Thereafter it fell into the lower divisions, but is currently enjoying another spell of relative glory. Attending a game at the impressive 80,000-seat **San Paolo** stadium is a memorable experience—all noise, color, and excitement—with tickets from around $65 for seats on the *curva,* among the more hard-core supporters (the so-called *ultra*), to $130 for a more central grandstand seat. Buy tickets online at *www.sscnapoli.it* or from selected Lotto outlets.

Visits to Pompeii, Paestum, and Herculaneum, three of Italy's most fascinating ancient sites

Excursions from Naples

A quiet scene in Mount Vesuvius National Park

Excursions from Naples

Several historic sites are accessible from Naples, including the fine Greek temples at Paestum and the Roman towns of Pompeii and Herculaneum. Mount Vesuvius buried the latter two sites under volcanic ash in A.D. 79, leaving them superbly preserved. The volcano itself, looming over the Bay of Naples, still lures visitors to this day.

The extraordinarily well-preserved Greek temple of Neptune at Paestum was built in 450 B.C.

The region around Naples has always been favored. The Greeks founded their first Italian trading post here, at Cuma (or Cumae), north of present-day Naples, around 750 B.C. They also created, among other things, the beautifully situated temple complex at ancient Paestum, one of the greatest and best preserved in Europe.

The Romans knew the area as *campania felix*, the happy land, after its balmy climate, easy living, and agricultural riches. Among their many cities here was Capua, so important in its day that its amphitheater was the second largest in the Roman world, after the Colosseum in Rome.

Other towns were more modest, occupied primarily by the empire's patrician and mercantile elite, who built palaces, holiday homes, and retirement villas. Herculaneum was one such wealthy enclave,

while Pompeii was a larger, more workaday town nearby. Though famous now, neither town was particularly well known in its day.

Today, the Neapolitan hinterland is not such a bucolic sight. Visitors fondly imagining that Pompeii and Herculaneum sit amid unspoiled countryside are in for a shock. Neither site should be missed, but be prepared for crowds and the urban blight that spreads around Naples. This applies also to the great palace at Caserta, another key excursion, built in the 18th century by Naples's Bourbon monarchs, and to Vesuvius. The volcano's upper slopes, while free of the modern world, are frequently swarmed with visitors undeterred by the half-hour hike to the summit.

All these attractions are easily seen from Naples in a day. Paestum is 56 miles

(90 km) south of the city, and though it can be visited on a day trip, it can also be part of a more far-reaching southern itinerary.

If you have time to make more than a day's excursion from Naples, or are driving south from Paestum, consider exploring one of Italy's newest national parks. The Parco Nazionale del Cilento protects Campania's loneliest corner, a rocky knuckle of mountains and rugged coastline between Eboli in the north and Sapri in the south.

Hotels in Paestum and on nearby beaches make an overnight stay possible. Organized tours run from Naples to Pompeii and other local sights, but it's also easy to get to those locations using buses or trains, notably the Circumvesuviana railroad, which serves both Herculaneum and Pompeii from Naples.

Consider purchasing an Artecard (tel 800 600 601, www.campaniartecard.it), which comes

in several versions and offers free or reduced rates on public transportation, as well as entry to many of Campania's attractions, including Pompeii and Herculaneum. They are available at the airport, some sights, and train stations. ∎

NOT TO BE MISSED:

Remains of ancient
Herculaneum 80–83

An ascent of Vesuvius 84–85

Ruins of Pompeii, one of
Europe's finest archaeological
sites 86–92

Three great Greek temples at
Paestum 94–95

Opulent Palazzo Reale at
Caserta 96

Parco Nazionale del Cilento, a new
national park 96

Herculaneum

Two Roman towns fell prey to Vesuvius in A.D. 79—Pompeii, a thriving commercial town, and Herculaneum, an exclusive residential retreat built to exploit the site's cooling sea breezes and far-reaching views across the bay, just 8 miles (12 km) south of Naples. Like Pompeii, Herculaneum remained buried until the 18th century and is still only partially excavated. Where it differs is in its more manageable size and the ease with which it can be explored.

Herculaneum's ruins are easier to explore than those of Pompeii.

Greek settlers probably founded Herculaneum around the fourth century B.C., two or three hundred years later than Pompeii. It was a smaller city than its neighbor—with just 5,000 inhabitants as compared with Pompeii's 20,000 to 35,000—but a far wealthier one, being a small fishing port and residential retreat devoted largely to exclusive villas, with fewer of the bars, stores, brothels, and other civic structures of Pompeii.

Much remains unknown about the site, primarily because most of it remains unexcavated. Given that much is buried 80 feet (25 m) beneath the modern town of Ercolano, it will probably remain so. This is not the site's only logistical problem, for while Pompeii was buried gradually in a relatively soft accumulation of dust, ash, and *lapilli* (fragments of pumice), Herculaneum was quickly covered by a river of volcanic mud. When this sludge combined with the torrential rains that followed the eruption, it formed a conglomerate of concrete-like resistance.

This covering has made excavation difficult since 1710, when workers digging a well for an expatriate Austrian

Italian Coral

Coral is something one associates with tropical reefs rather than the Italian coast, but the waters around Naples have long been renowned for their coral, especially a vivid red variety that lends itself to jewelry and sculpture. The heart of the still-flourishing industry is Torre del Greco, just south of Ercolano—the town's inhabitants are known as *corallini*, after the trade. Brave the suburban sprawl to visit one of the area's many workshops,

notably **APA Coral & Cameo** *(Via Cavallo 6, tel 081 881 1155, www.giovanniapa.com)*, generally open daily from 8.30 a.m., with free admission. Be warned that visits here are popular with tour groups, but if you are interested in buying coral jewelry or cameos, the quality is high. Also of interest is the small **Museo del Corallo** *(Piazza Luigi Palomba 6, tel 081 881 1360)*, generally open on weekdays by appointment.

prince found the first ruins. Various amateur and piecemeal excavations then took place until 1828, unfortunately accompanied by theft and botched research. Systematic work at the site began in 1927 and continues to this day, constantly redefining scholars' understanding of the ruins.

Over the last few years, for example, over 250 skeletons and carbonized bodies have been discovered near what once would have been the harbor (the sea has since retreated). This and other discoveries have undermined the long-held theory that the town's residents had time to escape, unlike most of their Pompeian compatriots. It appears that most of Herculaneum's victims were overwhelmed by the shock wave and surge of hot and poisonous gases from Vesuvius as they waited, in vain, to be rescued by sea. The survival of the bodies, and other organic matter, was due to the inert and swift-drying character of the mud that had covered them.

Getting There

Herculaneum lies in the uninteresting suburb of Ercolano, south of central Naples, and can be reached on the Circumvesuviana railroad from the station on Naples's Corso Garibaldi. Trains leave roughly every 30 minutes, and the journey to Ercolano Scavi station takes 20 minutes. A shuttle bus from Ercolano Scavi runs to the site entrance on Corso Resina. The alternative is a dreary ten-minute walk. Entry to the site is by individual ticket, Artecard (see p. 79), or a joint ticket, valid for three days, which also can be used for Pompeii and three other archaeological sites around Naples. Parking is difficult and driving is not recommended.

The Site

Orientation is straightforward. The excavated area is arranged on a simple grid of 11 blocks, or *insulae* (islands), centered on the Decumano Inferiore and Decumano Massimo (the names given to the main streets of

Herculaneum
🗺 79 B2
Visitor Information
✉ Via IV Novembre 82
☎ 081 857 5347
🕐 Closed p.m. daily, Sun., & Sat. Nov.–March

Herculaneum Archaeological Site
✉ Entrance at Corso Resina 6
☎ 081 732 4311
💲 $$$, plus fee ($$) for audio guide. Guided tours $$$. Combined ticket with Pompeii and sites at Boscoreale and Oplontis $$$$$.
🕐 Last ticket sold 3:30 p.m. Nov.–March, 6 p.m. rest of year

www.pompeiisites.org

most Roman towns) and three cross streets known as Cardine III, IV, and V. The best preserved buildings are found on Cardine IV and V. Allow two hours for a visit and note that houses open according to a rotating schedule, so some of the buildings described below may be closed on your visit.

From the site's entrance, follow the path along the excavations' southern edge, passing the remains of the **Palestra** (Gymnasium) on your right and the **Piscina** (Pool) on your left. Continue, as the route curves to the right, to reach what would have been the original waterfront, now the location of a tunnel that leads to the ancient town proper.

The first ruins are those of the **Terme Suburbane** (Surburban Baths), some of Europe's best preserved Roman baths. These are followed by

the elegant, two-story **Casa dei Cervi,** or House of the Stags (on Insula IV, Cardine V), named after the two sculptures of deer being attacked by hunting dogs (the statues are copies). In its day, this house, the most imposing of any on the site, would have possessed a prized seafront location, hence its generous terraces and rich decoration.

Farther down Cardine V on the left, near the junction with the Decumano Inferiore, stands the **Taberna di Priapo** (Priapus's Tavern), complete with a waiting room and private inner chambers. To its right, on the corner, is a grain shop or **Thermopolium** (fast-food outlet), identified by its marble counter and amphorae. Snacks here might have included chickpea soup, pork stewed in grape juice, and *mulsum,* an omelette-like dish flavored with onions and wine.

Almost opposite the Thermopolia, two columns mark the entrance to the partially buried Palestra, the venue for wrestling and other games. It is home to two pools, one of which has a copy of its original bronze fountain, while the other preserves inlets and amphorae probably used for fish farming. Farther down Cardine V on the right is a bakery, or **Pistrinum,** still with its oven and flour mills.

Cardine IV

Some of the site's most impressive remains stand at opposite ends of the Cardine

Part of a Roman fountain at Herculaneum. Entire streets were preserved under the debris from Vesuvius.

IV to the north. At the eastern end on its south side is the **Casa di Nettuno e Anfitrite,** named, like most houses at Herculaneum, after the chief archaeological treasure found at the location. In this case the find is a beautiful mosaic (the best on the site) portraying Neptune and Amphitrite in the nyphaeum (bath and fountain) at the rear of the house.

Across the street are the remains of the **Terme del Foro** (Forum Baths). Note the pipes, heating vents, separate sections for men and women, mosaics of marine life, and the shelves in the *apodyteria* area, used for depositing togas.

At the end of the street, turn right on the Decumano Massimo and take a few steps down to the **Casa del Bicentinario,** a patrician house whose scratched crosses in the upstairs rooms, perhaps used by servants or tenants, suggest early Christian occupation.

Returning to Cardine IV, walk west. Beyond the junction with the Decumano Inferiore on the right is the two-story **Casa del Tramezzo di Legno** (House of the Wooden Partition), with an intact wooden porch. The house takes its name from the carbonized wooden screen that separates the main atrium from the small *tablinum,* or office, where the house's owner would have conducted business with clients.

Almost next door is the **Casa a Graticcio** (House of the Latticework), a rare example of one of Herculaneum's poorer houses. Toward Cardine IV's western end on the left stands the **Casa dell'Atrio e Mosaico,** distinguished by its ravishing wall mosaics and store, still with goods on the counter.

INSIDER TIP:

Take the train and visit Herculaneum early in the morning without crowds; on the same train, you can continue to Pompeii.

—TINO SORIANO
National Geographic photographer

Outside the main site, opposite the café, is the **Villa dei Papiri** *(entry by reservation at www.arethusa.net),* built in A.D. 60, just 19 years before Vesuvius's eruption. John Paul Getty's villa-gallery above Malibu, California, was based on this building, which stretched for 820 feet (250 m) along the seafront. It takes its name from the 1,800 carbonized papyrus *(papiri)* scrolls found here in the 18th century.

For years scholars hoped that this library would yield lost masterpieces by Greek masters such as Aristotle. Most of the scrolls, however, turned out to be works by lesser poets and scholars. Note that many of the treasures originally found at the villa, including 87 statues, are now in Naples's Museo Archeologico Nazionale (see p. 51). ■

Vesuvius

Italy has higher and more active volcanoes—notably Sicily's Mount Etna—but none as notorious as Vesuvio (Vesuvius), whose catastrophic eruption in A.D. 79 famously buried and preserved the Roman towns of Pompeii and Herculaneum. Today, the volcano is dormant and can be admired by visitors as a backdrop to the Bay of Naples or from the closer proximity of the crater's edge.

Mount Vesuvius, seen from Naples, is dormant but not extinct.

People living close to Vesuvius in the first century A.D. knew all was not well with the volcano. Although the brooding peak had been dormant for generations, an earthquake in A.D. 63 had provided a worrying portent of the subterranean forces that were gathering strength.

More immediate warning was issued in the days before the catastrophe, when the volcano began to release a plume of ash, a sign at first ignored by people living in its vicinity. But Vesuvius, or Vesubius as it was then called, means "the unextinguished," and perhaps residents should have taken heed. On the morning of August 24, A.D. 79, as the cone's ancient basalt plug collapsed, the volcano more than lived up to its name.

Vesuvius, unlike the slow-smoldering Etna, erupts with sudden force. On that day in A.D. 79, gas, pumice, and other debris were released with devastating effect. Shock waves and a cloud of super-heated gas surged down the mountain, reaching speeds of 50 miles (80 km) an hour and temperatures of 750°F (400°C). A vast cloud blotted out the sun.

In Pompeii, ash and cinders buried the city within hours and superheated gases asphyxiated the 2,000 inhabitants who had not fled. By evening, the volcano's inner walls had also collapsed, unleashing further destruction, including the torrent of volcanic mud that engulfed Herculaneum.

INSIDER TIP:

Don't skip a visit to the edge of the huge, dark crater. If your guide lights a piece of paper and introduces it into a crack, thousands of rivulets of smoke will rise from the porous rock.

—ILARIA CAPUTI
National Geographic contributor

By the time the dust settled, Vesuvius was a different volcano. A large portion of the original 7,500-foot (2,300 m) summit, Monte Somma, had been blown away, the eruption having created a second cone inside the Somma crater. Today, what you see from below are the remnants of the Somma crater, now just 4,203 feet (1,281 m) high, with the new crater—650 feet (200 m) deep and 4,900 feet (1,500 m) around—inside it.

Not that Vesuvius has been idle. There have been periods of calm—very little happened between 1306 and 1631, for example—but 18 major (and many minor) eruptions have shaken the ground since A.D. 79. The last occurred in 1944, when the volcano lost its once distinctive *pennacchio*, or ashy plume. Another eruption, say the statisticians, is overdue. Some 700,000 people live in the red zone of greatest danger.

Don't hold off visiting on that account. About 200,000 people a year make the ascent, and much of the area is protected as a national park and UNESCO Biosphere Reserve. Park authorities have started to mark trails on the slopes away from the usual visitor trail to the summit. May and June are lovely times to visit, when the fertile lower slopes are in bloom. The views are sublime.

You can take an organized tour from Naples or a Circumvesuviana train to Ercolano station (15 mins.), then a cab or shuttle bus such as Vesuvio Express *(tel 800 880 007, www.vesuvioexpress.it)*, not the overpriced "private" buses touted on the street, to the park entrance, café, and visitor center *(www.vesuviopark.it)* at 3,106 feet (1,017 m). From here it is a 1-mile (1.5 km) walk and 838-foot (264 m) climb to the summit. Wear sturdy shoes and have a sweater and jacket. A fee is payable (*$$*) and a guide required. The volcano's slopes are closed in fog and other bad weather.

EXPERIENCE:
Astroni Crater

Some volcanic areas around Naples provide natural greenery that you can explore, birder's binoculars in hand. At the Campi Flegrei, or Phlegrean Fields, west of Fuorigrotta, one of the highlights is the Astroni crater near Agnano, which has a floor dotted with lakes and slopes garlanded with vegetation. The area is a World Wildlife Fund–monitored reserve, the **Riserva Naturale Cratere Degli Astroni** (*Via Agnano Astroni 468, tel 081 588 3720, www.wwf.it*), with a picnic site by the main lake, woodland trails, and observation blinds for birders.

Pompeii

But for a famous cataclysm, Pompeii (Pompei in Italian) would have been just another minor Roman colony lost to time. Instead, the town's fate—being buried by the eruption of Vesuvius in A.D. 79—was posterity's fortune, bequeathing to the world the best preserved remains from antiquity and providing an insight into the minutiae of first-century life.

A variety of public and private buildings are preserved in the ancient Roman city of Pompeii.

Pompeii
 79 B2
Visitor Information
 Via Sacra 1
 081 850 7255
🕐 Closed Sat. p.m.
    & Sun.

One of the many ironies of Pompeii is that the town was never as famous in its own day as it is in ours. The settlement probably began life as an Osci outpost in the seventh century B.C., part of a network of coastal villages belonging to this indigenous Italic tribe. A century later it became a Greek and Etruscan trading post and later fell to the Samnites, who controlled it for 200 years until they were defeated by the Romans in 290 B.C. After 80 B.C., when it attained

the status of a Roman colony, the town prospered quietly, a midsize, walled backwater covering around 160 acres (55 ha) and with a population of between 20,000 and 35,000 inhabitants. Its only other event of historical note came with an earthquake in A.D. 62, the damage from which had more or less been repaired when Vesuvius consigned the town to the ashes 17 years later.

There the site remained for more than 1,500 years, buried and forgotten. The first hints as to its existence came by accident in 1592, during the construction of a canal by architect Domenico Fontana. But the remains of the few frescoed buildings he discovered were thought to be part of Stabia, another Roman settlement, and little more happened until 1748, when the first of several haphazard excavations took place under the auspices of Charles of Bourbon, the king of Naples. Many of these excavations, however, involved cavalier work that badly compromised parts of the site, its remains, and the archaeological data that might have been recovered by more modern methods. Many treasures were also looted, and even the excavations of Giuseppe Fiorelli, who worked for the Italian government from about 1860 and uncovered most of the site, left much to be desired.

What did survive were the streets, houses, and other buildings of the Roman town, all but unaffected by the passage of time, the effects of the elements, and the pilfering of stone for building. As the diarist Henry Matthews wrote in 1820, "Nothing is wanting but the inhabitants," adding that a "morning's walk through the solemn streets of Pompeii will give you a livelier idea of their modes of life than all the books in the world."

Getting There

The Circumvesuviana railroad runs from Naples's Stazione Circumvesuviana on Corso Garibaldi (off Piazza Garibaldi) to the Pompeii–Villa dei Misteri station, next to the site's main entrance at Porta Marina. Travel time is 45 minutes. By car, take the Pompei Ovest exit on the A3 *autostrada* (expressway) and follow signs for Pompei Scavi.

Pompeii's contemporary difficulties revolve around the fact that so many people wish to enjoy this insight into the past. Up to 2.5 million visitors a year tramp through the site, compounding the problems of erosion, poor staffing, and lack of funding. The troubles reached such a point that in 2001 Pompeii was placed on a list of imperiled World Heritage sites. Since this wake-up call, things have improved slightly, but as many as 45 out of the 70 major buildings on the site may be closed at any one time for restoration or to prevent wear and tear.

What no one has been able to improve are Pompeii's surroundings, and you should be prepared for the considerable urban desecration that spoils the site's environs, not to mention the proximity of busy roads and the less-than-lovely modern town of Pompei. Depending on when you

Pompeii Archaeological Site

- Entrance at Piazza Porta Marina; also Piazza Esedra & Piazza Anfiteatro
- 081 857 5347
- Last ticket sold 3:30 p.m. Nov.–March, 6 p.m. rest of year
- $$$, audio guide

www.pompeii sites.org

www.pompei turismo.it

Private Villa Visits

Four major villas and a bath complex at Pompeii normally closed to visitors can be seen by pre-booking a visit at *www.arethusa.net*. Reservations can be made up to the day before a visit and no extra fee is payable above that paid to enter the main site. Confirmation is by email. Tours run every 30 minutes in groups up to a maximum of 15 people.

Witness to Destruction

"The falling cinders grew thicker and hotter... it was day everywhere else, but here a deeper darkness prevailed ... Vesuvius was blazing in several places, with spreading and towering flames. The common people followed us in the utmost consternation ... You could hear the shrieks of women, the crying of children, and the shouts of men; some praying to die, many lifting their hands to the gods, but the greater part imagining there were no gods left and that the last and eternal night had fallen ... Then in the gloom we beheld the sea, the water sucked back and the shore enlarged, holding many sea creatures captive on the dry sand. On the other side was a black and dreadful cloud bursting out in gusts of serpentine vapor ... Finally a watery sun appeared, the light lurid, every object in our frightened gaze changed, covered with a drift of ashes, like snow."

—Part of an eyewitness account of the A.D. 79 eruption by Roman writer Pliny the Younger, then age 17

visit, you should also be prepared for the heat—there is little shade—and come equipped with hat, sunscreen, water, and comfortable shoes. The site is large—it takes 25 minutes to walk from the amphitheater to the Villa dei Misteri at its opposite extremities—and you will need two hours for even the most superficial of visits. Concentrate first on the main sights described below, and don't become bogged down with the lesser streets, where one house looks much like another.

Afternoons are usually quieter, and off-season visits, especially in winter, the least crowded of all. Do not accept the blandishments of unlicensed guides or offers of special parking spots. Official guides, along with themed or evening guided tours, can be arranged through the Ufficio Scavi office; you will find this near the site's main entrance by the Porta Marina at the ruins' western (seaward) flank. Two-, four-, and six-hour audio-guide itineraries are also available.

The Site

Porta Marina is one of Pompeii's eight original gates, with separate entrances for pedestrians (on the left) and animals and carts (on the right). Once it was much closer to the sea, hence its name, but the coast is now some distance away. Although the gate led directly to the hub of the town, its steep approach meant that most carts probably used gates elsewhere around the walls.

Walking from the gate down Via Marina, you pass the **Tempio di Venere** (Temple of Venus) on the right. Originally this was one of the town's most sumptuous temples, but its prominent position made it subject to theft over the years. Farther down the street on the left is the **Tempio di Apollo** (Temple of Apollo), Pompeii's oldest religious building. On the right, opposite the temple, is the **Basilica,** one of the most important civic buildings. The rectangular structure accommodated the law courts, city hall, stock exchange, and other public offices.

The Basilica abuts the rectangular **Foro,** or Forum, the town's main square, with a colonnade and loggia running along three of its sides. With your back to Via Marina, the ruins of the **Tempio di Giove** (Temple of Jupiter) stand to the left, still displaying one of the temple's two triumphal arches. Jupiter was the most important god in the Roman pantheon, and it was the custom in most Roman colonies to place a temple to the deity (along with Juno and Minerva, two other leading deities) in the town's main public space.

Directly ahead of you, on the corner of the Forum and Via dell'Abbondanza, stands the **Edificio di Eumachia,** a wool factory and the headquarters of the wool and textile guild. Note the decorated portal and the small room inside on the right, whose overlapping basins were designed to collect the urine (used in the woolmaking process) of obliging passersby. In the far top left corner, between the Forum and Via degli Augustali, a three-columned portico marks the entrance to the former **Macellum,** a covered meat-and-fish market.

Exit the Forum to the left (on its north side by the café), passing the **Tempio di Augusto Fortuna** on the right and the small **Terme del Foro** (Forum Baths) on the left (on opposite corners of Via della Fortuna). Opposite the baths is the **Casa del Poeta Tragico,** best known for its famous floor mosaic of a chained dog and its accompanying warning, *Cave canem*—Beware of the dog. Turn

right on Via della Fortuna, and one block up on the left is the **Casa del Fauno** (House of the Faun), one of the site's largest and most sophisticated houses. It has two atria (inner courtyards) rather than the usual one, and it is known for the million-tesserae mosaic found here, thought to depict the 333 B.C. Battle of Issus between Alexander the Great and the Persian leader Darius III. The original (like the statue of the faun that gave the house its name) is in Naples's Museo Archeologico Nazionale (see p. 50). A project is under way to re-create the mosaic inside the house. The building also had two peristyles (porticoes running along a central courtyard) and four *triclinia* (dining rooms), one for each season.

Casa dei Vettii & Beyond

Take either of the streets off Via della Fortuna alongside the Casa

The casts of bodies captured where they fell in A.D. 79 are some of Pompeii's most compelling sights.

del Fauno and you reach the parallel Vicolo di Mercurio, where a right turn brings you quickly to the **Casa dei Vettii** (House of the Vettii). This was once the home of merchant brothers who grew rich in the wine trade, and it preserves

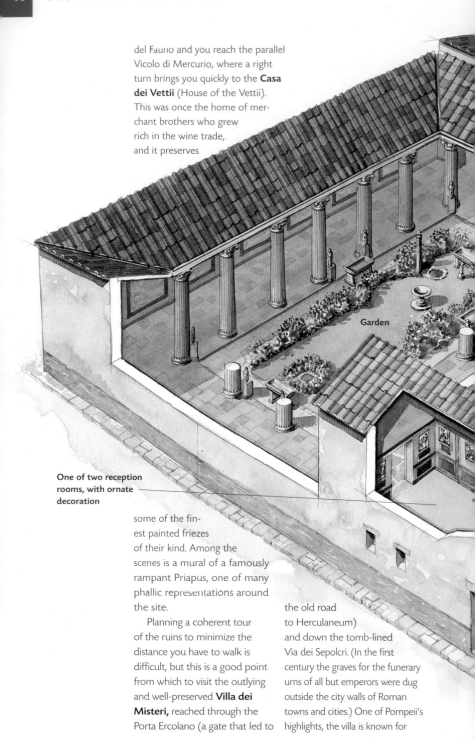

Garden

One of two reception rooms, with ornate decoration

some of the finest painted friezes of their kind. Among the scenes is a mural of a famously rampant Priapus, one of many phallic representations around the site.

Planning a coherent tour of the ruins to minimize the distance you have to walk is difficult, but this is a good point from which to visit the outlying and well-preserved **Villa dei Misteri,** reached through the Porta Ercolano (a gate that led to

the old road to Herculaneum) and down the tomb-lined Via dei Sepolcri. (In the first century the graves for the funerary urns of all but emperors were dug outside the city walls of Roman towns and cities.) One of Pompeii's highlights, the villa is known for

Casa dei Vettii (House of the Vettii)

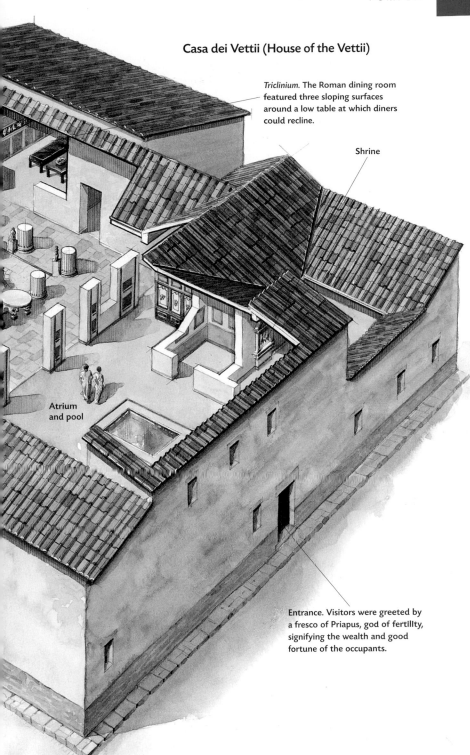

Triclinium. The Roman dining room featured three sloping surfaces around a low table at which diners could recline.

Shrine

Atrium and pool

Entrance. Visitors were greeted by a fresco of Priapus, god of fertility, signifying the wealth and good fortune of the occupants.

Oplontis

Oplontis (Oplonti in Italian) is the third of the main archaeological sites south of Naples *(Via Sepolcri, 081 862 1755, www .pompeiisites.org, $$; entry also by Artecard or combined ticket with Pompeii and Herculaneum),* **and though in a run-down area, offers an intimate and pleasing antidote to Pompeii and Herculaneum. A first-century villa, it may have belonged to Sabina Poppaea, second wife of the Emperor Nero, and is celebrated for its superb frescoes. Visit by cab from Pompeii or take the Circumvesuviana railroad to the nearby Torre Annunziata station.**

its magnificent *triclinium* (dining room) fresco cycle, one of the largest surviving from the ancient world. It is thought to depict a young girl—probably a bride—being initiated into the mysteries *(misteri)* of the Dionysian cult.

Walk back to the Forum and take Via dell'Abbondanza, ancient Pompeii's main street, whose range of stores, bars, houses, and other remains provides a multifaceted glimpse of Roman life. The stores are recognizable by their broad facades (for ease of public access), while private homes had narrower and more secure entrances. Taverns would have had large pots to store wine; circular cavities cut into the marble bars to keep drinks cool are still visible.

At Via dell'Abbondanza's second major junction, turn left on Vicolo del Lupanare (Street of the Brothel) to see the **Lupanare Africani et Victoris** on the corner of Via del Balcone Pensile, one of the city's 24 official brothels. Frescoes above each doorway illustrated the specialty of the woman working

there. Also on view are 120 pieces of graffiti etched into the walls by clients. Prostitution was part of everyday life, without stigma in the Roman world of the time.

Return to Via dell'Abbondanza and cross over onto Via dei Teatri. Entering the Triangular Forum, you will find your way to the **Teatro Grande** (left), a 5,000-seat open-air theater, and the 800-seat **Teatro Piccolo,** or Odeon, the name given to a smaller covered theater. On Via dell'Abbondanza, beyond the corner with Vicolo del Lupanare on the left, stretch the ruins of the **Terme Stabiane,** the town's main bath complex. Several of Pompeii's famous body casts are here. Also look for the textile workshop of **Verecundus** (Nos. 5–7) and the **Fullonica Stephani** opposite, a laundry. Two blocks down is a *thermopolium,* one of the town's 89 takeout food kiosks.

Moving down Via dell'Abbondanza, a right turn takes you to the **Casa del Menandro,** another outstanding patrician house adorned with mosaics and wall paintings. Note that you may need a numbered voucher from the Ufficio Scavi for timed entry to this house. Back to Via dell'Abbondanza, two more fine houses, both with beautiful gardens, are on the right toward the end of the street: the **Casa di Loretius Tiburtinus** (also called di Ottavio Quartione) and the **Villa di Giulia Felice.** Closing the eastern end of the site is the 20,000-seat **Anfiteatro,** one of the oldest and best preserved Roman amphitheaters in existence. ∎

EXPERIENCE: Touring Pompeii & Herculaneum

Pompeii and Herculaneum are large and complicated sites, and you can add to your experience of both by joining a small, private tour. Not only will you enjoy a more relaxed trip—the tour operator will usually arrange ticketing—but guides, often experts in their field, will furnish you with more in-depth historical information on the sites. The most straightforward tours are half- and full-day excursions from Naples, where there is a vast choice of companies, many incorporating both sites, along with Vesuvius or other archaeological sites.

If you choose an excursion, your hotel concierge can advise on the best local companies, but be aware that you will often be in large bus-tour groups. Some smaller companies can arrange hotel pickups, or will meet you off a cruise ship or at Naples's main railroad station. You can book such trips online through **Viator** *(www .viator.com)*, with three-hour tours *(starting at 10:30 a.m)*, including hotel pickup and drop-off.

If you prefer a private tour, contact the locally-based **Tredytours** *(Via Cristoforo Colombo 106, Meta, Naples, tel 081 534 1600, www.tredytours.com)*, which can provide guides, transportation, hotel or cruise-ship pick-ups, and a variety of tours to Pompeii and/or Herculaneum.

Multiday Tours

Many tour operators outside Italy offer cultural itineraries that include Pompeii as part of a longer tour of the country, but relatively few offer more specialized tours that allow more time at both sites and place them more firmly in a local context.

Two that do just that are the highly regarded U.K.-based **Martin Randall** **Travel** *(tel 44 [0] 20 8742 3355, www.martinrandall.com)* and **Ace Study Tours** *(tel 44 [0] 1223 835 055, www. acestudytours.co.uk)*. Both are dedicated cultural and educational tour operators with expert lecturers and small group sizes.

Sites Visited

Martin Randall Travel offers a six-day "Pompeii & Herculaneum" tour, based in Vico Equense, including a full-day tour of Pompeii and Paestum; a day at Herculaneum and in Naples's Museo Archeologico Nazionale; and a day exploring lesser known sites in the Bay of Naples.

Ace Study Tours offers two similar six-day tours annually in spring and fall, with full-day visits to Pompeii and Herculaneum, along with days devoted to Naples and particularly to the Museo Nazionale Archeologico, as well as Paestum, and the minor sites at Cumae, Pozzuoli, and elsewhere. The tour includes a visit to Velia, a former Greek colony that includes both classical and medieval buildings.

A spa from Pompeii looks ready for business.

Paestum

"Inexpressibly grand," wrote the poet Shelley of Paestum, southern Italy's most evocative and romantic archaeological ensemble. Center stage at the site goes to three almost perfectly preserved Doric temples, widely considered the greatest in the ancient Greek world—finer even than those of Greece itself. Much of Paestum's charm, however, derives from its flower-filled meadows and the rural beauty of its tranquil setting.

The remains of the Tempio di Cerere (Temple of Ceres), dedicated to Athena

Paestum

🄰 79 C1

Visitor Information

✉ Via Magna Grecia 165

☎ 082 881 1016

www.infopaestum.it

Paestum began its life as Poseidonia, the city of Poseidon, a colony founded by Greeks in the sixth century B.C. Absorbed by Romans in 273 B.C., when it took its present name, it was almost completely abandoned because of malaria and a devastating Saracen raid in A.D. 877. It then lay hidden amid the undergrowth for hundreds of years until its discovery during road construction in the 18th century, when excavations brought its magnificent temples and other ruins to light again.

Paestum is about 55 miles (90 km) south of Naples. By car, follow the S18 south of Salerno. Only local trains from Napoli Centrale stop here, via Salerno. There are also frequent buses that run from Salerno's Piazza Concordia.

The grandest and best preserved of the temples is the **Tempio di Nettuno,** or Temple of Neptune (fifth century B.C.). The temple's entablature and pediments have survived nearly intact, but the roof is missing. Almost alongside it stands the **Tempio di Hera,** the earliest of the temples, also known as the Basilica after being wrongly identified by 18th-century archaeologists.

In a more isolated position, at the site's northern extreme, stands the **Tempio di Cerere** (Temple of Ceres), a structure actually dedicated to the Greek goddess Athena and probably built sometime between the construction of its two neighbors.

Paestum's other Greek and later Roman remains are less striking, but it is still well worth exploring the site simply to soak up the atmosphere. For a good overall picture of the area, you could walk the line of the colony's former walls, a distance of just over 2 miles (3 km).

Tomb of the Diver

Also be sure to visit the **Museo Nazionale,** a museum of finds from the site located to the east of the temples (*tickets for the temples also valid for museum*). Its most treasured exhibits are the wall paintings of the Tomb of the Diver (480 B.C.). These pictures may be the only surviving examples of Greek mural painting from this period. The pictures—five in all—originally formed part of a coffin: Four of them show

scenes of a funeral banquet and the songs, games, musicians, and companions that would accompany the deceased in his journey into the next world.

The fifth panel, which probably formed the coffin's lid, is the most famous of the wall paintings and shows a naked diver—hence the tomb's name—diving into a blue sea. The scene may represent an unusual allegory of the passage from life to death.

Paestum Festivals

The wide-ranging summer Paestum Festival of music, dance, and other performing arts was founded in 1989, and despite having lapsed in the last decade has recently been resurrected. Visit *www.festivaldipaestum.it* for dates and program. And artichoke lovers can feast on a local speciality during a spring festival; visit *www.festadelcarciofo.it.*

Paestum by Night

In past summers it has been possible for visitors to the site to join nocturnal tours ("Passeggiate Notturne tra i Templi") of Paestum's temples (*generally twice nightly Aug.*), enjoying the magical sight of the floodlit ruins at close hand. These tours do not take place every year, so contact the visitor center for the latest details. ∎

Zona Archeologica
- ✉ Via Magna Grecia 913
- ☎ 082 872 2654
- 🕐 Open 8:45 a.m. –1 hour before sunset. Last admission 2 hours before sunset
- 💲 Archaeological area $$, audio guide $$

Museo Nazionale
- ✉ Zona Archeologica
- ☎ 082 872 1113
- 🕐 Closed 1st & 3rd Mon. each month
- 💲 $$

More Places to Visit around Naples

Caserta

It's a dour journey through Naples's suburbs, but Caserta, 12 miles (20 km) north of the city, is worth the trip. The town was an insignificant backwater until 1752, when Charles III, Naples's first Bourbon king, began what would become one of Europe's grandest royal residences. Charles commissioned architect Luigi Vanvitelli to create a building that would rival Versailles and more or less succeeded, for the Reggia, or **Palazzo Reale** (Via Douet 22, tel 082 327 7380, www.reggiadicaserta.altervista.org, closed Tues., palace $$$, park $, combined ticket $$$),

---

EXPERIENCE:
Discover Underwater Ruins

From the port at Baia, 12 miles (19 km) west of Naples, take a glass-bottomed boat (tel 349 497 4183, www.baiasom mersa.it for reservations, tours Sat. & Sun. April–Sept. 10 a.m., 12 p.m., 3 p.m., $$$) to view the **Parco Sommersa di Baia,** the submerged ruins of a former Roman colony. Scuba-diving tours of the ruins can also be arranged.

---

has five stories, 43 staircases, 1,790 windows, and 1,200 rooms, all arranged around four monumental courtyards. The extensive gardens are equally dazzling. You could easily spend a day touring the palace and visiting nearby Casertavecchia and Santa Maria Capua Vetere (see right). Buses run regularly from Naples's Piazza Garibaldi and trains from the city's Stazione Centrale. Travel time is 30 minutes; the palace is a five-minute walk from Caserta's railroad station.

Map 79 B3   ☒ **Visitor Information** Piazza Dante 43   ☎ 082 332 1137, www.eptcaserta.it

Around Caserta

Picturesque **Casertavecchia** (Old Caserta), just northeast of the modern town, is worth a short visit if you have time, primarily for its 12th-century cathedral, **San Michele Archangelo,** one of the finest Romanesque churches in the region. From Caserta Vecchia, the SS87 curves west toward Capua, passing close to another fine church, **Sant'Angelo in Formis** (tel 082 399 8891, by appt.), built in 1073 and adorned with frescoes. If the church doesn't appeal, take a cab or the train one stop west to **Santa Maria Capua Vetere,** inhabited since at least the ninth century B.C. In its day this was one of the most important cities in the Roman Empire. The Via Appia, the great road from Rome, was built in 312 B.C. to link the capital with Capua. The city had the empire's second largest **amphitheater** (Piazza 1 Ottobre, tel 082 379 8864, closed Mon., $) after the Colosseum, and parts of it survive to this day. The entrance ticket also gives admission to a **Mithraic temple** (Via Morelli) and the **Museo Antica Capua** (Via Roberto d'Angio 45, tel 082 384 4206, closed Mon., $), with archaeological finds.
Map 79 B3

Il Cilento

If you would like to take a little more time to explore some of the wilder territory south of Naples, consider a visit to one of Italy's most recent national parks. The **Parco Nazionale del Cilento** inhabits a portion of Campania between Eboli and Sapri. The best coastal landscapes are around Punta degli Infreschi near Palinuro in the south, while the finest hiking is in the small but dramatic Alburni mountain range to the north. The limestone region also contains many caves, with the best open to the public close to Pertosa and Castelcivita.
Map 79 B3   ☎ www.parks.it

Some of the most beautiful landscapes in Europe: the Costa Amalfitana, or Amalfi Coast, and the islands of Capri and Ischia

Amalfi Coast & the Islands

Fishing boats on the island of Capri

Amalfi Coast & the Islands

The Amalfi Coast, part of the Sorrentine Peninsula, is a romantic and balmy enclave of towering cliffs, sea-tumbling villages, lemon groves, corniche roads, luxuriant gardens, and magnificent vistas over turquoise waters. Scattered offshore is a trio of islands—Capri, Ischia, and Procida—that is more beguiling still. Lovely, chic towns such as Ravello and Positano draw crowds, but their lure is irresistible, especially in the off-season.

The Sorrentine Peninsula is a mountainous, cliff-edged crook of land that forms the southern arm of the Bay of Naples. At its tip is the island of Capri (pronounced CA-pree), a seductive and much celebrated retreat that looks across to the islands of Ischia and Procida, the sentinels at the bay's northern limit.

Much of the peninsula's northern coast is unremarkable, still touched by the development that blights much of the countryside

south of Naples. Only midway along the coast, just before the town of Sorrento, do things improve. The peninsula's southern coast, by contrast, is an almost constant delight, for this is the Amalfi Coast proper, a little patch of paradise named after its main town.

Many people base themselves on this southern coast, with Amalfi, Positano, and Ravello the most coveted destinations. One should know, however, that this is among

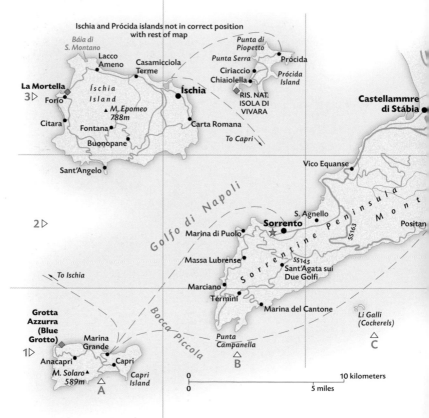

Europe's most popular and expensive vacation spots. Although it's less pretty than its southern counterparts, Sorrento has a far larger selection of mid-range hotels, and it is close enough to the sights to serve as a practical base. Ravello, located inland, is the best base of all, with the loveliest views and several fine, five-star hotels.

In an ideal world you would visit the coast and the islands in spring or early fall *(April–May or Sept.–Oct.),* avoiding high summer, when the tiny beaches, ferries, and famous corniche road around the coast are overwhelmingly busy. Off-season, and when explored at a leisurely pace (allow at least 4 days), the area's famous charms are readily apparent.

Above all, don't visit Capri merely as a day-tripper, and don't make the mistake of thinking Ischia will be a quieter version of Capri. Ischia has its attractions, namely its thermal spas, but

NOT TO BE MISSED:

Duomo and Chiostro del Paradiso, Amalfi **101–102**

Views and villa gardens of Ravello **104–107**

Sentiero degli Dei and other mountain hiking trails **109**

Driving the Amalfi Coast **110–113**

Hiking on Capri **116**

La Mortella gardens, Ischia **123**

Capri is more popular, and for good reason.

Nor should you be so bewitched by the sea and the coast that you fail to explore the Monti Lattari, the rugged mountains that run the length of the peninsula. Relatively few people venture inland, and so miss out not only on spectacular views, but also on some glorious walking along age-old trails. Maps are widely available, trails are marked, and visitor centers carry details of the major hikes. ■

Amalfi

In its day Amalfi was one of Italy's most important maritime powers. A thousand years later it is still the best known town on the Amalfi Coast, but for different reasons. A reasonable base or lovely stopover, it has a superb cathedral, a tempting labyrinth of picturesque streets, and a fine, mountain-ringed setting that can be explored on foot or admired from the sea.

Picturesque Amalfi, the coast's largest town

Amalfi

🏔 99 E2

Visitor Information

✉ Via delle Repubbliche Marinare 27

☎ 089 871 107

🕐 Closed Sun. & p.m. in winter, 1–3 p.m. in summer

www.amalfi touristoffice.it

Looking at Amalfi today, a tiny town squeezed between the sea and the mountains, it is hard to comprehend its powerful past. After declaring itself independent of Naples in 839, the town used its strategic position, a fine harbor, and an easily defended site to carve out a trading niche that over 200 years developed the coastal location into the main trading port of southern Italy.

Centuries before the rise of Pisa, Genoa, and Venice, Italy's other medieval maritime superpowers, Amalfi's merchants ranged far and wide, establishing trading outposts and Amalfitan communities across Africa, Byzantium, and Asia Minor. Its coins were used and accepted across the known world. In 1020, traders from Amalfi established the Hospice of St. John in Jerusalem, later to become the headquarters of the Knights Hospitalers of St. John. In time, the Hospitalers became the Knights of Malta, whose distinctive Maltese cross symbol can still be seen carved on street corners around the town. According to Boccaccio, author of the *Decameron* (partly set in Amalfi), the town was "full of gardens, fountains, and rich men."

Eventually, Amalfi's enclosed surroundings were its downfall, providing insufficient room to create a city commensurate with its mercantile reach. The Normans assumed periodic control after 1073, the Pisans—then the rising force in the Mediterranean—sacked the port in 1135, and a seaquake in 1343 destroyed large swaths of the old town. The Black Death of 1348 proved the final straw.

Even if you don't stay in Amalfi—though there are plenty of first-class hotels and several charming restaurants—or shop or swim here, you should definitely spend an hour or so exploring. Allow longer if you wish to tackle one or two of the easy trails that run up the narrow valley behind the town.

The Town

First impressions of Amalfi are not favorable. The seafront and small port, plus the narrow, stony beaches to either side, have a faded and workaday look. At the heart of this area is **Piazza Flavio Gioia,** named after the man who purportedly invented the magnetic compass. (Modern scholars think it is more likely that Amalfitan seafarers were the first Europeans to use the device, probably copied from the Arabs.)

A small portal, Porta Marinara, leads you from the waterfront into the far more congenial **Piazza del Duomo,** the town's busy and attractive heart. The square contains some delightful cafés, especially Pasticceria Andrea Pansa *(Piazza del Duomo 40),* since 1830 a perfect place to take in the passing parade and to admire the **Duomo** *(tel 089 871 059, closed lunchtime).*

The town's greatest pride, the beautiful cathedral has its roots in the ninth century, though the Romanesque bell tower dates

Coastal Transit

Train and bus travel in Sorrento and along the Amalfi Coast can be eased by using the Unicocostiera pass (valid for 45 or 90 mins., or for 1 or 3 days). If you intend to use transit a lot to make other excursions in and around the city of Naples, try the transit pass (www.unicocampania.it). The 3T Tourist Travel Ticket ($$$$$) allows three days' unlimited travel on all participating transit, including the Alibus shuttle to and from Naples's airport and the EAVBUS for Vesuvius.

from 1276 and the interior was extended and given a baroque gloss (now partly removed) during the 16th and 18th centuries. The impressive flight of steps is also comparatively recent, while the facade and lovely porch were rebuilt in 1891 to replace the

BOAT TRIPS: Boats run regularly from Amalfi's **Marina Grande** to the nearby beaches of Duoglio and Santa Croce and to the Grotta dello Smeraldo. *(089 873 190, www.coopsantadrea.com)*

**Palazzo del
Comune**

⊠ Piazza
Municipio,
entrance off
Corso Roma

☎ 089 873 6211

⊕ Closed Sat.,
Sun., & p.m.
daily except
Tues. & Thurs.

**La Valle dei
Mulini**

⊠ Salita Chiarito 9
Amalfi

☎ 089 873 211

13th-century original, which collapsed in 1861. The magnificent
bronze doors, however, are original and date from around 1066.

The church's interior is less
impressive, save for some ancient
columns, a mother-of-pearl cross
(brought back by Crusaders
returning from the Holy Land),
and the pair of *amboni* (pulpits)
flanking the altar, all remnants of
the early church. Far more beautiful is the **Chiostro del Paradiso**
*(closed Jan.–Feb. & 12:45–2:30
p.m. Nov.–Dec., $),* a lovely cloister
of palms, Moorish arches, and
ancient Roman sarcophagi.
Entered from a door on the left
of the porch, it was built in 1266
in Arab-Sicilian style as a cemetery
for Amalfi's wealthiest citizens.

Off the cloister is the **Cappella
del Crocifisso,** part of the oldest
church on the site, with traces of
14th-century frescoes and cases
containing various ecclesiastical
treasures. Steps from the chapel
lead to the **crypt,** which contains

what are alleged to be the relics of
St. Andrew (Sant'Andrea), stolen
in 1204 during the Fourth Crusade
and the Venetian-led sack of
Constantinople. The relics inspire
a devoted following, the more so
because twice a year the saint's
tomb exudes a liquid known as
manna di Sant'Andrea with allegedly

INSIDER TIP:

**Limoncello makes a
great gift for house
sitters and friends: Try
some from the shop
La Valle dei Mulini.**

—SUSAN STRAIGHT
National Geographic Books editor

miraculous properties. The first
event occurs on June 27, the day
on which Andrew's intercession
saved the town from a pirate
attack, and the second on November 30, the anniversary of the
saint's death.

Nearby, drop into the **Palazzo
del Comune** (City Hall), located
just east of the cathedral. The
Museo Civico here contains a
majolica panel with scenes from
Amalfi's history and an early
copy of the Tabula Amalfitana, a
maritime code written in Amalfi
in the 11th century and followed
throughout much of the Mediterranean until 1570.

Museo della Carta

Be sure to explore the warren
of streets off **Via Genova,** the
main street that wends up the
narrow valley above Amalfi.

Limoncello

Limoncello is a lemon-flavored digestif—
best drunk ice cold—that has always been
made on the Amalfi Coast. These days it is
trendy, and ubiquitous across Italy, but is
often served in badly made versions that
use lemon syrup rather than real lemons.
Some of the best, though, still comes
from the Amalfi region. On Capri, choose
from a wide selection at the **Capannina
Più** store *(Via Le Botteghe 39–41, tel 081
837 8899, www.capannina-capri.com, closed
Sun. in winter),* which also offers over 700
wines; or look for the Shaker brand, made
by a company that uses local lemons and
is based in **Vietri** *(Corso Umberto I 35/A, tel
089 761 717, www.shaker.it).*

Continue up this street (which later becomes Via Capuano) and you come to the Museo della Carta (Paper Museum) on your left. The upper part of the museum and the store are only moderately interesting, but be sure to join one of the fascinating tours of the old paper mill below for demonstrations of how Amalfi's traditional paper was (and still is) made.

Paper has been important in the town for centuries, and Amalfi was probably one of the first places in Europe where paper in the modern sense was made. The town's form of rag-made paper, as opposed to that made from pulp, is known as *bambagina*. The name is a corruption of the Arab town El-Marubig, where the technique of using scrap cotton, linen, and hemp to make paper was first perfected. Today, the paper is sold in exclusive stores worldwide, and it is still used by the Vatican, among others, for official correspondence.

Romanesque, Arab, and Sicilian motifs distinguish the architecture of the cathedral's Chiostro del Paradiso.

Valley Hikes

Continue up the main street beyond the museum, keeping right, and eventually the road becomes a trail up the narrow river valley. Follow this trail for a leisurely hour and you come to the **Valle dei Mulini,** named after the area's many flour and paper mills *(mulini),* built here to harness the Canneto River's power. Continue on the steepish trail, winding through citrus groves and past waterfalls to the upper valley, much of which is protected by a nature reserve. Here you enter the **Vallone delle Ferriere,** named after the area's former ironworks *(ferro—iron).* Allow four to six hours for the 7.5-mile (12 km) roundtrip. Another trail from Amalfi runs to the village of **Pogerola** (be warned that it has more than 1,000 steps); yet other trails join a high-level path all the way to Positano. ■

Museo della Carta

✉ Palazzo Pagliara, Via delle Cartiere 23

☎ 089 830 4561

🕐 Closed Mon. & Thurs. mid-Nov.–March

www.museodella carta.it

Ravello

The Amalfi Coast has many lovely vistas and villages, but none are quite as alluring as Ravello. Hidden in the hills above Amalfi, it is a romantic little retreat of gardens, pretty streets, venerable palaces, and some of the most sweeping and beautiful views in all of Italy.

Ravello
🅰 99 E2
Visitor Information
✉ Via Roma 18
☎ 089 857 096
www.ravellotime.it

Ravello may have been founded in the fifth or sixth century, but documentary evidence of the town dates to the ninth century, when it is recorded as being subject to Amalfi. Its

Sweeping views and fragrant villa gardens make Ravello the loveliest of the villages on the Amalfi Coast.

brief heyday came in the 13th century, when Amalfi's richest families, attracted by Ravello's lofty position, came here to build villas and palaces. Many of these grand homes survive to this day, a number of them converted into luxury hotels.

In later years, the glorious views and romantic setting attracted numerous writers and musicians, including Wagner, Liszt, Virginia Woolf, and many more. French writer André Gide described it as "closer to the sky than the sea," and the British novelist D. H. Lawrence wrote part of *Lady Chatterley's Lover* here.

Recently, the glitterati who found Positano losing its chic appeal in the face of tourism also moved in, hence the town's many luxury hotels. These, along with Ravello's intrinsic charm, make this the best overall base for the Amalfi Coast. If you are thinking of driving here for the day, note that parking is difficult and expensive, and that it can be better to take a cab or one of the regular buses here from Amalfi or elsewhere.

However you approach from Amalfi, the road is twisting and scenic, climbing sharply and passing rows of vines and craggy slopes before reaching Ravello's first little church, **Santa Maria a Gradillo**. This 11th-century Romanesque gem, with its distinctive bell tower, airy interior, and intertwined apses, provides a foretaste of the Moorish and Sicilian architectural flourishes that you'll see all over the town. These motifs were introduced by families who had grown rich trading in Sicily and in the Arab dominions in Spain, Asia, and North Africa.

The Duomo

The road up from the coast eventually arrives at **Piazza del Vescovado** (which has a large parking lot) and the adjoining **Piazza del Duomo.** Here you'll discover the Duomo (Cathedral), which is dedicated to San Pantaleone, Ravello's patron saint. Founded in 1086 by Orso Papiro, the first bishop of Ravello, the Duomo was largely sponsored, like much else in Ravello, by the Rufolo family, a wealthy banking dynasty. Although given a baroque makeover in 1786, it was stripped of its additions in the 1980s, when the austere beauty of the lovely 12th-century Romanesque original was once again revealed.

The first thing you notice are the central bronze doors, designed in 1179 by Barisano da Trani, who was probably influenced by the similar doors of Amalfi's cathedral. The 54 bronze reliefs were cast in Constantinople and depict scenes from the Passion, along with portraits of saints and warriors.

The church's interior has even more splendid treasures, starting with the Ambone dell'Epistola, the low pulpit on the left of the central nave, donated by Costantino

---

EXPERIENCE: Diving on the Amalfi Coast

The Amalfi Coast may not offer divers the greatest underwater experience, as fish numbers and variety are relatively limited (locals suggest offshore, and the **Punta Campanella** marine reserve in particular). But few places in the world offer such a wonderful environment in which to dive: the many tiny coves, cliffs, and caves make up one of Europe's finest marine landscapes. Excursions and equipment rental can be arranged through **Diving Nettuno** (*Via Vespucci 39, tel 081 808 1051, www.divingsorrento.com; 3 guided dives daily, closed Nov.–March*), based near Marina di Campone at the **Villaggio Nettuno** (*www.villaggionettuno.it*), where accommodation is available; and at the **Centro Sub Costiera Amalfitana** (*Via Marina di Praia, tel 089 812 148, www.centrosub.it; 2 dives daily in high season, night dives by request*), based at Praiano.

Rogadeo, the second bishop of Ravello, in 1130 or 1131. Richly adorned, it features two delightful mosaics from the story of Jonah and the whale: Jonah being swallowed by the whale (on the right) and reappearing from the whale's maw (on the left). Jonah's story was a favorite with artists in Campania, these two episodes serving as symbols of the Resurrection. On the nave's right stands the beautiful high pulpit, with its distinctive six lions, created in 1272 for Nicola Rufolo by Nicolò da Bartolommeo.

To the left of the main altar is the **Cappella di San Pantaleone,** created in 1643 to display a vial of the saint's blood. Like the blood of San Gennaro in

The Ravello Gardens

But for its steep terrain, Ravello might have been designed with gardens in mind: It has sheltered, south-facing slopes to nurture an almost subtropical abundance of flora, and far-reaching views of sea and mountain to complement nature's work. Even the terrain has become a virtue, thanks to terraces carved out over centuries, a natural stage for belvederes. The gardens of the Villa Rufolo a short walk from the Duomo are the most accessible, but those of the Villa Cimbrone, a little farther from the town center, are perhaps the most romantic. The American writer Gore Vidal, who lived in Ravello for years, when asked for the most beautiful place he had seen on his travels, replied: "the view from the belvedere of the Villa Cimbrone on a bright winter's day when the sky and the sea were each so vividly blue that it was not possible to tell one from the other."

Naples, Pantaleone's blood is said to liquefy on the anniversary of the saint's martyrdom on July 27, 305. The cathedral's crypt ($) contains a small collection of architectural and other fragments, the highlights of which are a silver bust depicting St. Barbara and an exquisite bust of Sicelogaita della Marra, the wife of Nicola Rufolo.

Along a lane that leads from the side of the Duomo is the first of Ravello's two outstanding gardens, the **Villa Rufolo** *(Piazza Vescovado, tel 089 857 621, www .villarufolo.it, $$)*, created for the Rufolo family between 1270 and 1280. By the time it was bought by a Scot, Francis Reid, in 1851, the main villa and the garden were in virtual ruin. Reid's restoration was an architectural mélange, but the gardens reemerged to delightful effect. They have been publicly owned since 1975.

The gardens famously provided the inspiration for the Klingsor garden scene in *Parsifal*, the last opera (1880) by German composer Richard Wagner. The gardens' main terrace is named the Terrazza Wagner in the

INSIDER TIP:

Climb the steps from Minori to Ravello: You'll pass picturesque courtyards and homes that have stood for hundreds of years.

—SUSAN STRAIGHT
National Geographic Books editor

composer's memory, and from a height of 1,115 feet (340 m) it affords one of the most famous views in Italy. If you have seen pictures of the panorama of the Amalfi Coast, framed by the country's most-photographed umbrella pines, then here is the real thing. The garden provides a fine setting for performances in the highly regarded **Festival di Ravello,** a series of classical concerts held here and elsewhere between March and early November *(tel 089 858 360, box office 089 858 422, www.ravellofestival.com)*.

If the view from the Villa Rufolo is magnificent, then the panorama from the **Villa Cimbrone** *(Via*

Santa Chiara 26, tel 089 857 459, www.villacimbrone.com, $$), with Ravello's second principal garden, is perhaps better still. Now a fine hotel, the villa lies south of the town center and can be reached only on foot (a 10-min. walk). The gardens are open to nonresidents, offering a more romantic retreat than the Villa Rufolo—all creamy camellias, roses, and exotic blooms. The villa's guise is a pastiche from the early 1900s, when Lord Grimthorpe, the designer of Big Ben's clockface, renovated it. The gardens' most celebrated view can be enjoyed from the **Belvedere Cimbrone,** its line of statues framing the coast far below.

In the town, similar vistas open up around unexpected corners. Climb the stepped lanes from Piazza del Duomo, for example, and venture along Via San Giovanni del Toro for the panorama

from the Belvedere Principessa di Piemonte. The street also contains **San Giovanni del Toro** *(Piazzetta San Giovanni del Toro 3, ask at visitor center for hours),* a lovely Romanesque church begun in 1065 that boasts an Arab-Sicilian bell tower and 12th-century pulpit.

Be sure to visit the ancient and easygoing village of **Scala** a mile or so down the coast from Ravello. It has another fine cathedral and is the starting point of several marked trails. These include Trail 51 to the peak of **Il Castello** (2 hours) or the easier walk to the hamlet of **Minuto.** From Ravello you can also walk to **Minori** via Torello, a 30-minute downhill hike that starts in the little alley by the Villa Rufolo. Also easy is the 5.6-mile (9 km) walk to the **Monastero di San Nicola.** The visitor center carries details of local hikes. ∎

Sentiero degli Dei near Positano. Hikes long and short are among the highlights of a trip to the Amalfi Coast. Many trails follow ancient tracks between remote villages.

Positano

Viewed from afar, Positano is one of Italy's most memorable little villages, thanks to its magnificent position, the best of any coastal town in the country. It is a medley of towering cliffs, the vivid green of lemon trees, and the impossibly picturesque tumble of pastel-colored houses falling steeply to the sea.

Once a sleepy fishing village, Positano has become a resort of chic hotels and expensive boutiques.

Positano
98 C2

Visitor Information
✉ Via del Saracino 4

☎ 089 875 067

🕐 Closed Sun. & p.m. daily Nov.–March

www.aziendaturismo positano.it

Positano enjoyed a brief period of maritime success in the 12th and 13th centuries, but never enough to rival Amalfi. Instead, Positano's moment of glory came in the 1960s, when it became –along with Capri and Rome's Via Veneto—one of the chic retreats favored by the *dolce vita* set. Before then it had been known only to a handful of outsiders, among them artists such as Pablo Picasso and writers like John Steinbeck.

Something of the flavor of the 1960s survives to this day, notably in the rather dated interiors of even the best hotels, which now have an almost retro chic, and in the many boutiques, some of which would not have been out of place in the Carnaby Street of swinging London in 1967.

Today, Positano is far from the sleepy and undiscovered fishing village of a generation ago. In summer, the approach roads seethe with drivers searching for a parking spot, and the steep lanes and tiny waterfront heave with day-trippers ferried from Naples and neighboring towns. Out of season, though, in winter, spring, or fall, the village has charm to spare, from the almond trees in blossom to the citrus groves heavy with fruit or a hot chocolate sipped in a waterfront bar.

In summer Positano is best admired from afar, from the curve of the SS163 road by the entrance to the San Pietro Hotel a mile or so to the east, or from the Belvedere dello Schiaccone viewpoint on the same road a mile or so to the west.

Close up, however, the village does have its moments. The steep, pedestrian-only lanes, often shaded with vines and trailing bougainvillea, are charming and fun to explore. Be sure to wear comfortable shoes, because unless you use the shuttle bus that circles the village from top to bottom, this is a place with a lot of steps and steep streets.

Most roads lead eventually to the **Marina Grande,** the waterfront, which has a small and pebbly gray-sand beach (with public and pay areas) and water that isn't particularly appealing for swimming. To the right as you face the sea, steps above the quay climb to a promenade that runs

to a smaller beach at **Fornillo,** a pretty stroll of a few minutes. Just above the marina is **Santa Maria Assunta** (Piazza Flavio Gioia), the town's main church, with its distinctive majolica-tiled dome and a much venerated 13th-century icon, the Madonna Nera, above the high altar. Just to the west is another pretty church, **Santa Caterina** (Via Pasitea), a companion to the **Chiesa Nuova** (Via Chiesa Nuova) in the upper part of the town, which is known for its striking tiled floor.

Like most villages on this coast, Positano is also a base for (or close to) a variety of trails. With most of these hikes it is sensible to take a cab to the upper trailhead and then walk down to Positano, thus avoiding a climb on steep grades. This is not appropriate, however, for the area's best known hike, the **Sentiero degli Dei** (Path of the Gods), which is actually a series of old shepherds' tracks following the ridges and contours of the hills high above the coast from Positano to Praiano. This walk starts from the hamlet of Nocello, easily reached by cab or local bus in a few minutes from Positano. ∎

Boat Excursions

It is possible to take boat excursions from many points on the Amalfi Coast. Note that ferries and hydrofoils linking the towns, or connecting to Naples and the islands, are often covered, and offer only restricted viewing. In Amalfi, contact Coop Sant'Andrea (tel 089 873 190, www.coopsantandrea.com) for trips to the Grotta dello Smeraldo (see p. 113) or nearby beaches at Duoglio and Santa Croce. In Positano, visit Gennaro & Salvatore (Via Trara Genoino 13, tel 089 811 613, www.gennaroesalvatore.it, no credit cards) on the main beach for day trips to Capri and along the coast, the Grotta dello Smeraldo, and the Li Galli islets.

A Drive along the Amalfi Coast

This scenic ramble from Sorrento to Salerno takes in the finest mountains, views, villages, and seascapes of Italy's most celebrated coastline.

The road along the Amalfi Coast is one of Italy's loveliest but also one of its busiest, at least in summer. It is also often tortuous and hair-raising, the price for sublime views being numerous switchbacks and plunging drops to the sea, often with only flimsy-looking roadside barriers between you and oblivion. Writer John Steinbeck and his wife Elaine Scott described a ride along the road in 1953, when they "lay clutched in each other's arms, weeping hysterically," as their driver guide, Signor Bassani, one hand on the wheel, blithely regaled them with tales of the region's history.

As ever here, try to travel in the off-season (April–May or Sept.–Oct.) and avoid morning, lunchtime, and evening rush hours. Allow plenty of time to explore the smaller roads at the peninsula's westernmost tip and the mountain roads that climb from the coast. Note, too, that although the drive may seem relatively short, the many bends and switchbacks make it feel longer. The best bet is to break the drive with overnight stays or allow plenty of stops for exploration en route.

Start at **Sorrento** ❶, a genteel town of sedate hotels popular with families and visitors on package tours. Although larger and less dramatic than towns on the peninsula's southern coast, it makes a good, homey, and less expensive base for exploring the region than Amalfi, Ravello, or Positano. The main things

---

NOT TO BE MISSED:

Punta Campanella • Amalfi • Ravello

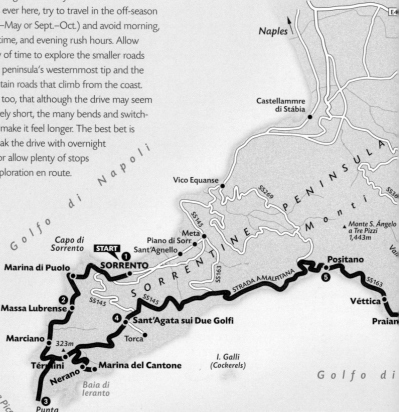

to see are the cloister of **San Francesco** *(Piazza San Francesco Saverio Gargiulo);* the **Museo Correale di Terranova** *(Via Correale 48, tel 081 878 1846, closed p.m. daily & Tues., $$$),* a small villa museum of local art and artifacts; and the **Museo-Bottega della Tarsia Lignea** *(Via San Nicola 28, tel 081 877 1942, closed Mon., $$$),* devoted to a large private collection of intarsia (inlaid wood) furniture. Contact the visitor center *(Via Luigi de Maio 35, tel 081 807 4033, www.sorrentotourism.com, closed Sun. except Aug.)* for further information.

Leave Sorrento not on the main SS145 highway, but on the minor coastal road that leads to Massa Lubrense, where you can pick up the little road and its spurs that provide access to Punta Campanella, the Sorrentine

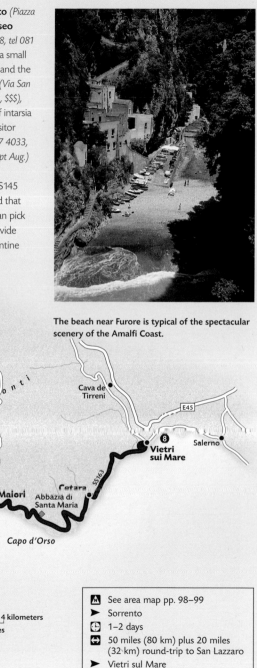

The beach near Furore is typical of the spectacular scenery of the Amalfi Coast.

🅰	See area map pp. 98–99
►	Sorrento
🕐	1–2 days
↔	50 miles (80 km) plus 20 miles (32 km) round-trip to San Lazzaro
►	Vietri sul Mare

Peninsula's ruggedly spectacular western tip. Compared to much of the coast, this is beautiful, empty, and mostly undeveloped country, all lemon trees, sea views, and coastal trails.

The road out of Sorrento leads first past the villages of **Capo di Sorrento** and an attractive turnoff right (north) down to the sandy beach at **Marina di Puolo**. Once in **Massa Lubrense ❷**, enjoy the view of Capri and the Bay of Naples from the overlook in Largo Vescovado and drop into the town's visitor center *(Viale Filangieri 11, tel 081 533 9021, www.massalub rense.it, closed Sun. Nov.–March & Sun. p.m. April– Oct.)* for details of the 20 or more marked and maintained hiking trails on and around Punta Campanella.

By car, continue on the road above the coast past the hamlet of **Marciano**, taking the dead-end road just before Termini to **Punta Campanella ❸**, named after its 1335 watchtower and bell *(campana)*, once rung to warn of pirate attack. The cape offers more delightful views of Capri. Return to the Termini road, pausing at **Termini** itself—a panoramic hamlet on a natural terrace at 1,059 feet (323 m)—and then perhaps take the twisting right-turn diversion

Too Close for Comfort

In an article for *Harper's Bazaar* in 1953, author John Steinbeck lamented that the Amalfi Coast road had been "carefully designed to be a little narrower than two cars side by side." It is much the same today. Buses often need the width of the road to maneuver; most announce their arrival with blasts of the horn, but on any bend it is best to anticipate an oncoming vehicle on your side of the road, and to proceed accordingly—that is, very slowly.

(5.5 miles/ 9 km round-trip) just beyond the village to the large beach and burgeoning resort at **Marina del Cantone.** En route you pass through Nerano, where an hour's hike on local Trail 39 (from the church) takes you to the **Baia di Leranto,** a stunning sandy bay otherwise accessible only by boat.

Retrace your tracks to Termini and drive onward (east) to **Sant'Agata sui Due Golfi ❹**, a village that, as its name suggests, commands views over two gulfs *(due golfi)*: those of Naples

Admiring the view near Sorrento, the start of the dramatic road around the Amalfi Coast

to the north and Salerno to the south. The best views are from the roof terrace of the convent of **Il Deserto** (*hours vary, usually closed a.m. daily, donation*), about half a mile (1 km) to the northwest. If the convent is closed, take the little road in the opposite direction to **Torca,** a hamlet with more glorious panoramas and a trail (No. 37) to the cove below at Marina di Crapolla.

The Costiera

Sant'Agata marks the start of the Costiera, or coast road proper, the SS145 (Strada Amalfitana), originally built in 1853 on the orders of the Bourbon ruler Ferdinand II to link the town with Salerno. From Sant'Agata follow the SS145 then the SS163 to **Positano** ❺ (see pp. 108–109), with views en route of the tiny islands of **Li Galli** (the Cockerels). The islets were once known as Le Sirenuse (the Sirens), after the notion that they were home to the Sirens of Homeric myth.

Beyond Positano, the road—now likely to be busier—stays closer to the coast, passing through **Vettica,** whose church, San Gennaro, has the colorful tiled dome and bell tower typical of local churches (the church square offers good views). Then comes **Praiano,** a quieter alternative to Positano, which marks the start of the road's most rugged reaches.

You'll reach some spectacular scenery at the **Vallone di Furore,** a dramatic gorge that opens to the sea 1.25 miles (2 km) beyond Marina di Praia. A short distance farther is the **Grotta dello Smeraldo,** or Emerald Grotto, a lesser rival to Capri's Blue Grotto. The cave, a popular visitor sight (*$$*), is reached by elevator or steps from the road and parking lot, and then by a short boat ride. It can also be reached on boat tours from Amalfi and Positano.

Continuing east, you pass the town of Conca dei Marini and then a junction for the minor road (SS366) north over the mountains to the peninsula's northern coast. You probably won't want to make the entire detour, but if time allows, it is well worth following this steep road through **Furore** (noted for its wines) and onto

the high plateau around **Agerola.** This is a different world from the coast, a pastoral upland of hamlets such as **San Lazzaro,** which offers more magnificent panoramas (make for the ruins of the Castel Lauritano for the best).

Returning to the coast the way you have come, continue east on SS163 to **Amalfi** ❻ (see pp. 100–103), Altrani, and the junction for the SS373 to **Ravello** ❼ (see pp. 104–107). If you wish to cut your drive short, continue on the SS373 north from Ravello and loop back to Sorrento (or continue to Naples) via Angri. Alternatively, return to the coast and follow the

---

EXPERIENCE:
Boat for Rent

The clue is in the name—the Amalfi Coast—and there's no doubt the best way to enjoy the special beauty of this region is from the sea. Rent a boat or take a boat tour to experience spectacular views of the area's cliffs, coves, beaches, and tiny villages. **Nautica o' Masticiello** (*tel 081 808 1443 or cell 339 314 2791, www.masticiello.com*), operates from Piazza del Cantone, Marine di Canone. **Lucibello** (*Via del Brigantino 9, tel 089 875 0032, www.lucibello.it*) in Positano also offers excursions and rents out a wide variety of boats.

---

coast road through **Maiori,** which has one of the area's largest and most developed beaches, and past the **Capo d'Orso.** A protected reserve, the cape is one of the loveliest parts of the coast, with a tempting trail to the Capo d'Orso lighthouse and nearby **Abbazia di Santa Maria Oleria** (also known as the Catacombe di Badia), a rock-cut abbey dating from the tenth century.

The drive then passes **Cetara,** a town known for its tuna industry, and concludes near Salerno at **Vietri sul Mare** ❽, widely celebrated for its ceramics and for the view from the church of San Giovanni Battista.

Capri

Capri is one of the most enchanting places in the Mediterranean, a beautiful little island with glorious sea views, pretty villages, lovely walks, luxurious hotels, and spectacular cliffs. Add to that its colorful history, and you'll understand why it has been the sybaritic home of artists and exiles for more than 2,000 years.

Fishing boats in the harbor at Marina Grande. Despite Capri's many visitors, the island retains a life of its own.

No one should forgo the considerable pleasures of Capri, but be aware that it has its annoyances, among them the sheer number of people who wish to indulge in the island's delights. If you come in high season—July, August, and weekends between May and September—you will join anything up to 6,000 day-trippers, 3,000 hotel guests, and 12,000 residents, all squeezed onto an island that measures just 4 square miles (10 sq km).

There are two solutions: Come outside high season (Capri virtually closes, in the best sense of the word, from November to March), or stay overnight, ensuring that you sample the island's evening strolls, al fresco meals, and other nocturnal delights without crowds.

Not that Capri is spoiled. For all visitors, the island's beauty, intimacy, and sense of nostalgic glamour remain. The sea shimmers and the sky is a glorious blue; frangipani and lemon groves scent the air; bougainvillea provides floral cascades of color; whitewashed villas dazzle against tree-swathed slopes; and cliffs plunge on a thrilling coastline. A rough terrain, traditional farming methods, more or less stringent development regulations, and the natural reluctance of residents to compromise their idyllic home all contrive to keep the worst excesses of modernity at bay.

The practicalities of a visit are straightforward. Regular ferries and hydrofoils serve the island from most points on the Campanian coast, notably from central Naples, Sorrento, Salerno, Amalfi, Positano, and the neighboring island of Ischia (see pp. 122–123). None takes more than about 50 minutes. Most services are year-round, though some—notably those from the Amalfi Coast—may be seasonal (April–Oct.). Most of the year you will not be able to bring a car onto the island, nor will you need to; there are buses, cabs, and two funiculars, and much of the island can be seen on foot. Indeed, easy hiking is one of Capri's great pleasures. Hotels should be reserved well in advance, as should tables at restaurants, especially if you wish to dine outside. Finally, note the pronunciation of the island's name—it's CA-pree, not Ca-PREE.

The elongated island runs east to west, with its main town, chic **Capri,** in the east and its only other town, the slightly more rustic **Anacapri,** in the higher western half. Between the two towns is 1,932-foot (589 m) **Monte Solaro,** the island's highest point. There are two mains sights: the Villa San Michele, which is a few moments' walk from Anacapri, and the Grotta Azzurra (Blue Grotto), located just below Anacapri near the island's northwest tip. Boat tours to the Blue Grotto and around the island (a trip highly recommended), and all ferries and hydrofoils, use

Marina Grande, the port area built in 1931 on the north coast below Capri town.

Arriving at Marina Grande

Be warned: Arriving in Marina Grande in high season is no fun. It's a drab place, at odds with the beauty and charm of the rest of the island, and you will have to run the gauntlet of your fellow visitors, hotel barkers, and trashy souvenir stalls. If you have booked a good hotel, someone should meet you and arrange for your luggage to be transported. Otherwise, you have four options. The first is to take one of the small orange SIPCC

INSIDER TIP:

In Anacapri, visit Santa Maria a Cetrella, which hosts the statue of a Madonna dear to the German poet Rilke.

—CAMILLA BOZZOLI
National Geographic translations

buses to Capri or Anacapri (you may have to wait in line); a second is to take a cab to your destination (again, you may have to wait your turn); a third is to take the funicular to Capri town (it departs on the west side of the port, on the right as you stand with your back to the sea); and the last option is to take a steep 10-minute walk up Via San Francesco to Capri town.

Capri
▲ 98 A1
Visitor Information
www.capritourism.com

Marina Grande Banchina del Porto
▲ 98 A1
Visitor Information
☎ 081 837 0634
🕐 Closed Sun. & 1:15–3 p.m. Nov.–Easter

Santa Maria a Cetrella
▲ 98 A1
Visitor Information
✉ Via Capodimonte
☎ 081 837 6218
www.cetrella.it

Capri Town

 98 A1

Visitor Information

 Piazza
Umberto I

☎ 081 837 0686

🕐 Closed Sun. &
1:15–3 p.m.
Nov.–Easter

Capri Town

Capri's main town is chic in the extreme. At its heart is Piazza Umberto I, the island's diminutive social hub, known to all simply as the **Piazzetta**—"Little Square." There are ways to avoid the square, but only the locals seem to know how. Otherwise all streets appear to lead here, making it, and its cafés and restaurants, a great outdoor summer salon. Invest in an expensive drink and settle back to enjoy the show. Streets in and around the square are filled with souvenir stores, but you'll also find a greater concentration of designer boutiques than any equivalent area in the world. Lose yourself in the alleys and lanes off these main thoroughfares, however, and you will begin to appreciate some of Capri's charm.

Start with Via Madre Serafina, a lane at the top of the steps by **Santo Stefano,** the baroque church on the Piazzetta's south side. Bear right and follow steep Via Castello and you eventually come to the **Belvedere Cannone,** a viewpoint that offers a panorama over Marina Piccola (a small harbor on the south side of the island) and the Faraglioni, a trio of great sea stacks to the southeast. Just around the Piazzetta from Santo Stefano is the 14th-century Palazzo Cerio, home to the **Museo Ignazio Cerio** (*Piazzetta Cerio 5, tel 081 837 6681, www.centrocaprense.org, closed Sun., Mon., & p.m. daily except Thurs., $*), with exhibits on the island's archaeological and natural history.

To the left of Santo Stefano, take Via Vittorio Emanuele past the Quisisana, the town's best known hotel. Continue down Via Federico Serena, then turn right on Viale Matteotti. The last street provides another lovely viewpoint, embracing olive groves, the sea, and the atmospheric **Certosa di San Giacomo** (*Viale Certosa, tel 081 837 6218, closed p.m. daily & Mon.*), an abbey reached via a

---

EXPERIENCE: Hikes on Capri

One of the loveliest ways to experience Capri is by hiking, escaping the crowds to walk trails scented with thyme and jasmine, following ancient tracks between villages. At times you'll enjoy sweeping sea views, at others vistas of the island's bucolic interior. All the trails are easy enough to follow, but if you'd like to learn more about the area as you hike, contact visitor centers about licensed guides.

One walk leads is Capri Town to the **Belvedere di Tragara,** continuing past Villa Malaparte (see p. 118).

More demanding is the 1,149-foot (350 m) climb on the **Passetiello** trail from beyond the hospital near Marina Piccola to the top of Monte Solaro via the Monte Santa Maria ridge and Santa Maria a Cetrella hermitage (details at the visitor center).

From Anacapri, you can walk to **Migliera** (45 mins.), taking Via Caposcuro from left of the Monte Solaro chairlift and following for 1.25 miles (2 km). Have lunch at **Gelsomina** and admire the views at the Belvedere Migliera at the path's end.

Designer stores typically found in Rome or Milan line the streets and alleys around the Piazzetta, Capri's chic social hub.

walled avenue at the eastern end of Viale Matteotti.

The Certosa, or Chapter-house, was founded in 1371 and suppressed by Napoleon in 1808. After this it was used as a prison and military hospital before falling into disrepair. Today, it serves a variety of municipal functions; it also offers a church, cloister, and pretty gardens open to the public.

Back on Viale Matteotti, continue west and you come to the **Giardini di Augusto,** the Gardens of Augustus, so named because they were laid out over the ruins of an ancient Roman settlement. This is your first brush with the island's ancient history. Capri has Greek or possibly Phoenician roots, its name deriving from the Greek *kapros,* boar, or *capreae,* a Romano-Italic word meaning "island of goats" (scholars dispute the precise origins). It first came

to relative prominence under the Roman emperor Augustus, who was captivated by the island. In 29 B.C., shortly before he became emperor, Augustus persuaded its owners, the Greeks of Neapolis (Naples), to exchange it for the larger and already Romanized island of Ischia, nearby.

The panoramic municipal gardens here were created as part of an estate belonging to Friedrich Alfred Krupp (1854–1902), a German arms manufacturer who also paid for the celebrated Via Krupp, a twisting path that winds down the cliff to Marina Piccola. The path is now open, having been officially closed for years as a result of landslides.

Marina Piccola has seafront cafés and several private beach clubs *(tel 081 837 0264, www .bagni-internazionali.com),* notably the Marina di Mulo and Marina

Anacapri

🔼 98 A1

Visitor Information

✉ Via Giuseppe
   Orlandi 59
☎ 081 837 1524
🕐 Closed Sun.
   Nov.–Easter

di Pennaulo, both favorite haunts in the jet-set heyday of the 1950s and '60s. The central area of beach around the Scoglio delle Sirene, a rocky outcrop, is free, and makes a good, popular place from which to swim. Via Krupp aside, Marina Piccola can be reached by bus or on Via Roma, Via Mulo, and Via Marina Piccola from Capri town.

Return to Capri town and the Quisisana Hotel (or walk from the

the belvedere and curves up and around the coast, past the Villa Malaparte, Grotta Matromania cave, and Arco Naturale rock arch. Toward the end of the path, at Le Grottelle, a bar-restaurant, you pick up Via Matermania (later Via Croce), which takes you back to town. This is a pleasing circular walk of about an hour.

An equally classic excursion is the stroll on the road and easy trail to the ruins of the once colossal

The church floor of San Michele in Anacapri is made up of more than 2,500 hand-painted tiles.

Piazzetta) to pick up Via Camerelle, a street that heads east from the hotel into Via Tragara, which is lined with hotels and more stylish stores. This is the route of the townspeople's *passeggiata,* or evening stroll, which ends in a lovely viewpoint at the **Belvedere di Tragara.** Most people turn and go back the way they have come (a 20-minute-or-so round-trip), but a paved path descends from

Villa Jovis *(Via Tiberio, tel 081 837 0634, $)* on the island's northeast tip, about 1.5 miles (2.4 km) from Capri town. From the Piazzetta take Via Botteghe, Via Fuorlovado, and Via Croce east (passing the pretty church of San Michele), and then follow signs.

In its day the villa was the most sumptuous of 12 palaces built on the island by Emperor Tiberius, one for each of the 12 most important gods in the Roman pantheon. Tiberius left Rome for Capri in A.D. 27 at the age of 68, bewitched by the island, and never returned. Numerous salacious stories surround his ten-year sojourn on Capri, tales of considerable sexual excess, though it's as well to remember that virtually all we know of Tiberius's last years come from the writings of Suetonius— and Tiberius, it is safe to say, was not Suetonius's favorite emperor. Don't miss the **Salto di Tiberio,** a 1,155-foot (333 m) precipice down which the emperor is said to have hurled those with whom he was sated or displeased.

Anacapri

Don't believe those who tell you that Anacapri is quieter and more "authentic" than Capri town. It certainly has a different air, thanks to its more rugged position at the foot of Monte Solaro and the more Arabic feel of its square whitewashed houses, but the number of visitors and designer outlets is more or less the same. You might prefer this as a base if you want to tackle some of the island's easy hikes, or if you want to stay in the glorious Capri Palace, the island's luxury hotel of choice.

Here the main square is **Piazza della Vittoria,** reached via a scenic, if occasionally hair-raising, road. Until the road was built in 1872, the great cliff wall it breaches meant that Anacapri and Capri town led virtually separate lives. The only link was the Scala Fenicia, an 882-step path built by

---

EXPERIENCE:
Villa Concerts

The sheer number of visitors can spoil trips to the Villa San Michele. Enjoy it in relative peace during one of the jazz or classical concerts (or occasional film presentations) held here during the summer. Performances take place weekly *(currently Fri.)* from June to mid-August, either on the 200-seat terrace or in the 60-seat chapel. Visit www.villasanmichele.eu for further information.

---

the island's first Greek settlers.

From Piazza della Vittoria it is a short walk northeast on Via Giuseppe Orlandi to the **Villa San Michele** *(Viale Axel Munthe 34, tel 081 837 1401, www.villasanmichele .eu, closed 3:30 p.m. Nov.–Feb., $$),* one of the island's main visitor sights. Built on the site of another of Tiberius's 12 villas, it was the creation of Axel Munthe (1857–1949), a Swedish doctor who achieved fame in Paris and Rome as one of the most popular society physicians of his time. He lived here between 1896 and 1910 and brought the villa, and with it the charms of Capri, to a wider audience with the publication of *The Story of San Michele* (1929). Written at the suggestion of American writer Henry James, the book was penned late in Munthe's life, when the doctor suffered from crippling insomnia and failing vision. It has been translated into more than 30 languages.

Munthe adored his house, "open to the sun, the wind and the voice of the sea," as he put it, and resembling "a Greek temple, with light, light everywhere." Others have been less enamored. British writer Bruce Chatwin observed in *Selflove among the Ruins* that "in Pasadena or Beverly Hills, Munthe's creation wouldn't get more than a passing glance."

Even if you remain unmoved by the house, it is hard to resist the charm of the gardens or the impact of the views. As ever, though, arrive as early as possible to avoid the crowds. Check with

embracing Vesuvius and the Gulfs of Naples and Salerno.

In Anacapri itself, the main things to see include the **Casa Rossa** *(Via Giuseppe Orlandi 78, tel 081 838 2193, closed Mon. & 1:30– 5:30 p.m. May–Sept., $)*, a folly built in 1876 by a former Confederate soldier, J.C. MacKowen, who wrote one of the first English-language guidebooks to Capri. Also leave time for **San Michele Archangelo** *(Piazza San Nicola,*

Lemons

Lemons are found everywhere on the Amalfi Coast: piled outside shops, growing on trees nurtured by the region's benign microclimate, and squeezed onto ancient terraces, or *macerine*, unique to the area's precipitous hillsides. Some of these terraces date from the tenth century, and are one of the reasons UNESCO awarded this coast World Heritage site status in 1997.

Several varieties are special to the region, notably the giant *ponsiri* and the smaller, thick-skinned, and almost sweet *profumati*, which can be eaten on their own in salads or desserts. Most locals have a few trees, but among the better commercial producers are the 320-plus members of the Solagri cooperative *(www.solagri.it)* based at Sant'Agnello di Sorrento.

the visitor center for details of the summer sunset concerts sometimes held on the grounds (see sidebar p. 119.) Also note that you can follow the Scala Fenicia steps from the chapel of Sant'Antonio just below the villa all the way down to Marina Grande.

The other essential excursion from Anacapri is up **Monte Solaro,** which you can approach as a hike or on the chairlift *(Via Caposcuro 10, tel 081 837 1428, www.capriseggiovia.it, $$)* from the south side of Piazza della Vittoria. The journey takes 12 minutes. Alternatively, ride up and walk down (or back to Capri town). The views, needless to say, are sublime,

tel 081 837 2396, closed p.m. Oct.– April), the town's baroque parish church (1719), distinguished by a pretty majolica floor (1761) made up of 2,500 *riggiole*, or Neapolitan-style ceramic tiles. The floor tiles depict the expulsion of Adam and Eve from Paradise. If you want to swim in relative peace, take an early bus to **Punta Carena** on the island's southwest tip.

Blue Grotto

The Blue Grotto, or Grotta Azzurra, is one of the best known sights in Italy, never mind Capri. The cavern's otherworldly blue light has mesmerized generations of visitors. It has been known since at least the time of Tiberius but was avoided by superstitious locals for centuries, only to be "rediscovered" in 1826 by Polish poet August Kopisch and German painter Ernst Fries. Given the number of visitors today and the rigmarole involved in seeing the grotto, it's debatable whether you should make the effort to see the cavern, at least in high summer. If in doubt, spend your money on a circular boat tour of the island instead.

First you must reach the grotto, which you can do by boat from Marina Grande or by bus or cab (or on foot in 45 mins.) from Anacapri to the parking lot above the grotto. Once you are at sea level and outside the cave, you have to wait to climb aboard a rowboat, the only way to enter the grotto owing to the low height of the cave entrance (under 3 ft/1 m, and becoming lower as the area sinks and the sea level rises). Technically you can swim in, but this is discouraged and not advised. Tours are canceled in seas with any significant swell. You must pay a fee to enter the grotto and a similar amount again for the rowboat; both of these fees are on top of the cost of the boat from Marina Grande, if that is the way you have come. At busy times, the lines of boats can be long, and because of the number of people wishing to experience the cave, you will have only a few minutes at most inside the cave.

Inside, the intense blue light reflecting off the cavern walls is certainly extraordinary. The effect is created by sunlight streaming through underwater fissures in the rock, with the red elements in the spectrum removed by the water. Morning is the best time to visit. ■

The entrance to Capri's Blue Grotto is so low that access is possible only in a small rowboat.

Ischia

Ischia plays second fiddle to Capri, but in parts it is just as enticing. Its rich, volcanic soils support exotic gardens and verdant landscapes, and its coastline—unlike that of its rival—is studded with fine sandy beaches. Most visitors come to the island for several days, less to sightsee than to sample thermal resorts that have been renowned since Roman times.

Sunbathers perch on volcanic rocks beneath the fortified ramparts of Ischia Ponte.

Ischia is five times larger than Capri and has five principal towns: Ischia on the east coast, where you will land; Forio, a resort on the west coast; Lacco Ameno and Casamicciola Terme on the north coast, both devoted to spas; and the pretty Sant'Angelo on the less populated south coast. At the island's heart is Monte Epomeo (2,582 ft/787 m), a volcano that last erupted in the 14th century and on whose slopes you will find quieter, little-visited villages such as Buonpane and Fontana (the trailhead for the 1-hour walk up the volcano).

Ischia town is filled with hotels, shops, and people. Its harbor is a former crater, an immediate hint as to the considerable volcanic activity that underpins the island. The main sight is the **Castello Aragonese** *(Piazzale Aragonese, tel 081 992 834, www.castelloaragonese.it, $$$),* once home to the court of Vittoria Colonna, a poet and humanist who numbered Michelangelo among her friends and frequent visitors.

Also diverting is the **Museo del Mare** *(Via Giovanni da Procida 2, tel 081 981 124 or 081 993 470, www.museodelmareischia.it, closed p.m. daily Nov.–March, & Feb., $),* a museum devoted to the sea, and film buffs might want to visit the **Palazzo Malcoviti** *(Vicolo Marina),* where much of the movie *The Talented Mr. Ripley* was filmed. **Cartaromana** to the south of the town is the best beach.

Moving north, most of **Casamicciola Terme** dates from after 1883, the year an earthquake razed the ancient town founded by the Greeks. This is a traditional spa town, devoted to serious cures rather than beauty and other regimes. Four of the island's most historic spas are here: the Manzi, Belliazzi, Elisabetta, and Lucibello.

Do your research if you are taking thermal treatments, for the island boasts more than 150 spas (plus 29 thermal baths, 67 geysers, and 103 hot springs), some traditional, some state-of-the-art. Most hotels and spas offer day packages to nonresidents.

Some of the grandest spas are in Lacco Ameno, notably the historic **Terme delle Regina Isabella** *(tel 081 994 322, www.reginaisabella.it)* and the more chic **Parco Termale Negombo** *(Baia di S. Montano, tel 081 986 152, www.negombo.it)* The latter is close to one of the island's best beaches, the **Baia di San Montano.** An equally exalted spa complex is the **Parco Termale Giardini Poseidon** *(tel 081 908 7111, www.giardiniposeidonterme.com)* in **Forio,** the island's largest but least touristy town, with 22 mostly outdoor pools and a large private beach. Other good beaches nearby include **Citara, Sorgeto,** and **San Francesco.** Forio is also at the heart of the island's flourishing wine industry.

Just north of the town is Ischia's main horticultural attraction, the garden of **La Mortella** *(Via Franceso Calise 39, tel 081 986 220, www.lamortella.org, closed Mon., Wed., Fri., & Nov.–March, $$$),* begun in the 1940s by British composer Sir William Walton and his wife, Susana, and designed by Russell Page, one of the 20th century's greatest landscape architects. Today, the gardens are an exotic delight, the more so if you are here for the concerts held most weekends between April and June and September and October.

INSIDER TIP:

Do as the Italians do, and rent a scooter to drive around Ischia: It's a great way to see the entire island.

—PATRICIA DANIELS
National Geographic Books editor

Forio has long attracted artists and writers, but today most discerning Italians head for **Sant'Angelo,** a former fishing village that is, relatively speaking, quieter and more relaxed than much of the island (though traffic on the approaches can be bad). It has a reasonable beach (Maroni), offers good views, and makes an ideal base. ■

Ischia Town
🄼 98 B3
Visitor Information
✉ Via Sogliuzzo 72
☎ 081 507 4211
**www
.infoischiaprocida.it**

More Places to Visit along the Amalfi Coast

Procida

Procida is the smallest of the inhabited islands in the Bay of Naples, covering an area of just 1.5 square miles (4 sq km) and with a population of about 11,000 (though this more than doubles in August). Despite the many visitors, it retains a certain charm, without coming close to the seductions of Capri or Ischia. Pleasant cafés and restaurants line the waterfronts, quiet lemon groves survive among the many houses, old and new, and the small **Vivara** nature reserve on the island's southwest tip provides a bucolic retreat. The **Castello,** a prison until the mid-1980s, dominates the approach to the harbor of Marina Grande, part of **Procida town,** the island's main settlement. Climb to the old quarter, the **Terra Murata,** for superb views of the bay, and make for the west coast between Chiaiolella and Ciriaccio for the best and most popular beach. For the quietest scenery and sea views, explore the lanes in the island's northeast corner between Punta Serra and Punta di Piopetto. Here is the now famous **Pozzo Vecchio** beach, one of the main locations in the 1994 movie *Il Postino,* starring Naples-born actor and comic Massimo Troisi.

🅜 98 B3 ✉ **Visitor Information** Via Vittorio Emanuele 173 ☎ 081 896 9628, *www .procida.net/proloco*

Salerno

An important center since the sixth century B.C., Salerno was the capital of Norman southern Italy until the royal court moved to Palermo in 1127. It was also renowned as one of Europe's leading medieval centers of medical learning; however, much of the town was destroyed in September 1943, when the Allies made it the bridgehead for their attack on the Italian peninsula. As a result, today's suburbs and waterfront are mostly dour, modern affairs, with only the old quarter retaining any interest. Much of the center has been rejuvenated by Oriol Bohigas, the Spanish architect responsible for transforming the Barcelona waterfront prior to the 1992 Olympics. For the casual visitor, the one great sight is the **cathedral,** founded in 845 and rebuilt by the Norman Robert Guiscard between 1076 and 1085. It has a lovely Romanesque portal, glorious bronze doors made in Constantinople in 1099, and an atrium of 28 ancient columns brought from Paestum (see pp. 94–95). Inside are two fine pulpits and Paschal (Easter) candlesticks (1173–1181), several medieval tombs, areas of Byzantine mosaic and pavement, and most remarkable of all, the alleged remains of the Apostle St. Matthew, which are kept in the crypt.

🅜 99 F2 ✉ **Visitor Information** Piazza Vittorio Veneto 1 ☎ 089 231 432, *www.salernoturismo.it* 🕐 Closed 1–4 p.m. & Sun.

The town of Vietri has produced its famous ceramics since the 15th century.

A gloriously varied region filled with sublime coastal landscapes, pastoral hills, and historic towns

Puglia

Details of the Romanesque cathedral of Conversano, near Bari

Puglia

Puglia—the heel of the Italian "boot"—is among Italy's largest regions, a rich agricultural domain overflowing with wine, wheat, and olive oil. Here you will find villages of white-washed houses stark against a turquoise sea and the sun-drilled brown of endless plains and heat-hazed hills.

A wedding outside the Basilica di San Nicola, Bari, one of Puglia's fine Romanesque churches

Puglia is a land rich in history, and thus in art, architecture, and cultural allure. Its ancient and unrecorded past belonged to early tribes such as the Messapians or Dauni. These were followed by the Greeks, who crossed the water from their homeland—little more than 60 miles (95 km) away—to found colonies that would become some of the most illustrious in the world. Later came the Romans, who built their first major road, the Via Appia, to link the area to Rome. Once established, the new invaders also introduced the agricultural prowess that has never left the area, along with the large *masserie*—feudal farmhouses-cum-fortresses—that still dominate much of the rural landscape.

Later still, the area's strategic position, so close to Greece, the Orient, and the Holy Land, attracted Byzantine and Saracen invaders. It also brought a short but intense period of prosperity,

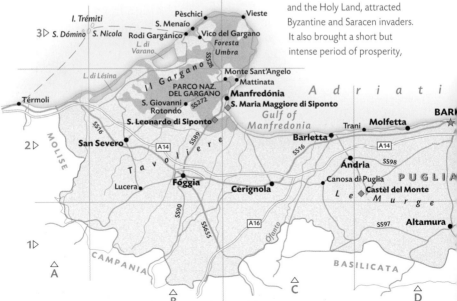

as countless pilgrims and crusaders used the region's many ports as points of embarkation for the Holy Land. At about the same time, in the 11th century, the arrival of the Normans saw the creation of Romanesque churches, one of Puglia's greatest glories. In the medieval era, riches came to Lecce, the region's most compelling large town, and with them a flowering of baroque architecture.

Art aside, your most enduring Puglian memories will probably be of its landscapes. You may find yourself recalling the endless plains of the north, the Tavoliere—the second largest in Italy, after the Po Valley—or the beautiful beaches and forests of the Gargano Peninsula; or the pastoral hills of Le Murge (the last made all the more compelling by the presence of the Castel del Monte, Europe's most mysterious fortress). Above all, there are the *trulli*, the curious ancient dwellings for which the region is famed.

Occasionally you will encounter the modern world, usually in the plain suburbs that girdle many a historic town. Don't be deterred. Puglia is a region on the cusp of discovery. Travelers are drawn by the recent appearance of fine new hotels, by low-cost flights from the rest of Europe, and, of course, by the age-old attractions at which Italy excels—art, food, climate, and sublimely beautiful landscapes. ■

NOT TO BE MISSED:

Il Gargano, especially the Parco Nazionale del Gargano and Peschici   **128–133**

Cathedrals of Bari and Molfetta **135, 137**

Fortress of Castel del Monte   **139**

Trulli structures of Alberobello and its surrounding countryside **140–145**

Hill town of Ostuni   **143**

Baroque facade of Santa Croce in Lecce   **149**

Mosaic floor of Otranto's cathedral of Santa Maria Annunziata   **153**

Il Gargano

The Gargano is the spur of the Italian boot, a beautiful peninsula that pushes into the Adriatic from the heat-baked plains of northern Puglia. A wonderfully varied scenic ensemble, its interior is covered in the Foresta Umbra, a protected enclave of ancient woodlands, while the coast is a stunning medley of cliffs, coves, beaches, azure seas, lagoons, fishing villages, and small resorts.

The coast near Mattinata is typical of the beautiful beaches and pristine seas of the Gargano Peninsula.

The Gargano's anomalous appearance—it is virtually the only mountainous intrusion on Italy's otherwise flat, sandy eastern coast—is a result of geological accident. In truth, it should be part of the Dalmatian shore across the Adriatic, the area to which its limestone and much of its flora and fauna belong. An alien on Italian soil, it is part of Central Europe, left behind when two geologic plates separated to form the Adriatic. For countless millennia thereafter it was an island, until silt deposited during the Ice Age connected it to the mainland.

Much of the area remains unknown to foreigners. Not so to the Italians, who long ago discovered its charms, and its beaches in particular. As a result, many of the coastal resorts are busy in summer. Note, too, that some beaches are owned by hotels, so access is not always straightforward unless you are a paying guest. Don't be deterred—if you come here outside of July and August, or drive or hike in the Foresta Umbra, you will barely meet a soul.

Sea and forest aside, there's plenty of incidental interest here as well, not least a selection of fine churches; the important pilgrimage site of Monte Sant'Angelo (see opposite), devoted to the cult of St. Michael the Archangel; and the still more important pilgrimage site of **San Giovanni Rotondo,** the erstwhile home of Padre Pio, a 20th-century monk whose piety and popular appeal saw him canonized in 2002 (see sidebar p. 130).

Routes through the Peninsula

Road and rail links enable you to approach the peninsula from the north or south and to follow any number of circular, or almost circular, tours that take in the best of the coast and the wooded interior. (The latter has been protected as a national park since 1991.) Approaching from the south, aim to start at **Manfredonia,** easily reached by fast road from Foggia. The town's environs are blighted by an oil refinery and light industry— an inauspicious start to the region—and you might drive right through were it not for a pair of fine churches on the town's approaches.

The first is **San Leonardo di Siponto,** on the south side of the SS89 from Foggia, 7 miles (11 km) west of Manfredonia. Begun near the end of the 11th century, it is a classic Puglian-Romanesque church, but it shows a mixture of Italian and Byzantine influences. These are most notable in the carvings of its exquisite doorway, where Eastern motifs are mixed with the sorts of animals, tendrils, and mythical creatures favored by Lombard and Tuscan sculptors of the period.

The second church, **Santa**

Maria Maggiore di Siponto, is on the south side of the same highway a couple of miles west of Manfredonia's town center. This building dates from 1023, but it was raised above a much older sanctuary that now forms the atmospheric crypt of the present church. Excavations to the left of the church have uncovered the remains of an even older Christian basilica, built over the ruins of a Roman temple of Diana. Pre-Roman tombs have also been found.

Evidence of such antiquity is hardly surprising, for the church was built on, or close to, the site of the ancient city from which it takes its name. Sipontum was already a flourishing port when it fell to the Romans in 194 B.C. A silted harbor, earthquakes, and malaria led to its downfall and the creation of a new town—present-day Manfredonia—in 1256.

Monte Sant'Angelo

Beyond Manfredonia, take the winding mountain road that climbs to Monte Sant'Angelo, or St. Michael's Mount, one

Il Gargano
🗺 126 B2 & B3

Manfredonia
🗺 126 C2
Visitor Information
✉ Piazza Libertà 1
☎ 088 458 1998
🕐 Closed Sun. & p.m. in winter, occasional p.m. opening in summer

San Giovanni Rotondo
🗺 126 B2
Visitor Information
✉ Piazza Europa 104
☎ 088 245 6240
🕐 Closed Sat. & Sun. in winter & p.m. daily except Tues. & Thurs.

EXPERIENCE:
Wildflower Vacations

Wildflowers are one of the Gargano's glories, and can easily be seen on hikes in the region in spring *(April–early May).* U.K.-based tour operator **Naturetrek** *(44 [0] 1962 733 051, www.naturetrek.co.uk)* offers two eight-day natural history vacations annually *(usually in April),* devoted to the peninsula's wildflowers, and its orchids in particular.

Monte Sant'Angelo

📍 126 C2

Visitor Information

✉ Via Reale Basilica 40

☎ 088 456 5520

www.proloco montesantangelo.it

of Europe's oldest and most important points of Christian pilgrimage. The town owes its existence to the Archangel Michael. A warrior angel and scourge of sinners, he is usually portrayed with a sword and scales in which he weighs the souls of the dead.

According to legend, Michael appeared three times in front of a local cave to St. Laurence, Bishop of Sipontum, on May 8 in A.D. 490, 491, and 493 (May 8 and

Lombards, warlike invaders from northern Europe who converted to Christianity, as well as during the Crusades, when knights came to pay homage before departing for the Holy Land. In the eighth century, St. Aubert, a French monk, took part of the angel's cloak to Brittany, in France, where he built the celebrated abbey of Mont St.-Michel.

Today, much of the plain-faced **Santuario di San Michele Archangelo** (*Via Reale Basilica*)

Padre Pio

Padre Pio (1887–1968) was born near Benevento, in Basilicata. At the age of 23 he became a Capuchin priest in Foggia, Puglia, before spending time as a medical orderly in Naples during World War I. After being discharged from the army with tuberculosis, he was sent to San Giovanni Rotondo in the Gargano to take the mountain air. In a monastery there on September 17, 1918, he developed stigmata—the wounds of Christ—that

allegedly never left him and caused lifelong pain. He became renowned for his healing powers, attracting a vast following, and was declared a saint in 2002. More than seven million pilgrims a year now come to San Giovanni, making it the world's second largest point of Christian pilgrimage, after Lourdes. An immense church, designed by Italian architect Renzo Piano, opened in the town in 2004.

September 29 are St. Michael's feast days). The angel also left his scarlet cloak at the bishop's feet, as well as the imprint of his foot, regaling the cleric with the words *Haec est domus specialis in qua noxialis quaeque action diluitur*—This is no ordinary house; here all sinful actions are washed away.

The cave duly became a place of pilgrimage and was eventually incorporated into a sanctuary and church, both of which have undergone numerous changes over the centuries. The cult and its warrior saint prospered in the eighth century under the

dates from after the 13th century, with more modern additions. The exception is the entrance to the old Romanesque-Gothic church, a structure that incorporates the original cave, reached by 86 steps. Its main portal is framed by the angel's words to St. Laurence and guarded by a pair of precious bronze doors, cast in Constantinople in 1076. Their 24 panels depict scenes from the life of the Archangel Michael, while inside the church the artistic highlight is a 12th-century throne of Leo II, onetime archbishop of Sipontum and Monte Sant'Angelo.

If you stop in the village of San Marco in Lamis, include a visit to the peaceful and impressive Convent of San Matteo.

—GIOVANNI GUGLIELMOTTI
Associazione Salerno IdeAperta

Across the road from the sanctuary, devote a few minutes to the ruins of the churches of **San Pietro** and nearby **Santa Maria Maggiore.** The latter dates from the early 12th century and preserves a beautiful main doorway (1198) and fragments of 14th-century Byzantine-style frescoes. Left of San Pietro, steps lead to the so-called **Tomba di Rotari,** long thought to be the tomb of a Lombard chieftain, but more likely a baptistery from the 12th century. Finally, clamber to the ruined **Norman castle** on the town's western flank for sweeping views over the rooftops.

Into the Woods

From Monte Sant'Angelo you have a choice of itineraries. One takes you west to San Giovanni Rotondo (see p. 129), returning to the coast near Mattinata. The other follows the SS528 road north through the best of the **Foresta Umbra** in the **Parco Nazionale del Gargano.** The latter route offers a firsthand view of the beeches, limes, oaks, chestnuts, and other trees that compose this wonderful expanse of relict woodland. Almost at the forest's heart, near the turnoff for Vico, lies the **Corpo Forestale,** a visitor center, where you can rent bikes and

Foresta Umbra
🏔 126 B3 & C3
Visitor Information
✉ Centro Visitatori, SS528
☎ 088 453 0311
🕐 Closed Nov.–March
✉ Ente Parco, Via Sant'Angelo Abate 121, Monte Sant'Angelo
☎ 088 456 1149 or 088 456 8911
www.parks.it
www.parcogargano.it

Convent of San Matteo
✉ Via Convento San Matteo, San Marco in Lamis
☎ 088 281 6716
www.biblioteca sanmatteo.it

The 11th-century church of Santa Maria Maggiore di Siponto

A fisherman rests on the beach at Peschici. Although the Gargano is a popular vacation destination, fishing and other traditional ways of life continue to thrive.

Peschici

📍 126 B3

Visitor Information

✉ Via Magenta 3

☎ 088 491 5362

Rodi Garganico

📍 126 B3

Visitor Information

✉ Piazza Luigi Rovelli 12

☎ 088 496 5576

pick up details of the region's many trails and other outdoor activities.

The forest's ecosystems have been called "a botanical museum of the Italian peninsula," a floral showcase that contains more than 2,000 species of small plants, shrubs, and trees. There are also 138 species of fauna that are "transadriatic"; they properly belong to the Balkans, descendants of creatures that existed when Italy and Central Europe were still joined.

The reasons for this biodiversity are various and disputed. Geographical remoteness has played a part, as has the isolation of the region—and its plant and other species—from the Apennines, the major mountain chain (and thus principal ecosystem) of the Italian peninsula. Then

there is the climate, which is mild and severe by turns, with additional inland and maritime variations. Also influential are the fertile soils, the varied topography of the region, and the fact that the forest has been state owned and protected since 1866.

Either of the two roads that strike north from the Corpo Forestale brings you to **Peschici,** perched above the sea and one of the smallest and nicest of the Gargano's resorts. (The route via hilltop Vico is best, if only because Vico itself is a pretty little village.)

Peschici began life in 970 as a defensive bastion against Saracen attack, its age still apparent in the attractive maze of venerable streets and white houses at its heart. To the resort's west lies a string of beaches, the relatively quiet resort of **San Meniano,** and another laid-back resort village, **Rodi Garganico,** originally a Greek settlement. Farther west still are several good beaches and the lagoons of **Lago di Varano** and **Lago di Lesina,** both noted bird-watching areas.

Vieste

Head east from Peschici and you pick up the promontory's coast road, quickly reaching Vieste, the area's most developed town, a place for beaches, relaxation, and nightlife. In the old town, look for the *trabucco,* a cantilevered arrangement of wooden beams and ropes used to fish for mullet. Found across the Gargano, the device probably dates from Phoenician times and is unique to the region. Fishermen lower a net from the device, wait for the mullet to swim in shoals above it, then winch the catch onto a platform. Also watch for the **Chianca Amara** (Bitter Stone) on Via Duomo, which marks the spot where 5,000 local people were beheaded when the Turks attacked the town in 1554.

From Vieste the road climbs through wooded and rocky landscapes, offering superb coastal vistas, with the beautiful contrast of green woodland and azure seas a constant backdrop.

Continue east and you will complete a circuit (and have seen the best of the region) that concludes close to Monte Sant'Angelo, a distance of about 95 miles (153 km). If time allows, fit in an excursion to the **Isole Tremiti** off the Gargano's northern coast, reached by regular ferries year-round from Vieste and in the summer from Vasto, Ortona, Termoli, and Manfredonia (embark from the last and you will enjoy lovely views of the Gargano's coastline). You can also make easy day trips to the islands by taking a boat from Rodi Garganico, just 8 miles (12 km) west.

The archipelago's principal islands are **San Nicola** and **San Domenico,** both packed in summer, but both renowned for their natural beauty and translucent waters. The diving, swimming, and other water sports are all first rate, but the less active can enjoy scenic boat trips, island strolls, and historical sights such as San Nicola's ninth-century Benedictine Abbey of Santa Maria al Mare. ■

Vieste

🗺 126 C3

Visitor Information

✉ Piazza Kennedy 1

☎ 088 470 8806

www.viaggiare inpuglia.it

EXPERIENCE:
Birding in the Gargano

The Gargano peninsula's varied habitats make it a birding destination. **Varano** and **Lesina** on the Gargano's north coast are southern Italy's largest lakes and one of the country's most important waterfowl sites. Huge numbers of resident and migrating birds can be seen, including cormorants, shovelers, pochard, coots, and red-breasted mergansers. Breeding birds here and elsewhere on the peninsula (notably the **Cesine nature reserve** east of Lecce and the salt flats near Margherita di Savoia) include vultures, honey buzzards, red and black kites, short-toed eagles, eagle owls, rollers, and middle-spotted and white-backed woodpeckers. Visit *www.parks.it* or *www.lipu.it,* the site of the Italian League for the Protection of Birds, for further information.

Bari

Bari is the capital of Puglia and the second city of southern Italy after Naples. A busy and bustling place, it is divided into an ordered but undistinguished modern city—full of broad boulevards and chic shops—and a tightly clustered Old Town that sits proudly on a rocky, castle-capped headland.

San Sabino, Bari's majestic cathedral, has the round arches typical of Romanesque architecture.

Bari

🅜 126 D2

Visitor Information

✉ Piazza Aldo
    Moro 33/A

☎ 080 524 2361 or
    080 990 9341

**www.infopointbari
.com**

Almost everything to see in Bari is in the tight maze of almost Arabic streets and alleys that makes up the **Città Vecchia** (Old Town). Until recently this area was largely run-down. These days, most of the old houses have been restored and numerous small bars, restaurants, and stores have opened, transforming the district, particularly at night, when the streets buzz with good-natured activity.

Bari's roots go back to the Bronze Age or earlier, with periods of Roman, Saracen, Lombard, and Byzantine domination; however, it was the arrival of the Normans in 1071 and the consequent boom in trade that fully established the city. Its status was further enhanced in 1087 when a group of Barese merchants in Antioch, learning that the Venetians intended to steal the sacred relics of St. Nicholas (then interred at Myra, on the southern coast of modern-day Turkey), preempted their rivals and stole the relics themselves.

Holy relics had great temporal and spiritual value in the Middle Ages, and after St. Nicholas's arrival in Bari it was only natural that a suitably splendid home should be created in which to house them. The result was the

French-influenced **Basilica di San Nicola** (*Piazza San Nicola, closed 12:45–4 p.m.*), one of the earliest and finest monuments of the Puglian-Romanesque architectural style. Begun circa 1087, the church was consecrated more than a hundred years later in 1197, though even then much of the building remained unfinished—hence its still slightly austere appearance.

The exterior highlight is the glorious carved main portal, a medley of Arab, Byzantine, and classical styles. Note the door to the left, the Porta dei Leoni, with its lively carving of knights on horseback. Inside, the eye-catching painted wooden and gilt ceiling dates from 1661–1674, but pride of place goes to the beautiful canopied ciborium (1150), the oldest in Puglia and the model for many similar tabernacles across the region. Almost equally magnificent is the Bishop's Throne (1089), used by Bishop Elia, the basilica's founder. The remains of St. Nicholas are found in the crypt.

Just south of the basilica stands Bari's cathedral, **San Sabino** (*Piazza Odegitria, closed 12:45–4 p.m.*), a virtual copy of San Nicola. Begun in 1170, it was designed to replace a cathedral destroyed when the Norman king William II razed the city in 1156 after a popular uprising (sparing only San Nicola). Like its near neighbor, this is a superb Romanesque building, still with its original wooden ceiling and another fine ciborium and episcopal throne. The strange, round building on the church's north side is known as the Trullo and was built in 1618 over the ruins of a baptistery destroyed by William in 1156.

North of both churches is the impressive modern **Museo Archeologico Provinciale** (*Piazza Umberto I, tel 080 523 5786, closed for restoration*), with a wide range of artifacts and ceramics dating from as far back as Neolithic times.

Bari's other major museum, the **Pinacoteca Provinciale** (*Palazzo della Provincia, Via Spalato 19, tel 080 541 2421, closed Mon. & Sun. p.m., $*), is in the new town along the Lungomare Nazario Sauro, but it is worth the journey. Its collection includes several major works by Venetian Renaissance masters such as Tintoretto and Veronese, as well as a good selection of southern Italian artists. ∎

St. Nicholas

Father Christmas, or Santa Claus, has his origins in St. Nicholas (San Nicola in Italian), the saint whose relics reside in Bari's Basilica di San Nicola. He is the patron saint of sailors and Holy Russia, among other things, but it is his role as a giver of gifts and as the protector of children for which he is best known. In one famous story, he resurrected three young boys killed by a butcher during a famine, and in another secretly left gifts of gold for three girls who, being without dowries, would have remained unmarried. The gifts, his association with the children, and his December 6 feast day saw him become a figure associated with Christmas in many cultures. In the United States, Santa Claus is probably a corruption of "San Nicholas" as adopted by early Dutch settlers.

Romanesque Puglia Drive

This drive begins in Bari, a busy port with a captivating historic quarter, and takes in Emperor Frederick II's great fortress at Castel del Monte and several towns celebrated for their fine Romanesque churches.

Begin in **Bari ❶** (see pp. 134–135), whose modern suburbs crowd in on the Città Vecchia, home to the late 12th-century cathedral of **San Sabino** and the 1087 **Basilica di San Nicola.** Both are supreme examples of the Romanesque architecture for which Puglia is famed. Such architecture flourished in the region for several reasons. First, the strong government of Norman, Swabian, and Angevin rulers over several centuries provided the stability and resources required to create buildings that often took more than a century to complete. Second, the region was a melting pot of ruling and other cultures, with the result that its buildings combined the architectural styles of Roman, Norman, Byzantine, Lombard, Arab,

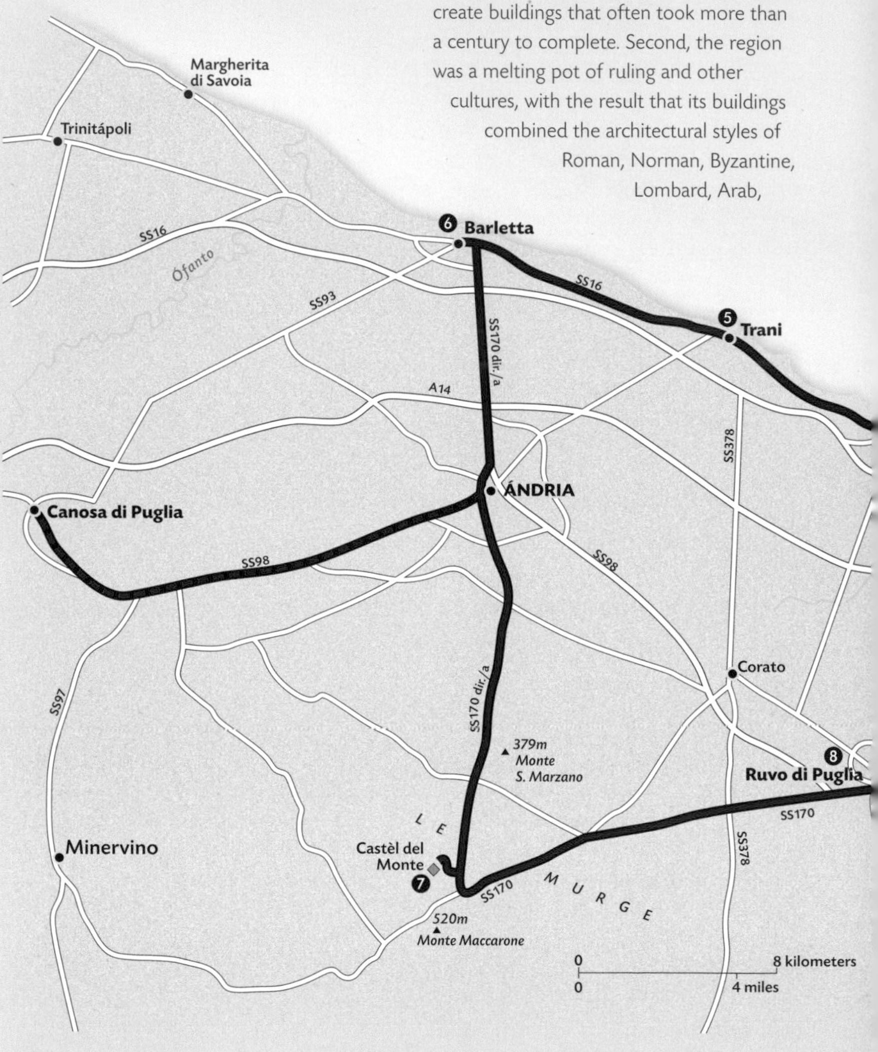

Margherita
di Savoia

Trinitápoli

SS16

Ófanto

SS93

❻ **Barletta**

SS16

SS170 dir/a

❺ **Trani**

A14

SS378

Canosa di Puglia

SS98

ÁNDRIA

SS98

SS170 dir/a

Corato

SS97

379m
Monte
S. Marzano

❽

Ruvo di Puglia

SS170

Minervino

Castèl del
Monte
❼

SS170

SS378

L E

M U R G E

520m
Monte Maccarone

| 0 | 8 kilometers |
| 0 | 4 miles |

NOT TO BE MISSED:

Molfetta cathedral • San Nicola cathedral, Trani • Castel del Monte • Ruvo di Puglia cathedral

and imported Tuscan and northern Italian craftspeople. Third, Puglia was at a major religious intersection, located astride several important pilgrimage routes—notably those leading to Monte Sant'Angelo (see pp. 129–131)—and close to ports used by pilgrims and crusaders.

Puglian Churches

No two Puglian churches are alike, but the variety, rich decoration, and sculptural acumen that mark them out as some of the glories of Italian architecture are bound by a few unifying strands. The earliest classical influences reached the region from Byzantium (the remnants of the old Eastern Roman Empire). At the same time, the

influence of Roman portraiture and the relief carving of classical sarcophagi also played their part.

Lombard sculpture from northern Italy contributed the carvings of lions, centaurs, and bizarre menageries usually found on and around a church's main portal. Architecturally, the Lombards contributed the high central naves (and lower aisles) of some churches, the three-sided apsidal ends, and the arched corbel-table below the roof. The Lombards were also responsible for the lovely lateral galleries formed of open arcades found in many local churches.

After exploring Bari, drive west on the SS16, perhaps pausing briefly at **Giovinazzo** ❷, where the late 13th-century cathedral was restructured in the baroque period but conserves a fine portal and crypt from the original Romanesque church. A few minutes farther west is **Molfetta** ❸, one of the area's most important fishing ports. Although unappealing on the outskirts, it is pleasant in its old center. There you will find a glorious

> ⛰ See area map pp. 126–127
> ► Bari
> 🕐 1–2 days
> 🚗 90 miles (145 km)
> ► Bari

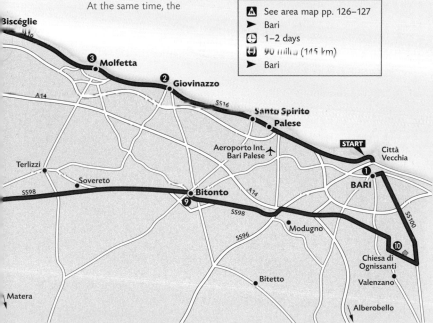

Begun by Frederick II in 1235, Bari's castle was completed by the Spanish in the 16th century.

cathedral *(Banchina Seminario, tel 080 396 9402)*, dedicated to the town's protector, St. Corrado, a Bavarian noble who retired to a hermitage nearby. It stands in a dramatic position virtually on the waterfront and was begun in the mid-12th century, its twin towers the only locally surviving example of a once common arrangement.

From Molfetta, continue west, with a short stop at **Bisceglie ❹**, another busy town with a splendid 11th-century **cathedral** *(Via Cardinale dell'Olio, tel 080 396 9402)* that has an especially lovely main portal.

Then push on to **Trani ❺**, a thriving port that in the cathedral of **San Nicola** *(Piazza Abate Elia)* boasts what is often called the "Queen of Puglian churches." The three apses that make up the rear of the church face the sea, a custom diffused along the Adriatic coast, both in Italy and the Balkans. The church was begun at the end of the 12th century, but it incorporates two earlier buildings: the chapel of San Leucio and the church of Santa Maria della Scala, both dating from at least the seventh century. Inside, the church contains 32

magnificent bronze panels (1175–1179) that once adorned the exterior of the main door.

Continue west to **Barletta ❻**, a drab town enlivened by **San Sepolcro** *(corner of Corso Giuseppe Garibaldi & Corso Vittorio Emanuele II, tel 088 333 3918)*, a Romanesque church founded in the 11th century and overlaid with a Burgundian-Gothic veneer 200 years later. Also visit the "Colosseo" north of the church, a statue that may represent the fourth-century Roman emperor Valentinian. Stolen from Constantinople by the Venetians, the figure washed up on the coast nearby; at 16 feet (5 m) high it is the largest surviving bronze figure from Roman antiquity.

From Barletta, strike inland on the SS170, perhaps pausing briefly at **Andria** to admire the richly carved portal of **Sant'Agostino** *(Via Porta La Barra, tel 088 359 2283)*, a church where the first hints of the Gothic style can be seen (note the door's slightly pointed, as opposed to rounded Romanesque, arch). A 14-mile (22 km) detour west on the SS98 takes you to **Canosa di Puglia,** where the outstanding Romanesque **Duomo di San Sabino**

(Piazza Vittorio Veneto, tel 088 361 1619) features
a beautiful carved pulpit and throne. In the
church's right (south) transept you can see the
Tomba di Boemondo (1111), the chapel-like
tomb of a Norman prince killed in the First
Crusade (note the superb bronze doors).

Castel del Monte

Otherwise, continue south on the SS170
from Andria to **Castel del Monte** ❼ *(tel
088 356 9997, $)*, one of southern Italy's
most memorable and mysterious sights.
A huge fortress visible for miles around, it
sits 1,790 feet (540 m) above Puglia's hilly
interior—a region known as Le Murge—its
purpose and distinctive design a puzzle to
generations of historians. Built between
1229 and 1240, it was the brainchild of
Frederick II, Holy Roman emperor and one
of the great personalities of the medieval
age. Everything about the building betrays
an obsession with mathematical harmony,
and in particular with the number eight:
The building is octagonal in plan and has
an octagonal courtyard and eight octagonal
towers, each of which contains two stories
of eight rooms each. Some claim that eight
is a symbol of the crown or the union of
God and humankind, others that the castle's

Lucera Castle

If you like the Castel del Monte, take
a detour about 53 miles (85 km) from
Canosa di Puglia to Frederick II's other
great Puglian fortress at Lucera *(Piazza
Padre Angelo, tel 800 767 606 toll-free in
Italy, www.comune.lucera.fg.it/castello,
closed Mon. & p.m. Nov.–March)*. The
second-largest castle in southern Italy
after Lagopesole in Basilicata, it was
built by Frederick for his court. The
walls are half a mile (1 km) long and
command magnificent views across
the Tavoliere plains to the uplands of
the Apennines and Gargano Peninsula.

---

proportions reflect some astrological con-
figuration of the heavens. That it had some
special significance is beyond question—it
was the only octagonal fortress among the
200 quadrilateral castles commissioned by
Frederick upon his return from the Crusades.

After your visit, turn left (east) on the
SS170 at the junction just south of the fortress
and follow signs to the 3,000-year-old village
of **Ruvo di Puglia** ❽, whose **cathedral** *(Via
Cattedrale, tel 080 361 5419)*, and its pretty
main portal in particular, again encapsulates
the best of the Puglian-Romanesque style. In
Greek and early Roman times, the town was
renowned for its distinctive red-black ceramics,
Puglian ware, examples of which can be seen
in the local **Museo Archeologico Nazionale**
*(Piazza Giovanni Bovio 35, tel 080 361 2848,
closed p.m. Mon.–Thurs.)*. From Ruvo, a good
road (the SS98) runs east to **Bitonto** ❾, a
town encircled by olive groves, and one whose
Romanesque **cathedral** *(Piazza Cattedrale)* bears
similarities to the cathedrals of Bari and Trani.

Conclude your drive by returning to Bari
or negotiate the muddle of roads south of the
city to find the **Chiesa di Ognissanti** ❿, just
off the SS100 northwest of Valenzano. This is
one of the earliest Romanesque churches in
the region (begun in 1062), an almost plain,
fortresslike rectangular building with three
shallow-pitched pyramidal cupolas. Set in
pretty, open country, surrounded by almond
trees and vines, it has a solitude and an austere
beauty—the same beauty that informs so many
Romanesque buildings—that make a fitting
conclusion to your tour.

Trulli Country

Across the dry, limestone hills of Le Murge, amid the pastoral countryside of the Valle d'Itria southwest of Bari, is one of southern Italy's most distinctive landscapes. Here, vineyards, oak woods, olive groves, and cherry orchards are dotted with *trulli* (see pp. 144–145), strange conical dwellings of mysterious origin that are virtually unique to this small corner of Italy.

Trulli dominate the old quarter of Alberobello in a region renowned for these unique dwellings.

Trulli country can be explored from any number of bases, though it is best to stay somewhere other than in the three busy main towns in the Valle d'Itria—Alberobello, Locorotondo, and Martina Franca. **Torre Canne** has a fine five-star hotel, the Masseria di San Domenico, and there are plenty of options in the Valle d'Itria countryside. You should also note that while most tour groups head straight for the towns, and Alberobello in particular, the most evocative trulli are often those in the rural areas, where they form a lovely and organic part of the age-old landscape. Therefore be prepared to leave the main roads between the towns, notably the SS172, and explore the smaller country lanes that meander between the fields.

However you explore, the heart of trulli country is small and easily seen in a day. The tour described below assumes starting in the west at Castellana Grotte, about 9 miles (15 km) southwest of Monopoli, and heading east to finish at Ostuni. A particularly pretty approach is to take the country road from Fasano to Castellana via Impalata, where the Loggia di Pilato on the east side of the village provides a beautiful overlook. If you are traveling without a car, the Ferrovia Sud-Est (FSE) railroad runs through the Valle d'Itria, connecting Bari with Castellana Grotte, Putignano, Alberobello, Martina Franca, and Cisternino.

Castellana Grotte, as its name suggests, is notable for its grottoes, part of an extensive system of caves and other karst features that stretches across the region's mainly limestone land-scape (see sidebar p. 143). The caves (tel 080 499 8211, www .grottedicastellana.it, closed p.m. daily Nov.–mid-March, $$$), the finest caverns in Italy open to the public, are just southwest of the village off the SS377. Tours take place roughly every half hour and are divided into 50-minute visits of just over half a mile (1 km) and two-hour tours of around 2 miles (3 km). The complex consists of five major caverns, its climax the Grotta Bianca, or White Cave, a dazzling array of ghostly white stalactites and stalagmites.

From Castellana Grotte, head southwest to the village of **Putignano,** where the first trulli begin to appear in significant numbers. Then take the SS172 or minor roads east, a route that reveals increasing numbers of trulli

and culminates in **Alberobello,** "capital" of the region and a UNESCO World Heritage site. There's no escaping the fact that this is a touristy spot. At the same time, the 1,500 trulli in and around the town make it somewhere that has to be seen. Just aim to come early or late to miss the worst of the crowds, and be sure to spend an equal amount of time in Cisternino and the trulli-filled countryside nearby.

Alberobello grew up around a sixth-century abbey and probably takes its name from a translation of silva arboris belli, after the oak woods that once surrounded it. Virtually all the trulli are concentrated in the southern part of the village, including a whole hillside

INSIDER TIP:

Every visitor to Puglia should tour the region of Alberobello, a countryside dominated by cone-shaped trulli.

—RICCARDO STRANO
Director, Italian Government Tourist Board North America

filled with these distinctive dwellings. Most are given over to food, wine, craft, or souvenir stores. Some are for rent, but if you want to stay in a trullo, it is better to rent outside the town (www .trullinet.com or www.tuttoalberobello .it; see p. 220). The **Trullo Sovrano** in Piazza Sacramento is the town's only two-story trullo, and at the top of the quarter the

Alberobello
🅰 127 E2
Visitor Information
✉ Pro Loco, Via Monte Nero 1
☎ 080 432 2822
🕐 Closed 1–3:30 p.m.
www.proloco alberobello.it

Martina Franca

🄰 127 F2

Visitor Information

✉ Via XX
　Settembre 3

☎ 080 480 5702

🕓 Closed Sun.,
　& p.m. except
　Tues. & Thurs.
　Oct.–April

modern church of **Sant'Antonio** (1926) is built in the form of a trullo. Note that here, as in much of the region, the trulli are mostly rebuilt or fairly recent—19th century or later.

From Alberobello it is just over 5 miles (8.7 km) to the area's second major town, **Locorotondo,** whose streets are arranged on a circular plan around a conical hilltop—hence its name ("round place"). Even without the nearby trulli, this would be a pleasing place, well worth a few minutes' exploration for the views over the fields and hills (Via Nardelli makes a particularly good vantage point). Note the oak woods in particular, fragments of what was once a much larger forest.

A short drive south of Locorotondo is **Martina Franca,** the third of the Valle d'Itria's main

centers, a place blighted by modern outskirts. At its heart, however, the town preserves an appealing historic core, dominated on its eastern margins by the **Palazzo Ducale** *(Piazza Roma),* built by the local noble Caracciolo family in the 17th century over the ruins of a castle dating from 1388. Today it is the town hall, whose few frescoed rooms are open to the public most weekday mornings during office hours. From Piazza Roma, Corso Vittorio Emanuele II leads west to **Piazza Plebiscito,** the main square, home to **San Martino,** a redoubtable baroque church. On the northern edge of the old center, the church of the **Carmine** *(Via Pergolesi)* provides another good outlook for views over the Valle d'Itria. Note that Martina Franca hosts one of Puglia's leading opera and classical

The limestone hills of Puglia contain numerous caverns, including the Grotte di Castellana, the finest cave system open to the public in Italy.

EXPERIENCE: Visiting the Caves

Much of central Puglia is composed of limestone, a permeable rock that often produces "karst" topography—that is, a landscape dotted with natural features produced by the dissolving action of water on limestone. The region's most dramatic karst features are the **Grotte di Castellana,** largely created over the millennia by a powerful underground river. Much of the complex closest to the surface was used as a garbage dump until its full extent was discovered by accident in 1938. Since its discovery, more than 14 million people have visited the complex.

The largest of the show caves open to the public is known as **La Grave,** over 330 feet (100 m) long by 165 feet (50 m) wide, and 180 feet (60 m) below

ground. It is the only section naturally linked to the surface, offering evocative, tree-framed glimpses of the Puglian sky from within the grotto. Equally striking is the light in the last of the major caves, the **Grotta Bianca,** where crystalline rock and alabaster-hued stalactites and stalagmites lend the cavern the intense white (*bianca*) color that explains its name.

Elsewhere, the tours of the cave touch on evocatively named speleological features such as the Cascata di Alabastro (Alabaster Waterfall) and Il Corridoio del Serpente (The Corridor of the Serpent). The tours ($$$) conclude with a visit to an on-site museum, the **Museo Speleogico,** which has displays related to the region's karst scenery.

musical festivals in late July and August, the **Festival della Valle d'Itria** (tel 080 480 510).

From Martina Franca drive northwest through Locorotondo to **Cisternino,** a prettier and more authentic sightseeing experience than Alberobello. It lies at the heart of some of the loveliest of all the pastoral scenery of the Valle d'Itria. Walk the lattice of small, almost Arabic streets and then take time to drive slowly to **Ostuni,** one of Puglia's most appealing hilltop towns, located on the eastern fringes of Le Murge and trulli country.

Known as the "white city" after its mantle of Greek-style whitewashed, flat-roofed houses, Ostuni sits on three hills. The highest contains the heart of the town, in whose network of twisting alleys you are guaranteed to become pleasantly lost. At

the top of the town, near Largo Castello, there are sweeping views over the countryside to the north. The town has pre-Roman roots; at periods during its history it has entertained monks from Syria and Egypt (in the 9th century) and seen the arrival of the Normans (in the 11th century).

Piazza Libertà, a large square on the southern edge of the old quarter, is an obvious place to start exploring. Locals gravitate here during the busy *passeggiata,* or evening stroll. From the square, curve uphill on Via Cattedrale to the **Duomo** (1469–1495), unexceptional inside but with a nice facade and late Gothic rose window. A few steps away is the **Museo della Civiltà Preclassiche della Murgia Meridionale** (Via Cattedrale, tel 083 133 6383, $), a small museum devoted to the region's pre-Roman history. ■

Ostuni
Ⓜ 127 F2
Visitor Information
✉ Corso Mazzini 8
☎ 083 130 1268

Trulli

Trulli are curious dwellings of mysterious origin. Round, single-story houses, barns, or stores, their age is uncertain, as are the reasons for their appearance. Unknown elsewhere in Europe, they are found scattered across much of the pretty pastoral countryside south of Bari, but especially in the towns and region around Alberobello and Martina Franca.

The word *trullo* (plural *trulli*) probably comes from the Greek *tholos,* meaning "cupola." The simple stone structures—using the vast quantities of limestone scattered across the region—have likely been built in Puglia for thousands of years. Yet almost everything about them is a mystery. The only simple things are their practicality and the way they are made. They are cool in summer, warm in winter, resistant to the elements, and cheap and easy to build. Many are still being created today: The domes, with their uncemented *chiancarelle,* or thin layers of stones, are easier to construct than they might appear.

INSIDER TIP:

Stay for the night in a rented *trullo*. The unique shape of the building creates a protective, almost holy feeling.

—ILARIA CAPUTI
National Geographic contributor

Most trulli are whitewashed, and many are topped with a cross, strange stone markers (a ball, cone, or combination of the two), or other symbols of unknown magical or superstitious significance. Roofs are often roughly painted with arcane hieroglyphics in white or gray.

But the trulli's simple practicality raises the issue of why they are absent across the rest of the Mediterranean, where conditions and building materials are often identical.

Some of the theories for the trulli's existence have their roots in peasant artfulness. During the 15th century, Ferdinand of Aragon prohibited his Puglian subjects from building permanent houses, the idea being that he could move a servile labor force where it was most needed. In response the Puglians—or so it is claimed—built loose-stoned houses that could be easily dismantled if their occupants needed to move or word came of an impending visit from one of the emperor's inspectors.

Another theory suggests that the houses were a sophisticated form of tax evasion—the Aragonese had imposed a levy on all houses except those that were unfinished, an exemption for which the Puglians could quickly qualify by removing (and later replacing) the trulli's loose-stoned roofs.

These theories are quaint, but in truth the origins of the trulli are probably more exotic still. The oldest surviving trulli probably date from the 13th century, though the majority are no more than 100 or 200 years old. Some current thinking, however, connects the buildings with similar structures in Mycenae in Greece, which would link them with a civilization almost 5,000 years old. Such links are not terribly far-fetched, for Puglia's ports are the closest of any in Italy to the Greek mainland. Furthermore, much of the region fell within the realm of Magna Graecia, the area of southern Italy and Sicily that was colonized by the Greeks between the eighth and third centuries B.C.

Unfortunately, this theory still doesn't explain why trulli are so limited in geographic extent. One or two could have been built as tombs or homes in Puglia by monks who settled in the region from the East, then copied and adapted by local people to everyday use. They would have been ideally suited to Puglia's scattered population. That no one really knows the trulli's origins, however, only adds to the allure of these most mysterious of buildings.

Trulli houses mix with more recent buildings in Alberobello.

Lecce

Lecce is known as the "Florence of the baroque," a sobriquet coined as testimony to an architectural flowering almost unequaled in southern Italy. Greeks, Romans, and Normans all left their mark here, but the most lasting legacy was that of the religious orders and the powers of Habsburg Spain. Those ruling denizens effected a sweeping transformation of the city in the 16th and 17th centuries.

Outstanding baroque architecture, as seen in the extravagant facade of Sant'Oronzo, has made Lecce famous.

Lecce's metamorphosis was fired by the fervor of the Counter-Reformation, financed by wealthy merchants, and helped by a sumptuous local stone. The city's baroque veneer was applied not only to its major civic and religious buildings but also to these buildings' many decorative details. Porches, pedestals, courtyards, windows, and balconies—especially balconies—are smothered in garlands of fruit, chubby statues, gargoyles, and intricately worked curlicues of stone. Almost every surface of a certain age is adorned with the light, golden, and close-grained local limestone—*pietra dorata*—whose easily worked but durable properties proved perfectly suited to carving.

Historic Lecce

Long before its baroque heyday, Lecce began life as a Messapian city, taking the name Lupiae under the Romans, who brought prosperity to the region by building an extension of the Via Appia (an important Roman road) from the port of Brindisi to the north. The town prospered further under Byzantine and Norman rule between the 6th and 11th centuries. By the

15th century Lecce was at the heart of trade in the lower Adriatic.

Today, the old nucleus of the Messapian and later Roman cities, with their concentric circles of streets, is still evident, captured within a set of bastioned walls built on the orders of Charles V in 1543. Although little of the walls remain—save for three of the original four portals—virtually all of what you want to see during a visit remains within their former embrace. Outside, beyond the old town's former limits, is an uninteresting modern city of 97,500 inhabitants.

Piazza del Duomo

The city's baroque heart is Piazza del Duomo, unusual by Italian standards in that it is almost completely enclosed, with just one easily missed entrance (created in 1761) on its northern flank off Via Vittorio Emanuele II. In the square's southeast corner stands the cathedral (1659–1670) or **Duomo di Sant'Oronzo,** which was rebuilt by the principal architect of the city's baroque transformation, Giuseppe Zimbalo (1620–1710). Created to replace an 11th-century cathedral on the site, the church is distinguished by its twin facades, the main one restrained and relatively sober, the other a more luxurious offering that deliberately resembles a grand retablo (large altarpiece) of a type common in Spain. The redoubtable

227-foot (70 m) campanile (1661–1682) is also the work of Zimbalo. Note that this square is particularly beautiful in the evening, when the buildings are floodlit.

To the right of the cathedral is the **Palazzo Vescovile** (Bishops' Palace) and its delightful loggia, built in 1428, when the lower arcade would have been filled with shops. It was reconstructed in 1632. Zimbalo's star pupil, Giuseppe Cino (1635/44–1722), built the glorious **Seminario** (Seminary) next to it between 1694 and 1709. Don't miss the richly decorated well in the courtyard, also by Cino.

Walk west from the Piazza del Duomo on Via Vittorio Emanuele

Lecce
127 G2

Visitor Information
Via Vittorio Emanuele II, 16
083 224 8092
Closed Sun. & Sat. p.m. Oct.–April
www.viaggiare inpuglia.it

EXPERIENCE: Special-Interest Vacations

You can get behind the scenes in Puglia by contacting a local tour company such as **Path** *(tel 860/881-2780 ext. 19277 in the U.S., or 340 080 9257 in Italy, www .experience-path.com).* You might take a self-guided hike or bike tour round small vineyards, stopping to visit ancient cantinas; or, from a base in Lecce, take part in introductory courses in cooking and wine appreciation; or climb on a Vespa for a breezy rural tour of quiet country roads. The emphasis is on meeting local people and sampling local producers. For a more sedate tour of villages, countryside, and cultural highlights, **Backroads** *(tel 800 462 2848, www.backroads.com)* offers six-day bike tours departing from Bari and visiting trulli country and beyond. To learn about local cooking from expert local cooks, contact the Puglia-based **Stile Mediterraneo** *(www.italycookingcourses.com).*

San'Irene

✉ Via Vittorio Emanuele II

☎ 083 230 8107

II and Via Giuseppe Libertini, and you pass a pair of pretty churches on the left (Santa Teresa and Sant'Anna) before coming to **Santa Maria del Rosario** *(Via Vittorio Emanuele II, tel 083 294 7040, closed 12–4:30 p.m. & Sun. p.m.)*, or San Giovanni Battista, Zimbalo's last and finest work (1691–1728). The church's cloister

INSIDER TIP:

You can drive across the peninsula near Lecce in just over an hour. In one day you can watch the sun rise over the east coast and set over the west.

—PATRICIA DANIELS
National Geographic Books editor

once held a tobacco factory, Lecce's snuff having been famous since the time of Emperor Napoleon, who would use no other.

Explore the sleepy maze of little streets to the north of Via Giuseppe Libertini and then retrace your steps, passing the graceful baroque church of **Sant'Irene,** built between 1591 and 1639 by the Theatine religious order. With the Jesuit church of the Gesù (a short distance north on Via Rubichi), built in 1575, this was one of Lecce's earliest baroque transformations. Externally the church is far less florid than many of its successors, but inside it has some of the city's most ornate altars, as well as a high altarpiece by

Oronzo Tiso (1726–1800), one of the last exponents of Lecce's baroque school of painting.

Piazza Sant'Oronzo

Continue east to Piazza Sant'Oronzo, Lecce's busy main square named after St. Orontius, the city's first bishop (appointed by St. Paul, no less). He was martyred in A.D. 66 or 68 during the persecutions by Emperor Nero. The square is a sprawling, rather curious space, largely because the sunken remains of a **Roman amphitheater** occupy much of its southern half. Built under Hadrian in the second century, the 20,000-seat arena would almost certainly have been at the center of a far larger complex, probably comprising baths, gyms, and other public and civic buildings.

At the square's heart is the **Colonna di Sant'Oronzo,** one of two Roman pillars that once marked the end of the Via Appia in Brindisi. It was brought here in 1666 and raised as a votive offering to St. Orontius, whose intercession was credited with having saved the city from a plague ten years earlier.

Close to the column is a pair of linked little buildings, the **Sedile** (or Palazzo del Seggio, dating from 1592) and the deconsecrated church of **San Marco** *(Piazza Sant'Oronzo, closed 1–4 p.m.)*, the latter built in 1543 and attributed to Gabriele Riccardi (1524–1582/84), whose work you will see again. Graced with lovely carved details, these structures are two of Lecce's gems, the former an erstwhile meeting place for the city's elders, the latter built as a chapel for Lecce's resident community of Venetian merchants (hence the lion in the lunette, symbol of St. Mark and of Venice).

In the piazza's southeast corner is another church from the 1590s, **Santa Maria delle Grazie** *(Via Fazzi, off Piazza Sant'Oronzo, tel 083 224 0159, closed p.m. daily).* Built, like Sant'Irene, by the Theatine Order, it is far more ornate than its near neighbor. In the strip of stores and bars to the left of the church is one of Lecce's most pleasant cafés, the Caffè al Vino, graced with a lovely old-fashioned interior. Beyond it to the east rises the lumpen bulk of the city's **Castello,** a 16th-century fortress built by Emperor Charles V, now containing offices. On the opposite, western side of the

square, note the name of the street—Via Augusto Imperatore—so called because it was here in 44 B.C. that Octavian (the future Emperor Augustus) was first proclaimed emperor after learning of the assassination of his great-uncle and adoptive father, Julius Caesar.

Baroque Extravagance

From the square, walk north on Via Umberto I to join the crowds admiring **Santa Croce** *(Via Umberto I, closed 1–4 p.m.),* the apotheosis of Lecce's vivacious baroque style. Begun in 1549 by Gabriele Riccardi, the completed church (150 years in the making) was the work of several architects, including the ubiquitous Zimbalo, who was responsible for much of the facade's pediment and rose window. Next to the church stands

Balconies and beautiful architectural details are found on virtually every historic building in Lecce.

the **Palazzo del Governo** *(interior closed to public)*, or Palazzo dei Celestini (1659–1695), the former residence of the city's governor.It began as a Celestine monastery, but was converted first by Zimbalo (responsible for the lower facade) and then by Cino.

Santa Chiara

Return to Piazza Sant'Oronzo and explore the knot of streets to the south, making a beeline for **Santa Chiara** *(Piazza Vittorio Emanuele II)*, attributed in part to Cino. Built in 1687, it stands on the west side of a little square with a charming garden and a statue of a rakish-looking King Vittorio Emanuele II. Santa Chiara has a diverting facade, but it takes second place to the interior, festooned with gilt and extravagantly decorated altars and columns.

The deeply incised carving of the altars is typical of Lecce's baroque style.

Note the little street to the church's left, Via Arte della Cartapesta, named after the papier-mâché figurines (usually of saints) that were made here and elsewhere in Lecce. This craft, along with wrought-iron work, brought the city much renown in the 17th through the 19th centuries. The street leads to the first-century A.D. **Teatro Romano,** the well-preserved remains of Puglia's only Roman theater. In its day the structure probably had more than the dozen surviving tiers of seats and could probably accommodate an audience of more than 5,000.

Return to Santa Chiara and continue south on Via d'Aragona, passing **San Matteo** *(closed Mon. a.m.)* on the right. This baroque church is distinguished

The ruins of Lecce's ancient Roman amphitheater dominate Piazza Sant'Oronzo, the town's vast central square.

by its curious facade, a hybrid that makes playful use of both convex and concave architectural conceits. The interior is worth a glance for its lavish decoration.

Museo Provinciale

Keep walking south and you come to Lecce's principal museum, the **Museo Provinciale Sigismondo Castromediano** *(Viale Gallipoli 28, tel 083 230 7415, closed 1:30–2:30 p.m. & Sun. p.m.)*. The museum's wide-ranging collection includes many reliefs and other items removed from the city's amphitheater and Roman theater, but it is best known for its ceramics; its Greek, Roman, and Puglian vases (the earliest dating from the sixth century B.C.); and a miscellany of Murano glass, ivories, enamels, coins, bronzes, and terra-cottas.

Among the paintings in the picture gallery (occasionally partially or completely closed), the highlights are a polyptych by the Venetian master Bartolomeo Vivarini (1430–1491 or later) and Oronzo Tiso's "Madonna with Saints Benedict and Ignatius." Look, too, for the portrait of St. Orontius by Giovanni Andrea Coppola (1597–1659).

If you are not yet sated with baroque architecture, walk a short distance west on Viale Gallipoli, take the first right on Via Cairoli, then the first alley on the left, and you come to the **Carmine** *(Piazza Tancredi)*, a vast and immensely ornate church, the whimsical last work of Giuseppe Cino.

The city's final major sight, the abbey church of **Santi Nicola e Cataldo** (1180), lies northeast of the old center at the end of Via del Cimitero, but it is well worth the detour. Inevitably, the Romanesque purity of the original Norman building, built by Tancred, the last Norman king of Sicily, has been compromised by later additions, but something of

Land of Plenty

Puglia produces 80 percent of the pasta consumed in Europe, more wine than all of Germany put together (or around 20 percent of all Italian wine), and more olive oil than all the other regions of Italy combined (or a third of total Italian production). The heart of this great food-producing region is the Tavoliere, near Foggia, the largest Italian plain south of the Po plain in northern Italy, and in a summer a vision of golden wheat fields. Puglia is also one of the main sources of sun-dried tomatoes, thanks to the region's high summer temperatures.

the facade's original glory can be gleaned from the superb 12th-century rose window and the ornamentation around the main portal. Inside, the arches and octagonal cupola show the Arab influences that colored Sicilian church architecture of the time. ■

Il Salento

Il Salento is the name given to the Salentine Peninsula, the southernmost tip of the Italian heel. Easily explored by car from Lecce, it offers a delightful medley of lovely coastal landscapes, a sun-bleached interior, villages of whitewashed houses, and two interesting historic towns—Otranto and Gallipoli.

Otranto's harbor festival is one of many regular events taking place in this charming village.

Il Salento
▲ 127 F2 & G2

San Cataldo
▲ 127 G2
Visitor Information
✉ Via Gidiuli 64
☎ 083 265 0139

From Lecce (see pp. 146–151), take the arrow-straight SS543 road northwest to the coast at **San Cataldo,** a pleasing resort with a sandy beach. Then turn south on the SS611, a picturesque road that shadows the shoreline. It passes a small nature reserve at Le Cesine *(tel 083 2631 3548),* south of San Cataldo, and the occasional ruined tower. Eventually you come to **Otranto,** which can also be reached by train (change at Maglie) or a fast road (SS16) from Lecce (23 miles/45 km).

Italy's most easterly town, Otranto was a Roman, Byzantine, and Norman port. Today, it is a popular summer resort, but it remains best known for a joint Turkish and Venetian attack in 1480. Twelve thousand local people lost their lives and 800 survivors were executed on the Hill of Minerva just south of the town (marked by a commemorative church and memorial). The Turkish commander, having sawed the town's archbishop in half, offered to spare the lives of the 800 if they renounced their

Christian faith. None complied, and all duly died.

The old town's main artistic attraction is in the cathedral of **Santa Maria Annunziata** *(Piazza Basilica, tel 083 680 1436),* begun in 1080. Its extraordinary mosaic floor (1163–1166) mixes pagan myth, historical fact, and Christian iconography. Elsewhere in the church, visit the chapel in the right (south) transept, which contains some of the bones of the martyrs of 1480. Also visit the church of **Santi Pietro e Paolo** on the stepped alley off Piazza Basilica, which is adorned with important early frescoes.

South of Otranto

South of Otranto, follow the SS173 road, which offers wonderful sea views and the chance to visit some of the many caves (notably the **Grotta Zinzulusa**) whose signposts dot the roadside. Cut inland and head toward Gallipoli (via Casarano), detouring to tiny **Patù** (2 miles /3 km east of Gagliano). Here is the celebrated **Centopietre,** a mysterious barrow, which may be a prehistoric sanctuary, a Greek mausoleum, or a medieval building of unknown purpose.

The modern portion of **Gallipoli** is uninspiring, but the lively old town across the bridge has a pretty tangle of whitewashed houses and alleys hung with fishing nets. The cathedral, castle, and small museum provide points of interest.

From Gallipoli take the coast road north to the resort of Santa Maria del Bagno. Then cut inland to **Nardo,** the first of a trio of attractive, little-known towns. In Nardo, still part-enclosed by ancient walls, see the **cathedral** *(Piazza Pio II, tel 088 387 2004)* and the octagonal *edicola,* or baroque monument, in Piazza Osanna, and stroll the pretty Piazza Mercato. To the east, **Galatina** offers magnificent 14th-century frescoes in the church of **Santa Caterina d'Alessandria** *(Piazza Orsini, tel 083 656 2304).* Finally, pause in **Copertino,** dominated by a castle *(closed p.m. daily, $)* built in 1535. ∎

Otranto
 127 H2
Visitor Information
- ✉ Piazza Castello 5
- ☎ 083 680 1436
- 🕐 Closed Sun. & 1–3/4 p.m.

Gallipoli
🅰 127 G1
Visitor Information
- ✉ Via Antoniettade Pace 86, Piazza Imbriani 10 (after 2011)
- ☎ 083 326 2529
- 🕐 Closed Sun. & 1–3/4 p.m

EXPERIENCE: The Tarantella

Tarantism is an illness supposedly brought on by a spider bite; it resulted in a frenzied dance, the tarantella, which supposedly cured the condition. This, in turn, inspired a ritualized folk dance and musical accompaniment, first in Naples, then across southern Italy, and especially in Puglia's Salento region, where the dance and music are known as *pizzica*. After dying out in the fifties, the tarantella folk tradition has recently enjoyed a revival.

To experience it, visit Galatina, 15 miles (24 km) south of Lecce, for the **Festa Patronale dei SS. Apostoli Pietro e Paolo,** held annually June 28–30 *(www .comune.galatina.le.it).* San Paolo (St. Paul) is invoked against bites from spiders and poisonous animals. Pizzica is danced and played here, and, increasingly, at other festivals in the region, such as in **Torrepaduli** *(www.festasanroccotorrepaduli.it).* Visit www.lanottedellataranta.it for details of similar events during August.

More Places to Visit in Puglia

Brindisi

Brindisi features prominently in southern Italy's commercial affairs, being the region's largest port and a major point of embarkation for ferries and cruise ships to Greece and beyond. In classical times it marked the end of the Via Appia from Rome. Across the centuries it has been a conduit for legionaries, traders, and pilgrims and crusaders to the Holy Land. Today, however, although it offers little for the casual visitor, it does contain a handful of interesting sights in the old center. Chief among these are the church of **San Benedetto** *(Via San Benedetto);* the circular church of **San Giovanni al Sepolcro** *(Via del Tempio),* built by the Knights Templar around the year 1000; and the **Museo Archeologico Provinciale "F. Ribezzo"** *(Piazza Duomo 7, tel 083 156 5508, closed Sun., Mon., & p.m. except Tues.).* The last has a rich collection of archaeological finds, including artifacts from pre-Roman necropoli in the city's outskirts.

🅰 127 F2 ✉ **Visitor Information** Lungomare Regina Margherita 43–44 ☎ 083 152 3072 or 083 156 2126

Taranto

Taranto is much like Brindisi, in that its long and distinguished history—it was once the first city of ancient Magna Graecia—is today obscured by a large modern city. Like Brindisi, Taranto is a major port and has long been home to a large part of the Italian fleet, for which reason it was heavily bombed in World War II. Its ancient heart survives—just—on a small island that commands the harbor entrance, home to a **Duomo** *(Via del Duomo)* founded in the 11th century but much altered since. The decorated chapel of San Cataldo is the main attraction. Also visit the colorful **fish market** *(Via Cariati)* and the warren of old, crumbling streets. The city's genuine star is the **Museo Nazionale** *(Corso Umberto I, 41, tel 099 453 2112, $$),* which has more than 100,000 exhibits from different eras; in archaeological terms, it is second in southern Italy only to the Museo Archeologico Nazionale in Naples (see pp. 48–51).

🅰 127 F1 ✉ **Visitor Information** Corso Umberto I, 121 ☎ 099 453 2392 or 099 453 2397

Padre Pio's image is found throughout Italy—here, in Taranto—a testament to his following.

Two of Italy's least known regions, wild places filled with ancient sites and sparkling seas

Calabria & Basilicata

Calabria's seas provide fresh seafood.

Calabria & Basilicata

In the popular imagination, Calabria and Basilicata are the essence of rural Italy: two remote regions of harsh, if breathtaking, mountainscapes; places with a traditional way of life and a proud but impoverished people hamstrung by years of emigration and the disdain of their wealthy northern neighbors.

A market vendor in Tropea, Calabria, purveys some of the region's luscious produce.

Well, up to point. Apart from the golden era of Magna Graecia and the Greek colonies that prospered on the Calabrian coast 2,500 years ago, history has passed the regions by or dealt them a cruel hand. Decline set in as early as the Roman period, forcing an ever dwindling population to the lonely villages of an interior marked by earthquakes, climactic extremes, and wilderness.

Today those same coasts and remote landscapes are the regions' chief glories. The 485 miles (780 km) of the Calabrian coast have seen a boom in agriculture and a proliferation of seaside resorts such as chic little Tropea and Maratea in Basilicata.

Inland, the story is the same. True, the landscapes can appear haunting, but it is precisely the qualities of silent vistas and brooding wilderness that make the countryside so compelling. The finest scenery is in the regions' three national parks, spanning the remote mountains of Pollino and Orsomarso in the north, the dulcet meadows and forests of Calabria's Sila uplands, and the utter wilderness of the Aspromonte in the south. Farther east, the lunar landscapes and cave dwellings of Matera provide some of southern Italy's most enticing sights.

The regions do not have the rich culture one associates with Italy. Even at the many Greek sites the remains are scanty, the treasures now residing in the archaeological museum in Calabria's regional capital, Reggio di Calabria. But there are still lovely things here, and fascinating cultural must-sees, from the regions' 500-year-old Arbëreshë (Albanian) villages and priceless illuminated manuscripts at Rossano to the Byzantine churches and Norman cathedrals of Stilo and Gerace. ■

A

B

C

Spinnazzola

Melfi

Altamura

Gioia
d. Colle

Alberobello

Ostuni

Martina
Franca

6 ▷

PUGLIA

A14

Pescopagano

Matera

Mottola

Massafra

SS7

Laterza

Potenza

Táranto

BASILICATA

SS407

Basento

Metaponto

Sala Consilina

Santa Maria
d'Anglona

Policoro

5 ▷

CAMPANIA

A3

Agri

Golfo di
Táranto

PARCO NAZ.
D. CILENTO
E VALLO DI
DIANO

Lagonegro

Pisciotta

Rivello

San
Severino

PARCO NAZ.
DEL POLLINO

SS92

Ionian

Fiumicello

Maratea

Sant.

S. Biágio

Porto

Marina di Maratea

Praia a Mare

Scalea

M. Pollino
2,246m

S. Dolcedorme

SS105

Terranova
di Pollino

SS106

Trebisacce

S. Lorenzo Bellizzi

Sibari

Castrovíllari

Coast

4 ▷

M. di
Orsomarso ▲
1,827m

Firmo

Diamante

Spezzano
Albanese

Rossano

Calabria

SS18

CALABRIA

Cirò Marina

Camigliatello
Silano

Páola

SS18

PARCO
NAZ.

San Giovanni
in Fiori

Riviera

Cosenza

A3

La Sila

Crotone

Amantea

D. CALABRIA

Rome

Naples

3 ▷

Nicastro

Catanzaro

SS280

Golfo di
S Eufémia

Golfo di
Squillance

Area of map detail

Pizzo

SS110

SS182

Soverato

Zambrone

I. Stromboli

Parghelia

Tropea

Vibo Valéntia

SS182

Serra San Bruno

2 ▷

I. Panarea

Capo
Vaticano

Joppolo

SS18

La Serre

Bivongi

Stilo

Nicotera

Rosarno

Gióla Táuro

I. Lipari

Tyrrhenian Sea

Palmi

A3

Taurianova

SS106

I. Vulcano

Costa Viola

Gerace

SS112

Locri

Messina

Aspromonte

SS184

▲ S. Montalto
1955m

Bianco

Ionian Sea

1 ▷

**Réggio di
Calábria**

SS183

Roccaforte
del Greco

Roghudi

E90

SICILY

Galliciano

Bova

0

50 kilometers

A20

E45

Mélito

0

25 miles

A18

Matera

Matera is one of Italy's most alluring sights, thanks to its extraordinary *sassi*, or cave dwellings—more than 3,000 houses and 150 cave churches that form the largest and most complex troglodyte city in the Mediterranean. A byword for grinding peasant poverty until the 1950s, they were awarded UNESCO World Heritage status in 1993 and today have been restored to become some of the South's foremost visitor attractions.

Despite its long history, Matera is firmly rooted in the present, with a vibrant culture.

Matera

157 B6

Visitor Information

- Via de Viti de Marco 9
- ☎ 083 533 1983
- 🕐 Closed Sat., Sun., & p.m. except Mon & Thurs.
- Via Ridola 60
- ☎ 083 531 1655
- 🕐 Closed 2:30–4 p.m.

www.aptbasilicata.it

Matera occupies a lofty site on the precipitous edge of the Gravina di Matera, one of the typical *gravine* (ravines) that characterize the low hills of eastern Basilicata. At the heart of the town is Piazza Vittorio Veneto, with another pivotal square, Piazza del Duomo, to the east. Modern Matera stretches north and west of the squares, while the area containing the sassi lies lower to the east, riddling two districts on

the slopes of the ravine: the northwest-facing Sasso Barisano and traditionally more impoverished northeast-facing Sasso Caveoso.

Both districts have ancient origins, dating back at least 7,000 years, when humans took advantage of the area's easily excavated tufa stone and inhabited the ravine's natural caves and early niche-cut dwellings. From Roman times until the arrival of the Normans in 1064, the town's history was one of subjection and invasion by Hannibal of Carthage, Goths, Lombards, Franks, Saracens, Byzantines, and others. After 1663 the town became the capital of Basilicata, ceding its title to the more central Potenza in 1806.

For most of this time, the sassi provided viable and, by the standards of the day, relatively civilized dwellings. An ingenious network of small canals provided water and dealt with sewage, and a warren of churches, small hanging gardens, and carved streets and alleys created a livable city. The problems began in the early 19th century, when an unsustainable increase in population led to the habitation of sassi previously reserved for animals or storage. Most of these new "homes" lacked natural light, ventilation, or running water.

The town's subsequent squalor and poverty—extreme even by the often appalling standards of the South—were brought to the attention of a wider world by the publication of *Christ Stopped at Eboli* (1945) by Carlo Levi, who had been exiled to the region for his political views by the Fascist government in the 1930s. Levi's marvelous but shocking book described the way of life in Matera and beyond, painting a picture of a place wracked not just by unimaginable poverty, but by dysentery, malaria, and tracoma, among other evils.

In the 1950s the government was finally shamed to action, and 15,000 of the town's inhabitants were forcibly rehoused. For years afterward the abandoned area fell into decay, a ghost town whose entrances were often sealed and whose bizarre secrets were known only to a handful of visitors. Now the place is reemerging and visitors are being welcomed, with sassi being turned into cafés, hotels, and chic designer homes. The area received a boost, of sorts, when actor and director Mel Gibson chose the sassi and the barren landscapes just outside of town to shoot the Crucifixion and other scenes in his 2004 movie, *The Passion of the Christ.*

Tours of the *Sassi*

If you decide not to explore the sassi under your own steam, you can pick up additional insights and see some of Matera's more well-hidden corners on a guided tour. Ferula Viaggi (*Via Cappelluti 34, Matera, tel 083 533 6572, www.ferulaviaggi.it*) **offers tours, as well as vacation packages in the town and cultural, hiking, cycling, and food and wine tours in Basilicata and Puglia. Details of other tours, including "The Passion Tour" of sites associated with Mel Gibson's 2004 movie** *The Passion of the Christ* **(shot locally), can be found at** *www .sassiweb.com/guided-tours.*

Visiting the Sassi

Until recently you might have been advised to hire a guide to navigate the sassi and to find the best concealed nooks and tiny churches. You still can do this if you wish, or you can join one of the many guided tours organized by different groups around town; however, armed with one of the newer and better maps, you can easily tackle the sassi area on your own.

**Museo Nazionale
Ridola**

✉ Via Ridola 24
☎ 083 531 0058
🕐 Closed Mon.
a.m.
💲 $

**Museo d'Arte
Mediovale e
Moderna**

✉ Palazzo
Lanfranchi
☎ 083 531 4235
🕐 Closed Mon. &
1–4 p.m.
💲 $

The sassi district can be entered from several points in the old town, some of which are signposted, including entrances just off Piazza Vittorio Veneto and Piazza San Francesco; there's also a signposted tourist

INSIDER TIP:

For an uncrowded experience, visit Matera in the summer, when most tourists prefer to go to southern Italy's beaches.

—TINO SORIANO
National Geographic photographer

itinerary that begins just south of Piazza del Duomo. A main street, the **Strada Panoramica dei Sassi,** winds through both quarters, but you need to leave this—and be prepared to negotiate plenty of steps and small lanes—to get the most out of a visit.

Cave Churches

Of the two districts, the **Sasso Caveoso** is the more picturesque. It also includes three of the more distinguished of the 48 **cave churches** *(chiese rupestri)* carved by monks between the 8th and 12th centuries. These are the rather over-restored **San Pietro Caveoso** *(Piazza San Pietro, $ or $$ for all 3 churches);* the tenth-century **Santa Lucia alle Malve** *(Via del Corso–Via la Vista, $),* distinguished by its Byzantine frescoes from 1250; and

the tenth-century **Santa Maria d'Idris,** the most impressive of the trio, thanks to its medieval frescoes and an older, linked chapel, **San Monte Errone,** which may date from the eighth century. (Be aware that although San Pietro is usually open to visitors, the other two churches have variable hours that depend upon staffing and budgets.) Also worth special attention is **Sant'Antonio,** four linked rock churches from 1200, later used as wine cellars, then houses.

Note that there are about a hundred or more cave churches in the countryside around the town, details of which can be obtained from the visitor center. To see some of these, and for excellent views of the town from a distance, take the Taranto–Laterza road onto the **Murgia plateau,** the area where much of Gibson's film was shot.

Just south of Santa Maria d'Idris is the **Casa-Grotta di vico Solitario** *(off Via B. Buozzi, $),* a typical cave house that has been restored (with the help of the family who once lived here) to its 1950s appearance, complete with rooms for manure, donkeys, and pigs.

A little west is the **Museo Nazionale Ridola,** devoted to archaeological finds from Matera's classical as well as its prehistoric past. A few steps to the south down Via Ridola is the **Museo d'Arte Medievale e Moderna,** with, among other things, paintings and ephemera associated with the writer Carlo Levi.

The Old Town

Matera's old center has several diverting churches and—now that money is flowing into the town—increasing charm, especially in early evening when the *passeggiata* is in full flow. Palaces and churches surround the central **Piazza Vittorio Veneto,** the place to enjoy a drink and a distant view of the sassi. You can also look down on recent excavations that have uncovered fragments of a castle, church, cistern, and other traces of Byzantine Matera.

From the piazza's southern flank, little Via del Corso runs east to the church of **San Francesco** *(Piazza San Francesco),* a mostly 17th-century baroque affair that incorporates two earlier chapels on the site. Its main altar features eight panels from a polyptych by the Venetian painter Bartolomeo Vivarini (1450–1499).

From San Francesco it's a short walk via Piazza Sedile and Via Duomo to the **Duomo** (1268–1270), whose exterior bears a pleasing facade in late Puglian-Romanesque style and a rather less alluring interior burdened with an excess of baroque decoration. Note the figure of the Madonna della Bruna between Sts. Peter and Paul above the facade's main doorway. The Madonna is Matera's patron protectress and is celebrated with a lively *festa* on July 23, her feast day.

Inside the cathedral, amid all the gilt, the highlights are the ancient nave columns, removed from a temple at Metaponto (see p. 165), and the wooden choir, carved in 1453. A door on the left leads to a courtyard and the earlier church of Santa Maria di Costantinopli. ■

The baroque church of Santa Chiara on Via Ridola features a carved and gilded wooden altar.

Cultural Crossroads

Few regions in Europe have remained unsettled by outsiders. Southern Italy, at the crossroads of the Mediterranean, has seen more visitors than most, from ancient Neolithic peoples to the emigrants from North Africa who in recent years have struggled to establish a foothold in Sicily. Two different peoples, however, have provided the South with its most enduring cultural heritage: the Greeks and the Arbëreshë.

Remnants of cultures that have resided in southern Italy include Santa Maria dell'Isola in Tropea.

More than 2,500 years, ago, the Greeks built an extensive network of cities across Sicily and the southern Italian coast. Their legacy is vast and far-reaching, from the great temples that can still be seen in Paestum and Sicily to the traditions of art, sculpture, and architecture they bequeathed to the Romans and thus to the modern world.

The Arbëreshë were Greece's neighbors, refugees from Arbëria, modern-day Albania. In the 15th century the Ottoman Turks turned their empire-building attention to Arbëria, their campaigns there forcing entire communities to emigrate to southern Italy. The first settled in Puglia in 1460, welcomed by the South's Aragonese rulers in thanks for the help given by Gjergi

Kastriota Skanderbeg (1405/12–1468), one of Albania's heroes, in defeating their rivals.

The Aragonese welcomed the immigrants only up to a point, however, giving them worthless land and forbidding them to build fortresses or other strongholds. The effects of this were threefold: The poor land meant the Arbëreshë, as they were known, were left alone; their lack of fortresses meant they never became, or were viewed as, a threat; and the natural hardships of forging a life in remote areas cemented and strengthened the natural ties of the isolated newcomers.

Today, Italy has almost 110,000 people of Arbëreshë descent, amounting to more than 50 distinct communities, some in Sicily or Le Marche in central Italy, but over two-thirds in northern and central Calabria. Here, 85 percent of the adult Arbëreshë population speaks a language with obvious Albanian roots, and one that is so distinctive and widespread that many street signs are bilingual. Devout Arbëreshë also observe an Eastern Orthodox rite, specially sanctioned in 1919 by Pope Benedict XV.

Language and religious observance aside, two of the other obvious manifestations of Arbëreshë culture are music—accordions are a great favorite—and a dazzling ethnic costume, the latter worn at weddings, Easter, and other religious or special festivals.

In the right parts of Calabria, you may be lucky enough to stumble across manifestations of Arbëreshë culture, including festivals in local

A detail of a column in Monreale, Sicily, shows the area's blend of Arab and European cultures.

dress, but to be sure of enjoying a unique spectacle, visit some of the key Arbëreshë villages during their Easter celebrations. The main villages include Acquaformosa, Eianina, Firmo, Santa Caterina Albanese, Spezzano Albanese, Santa Sofia d'Epiro, and especially San Demetrio Corone and Civita, where a folk dance through the streets on the Tuesday after Easter celebrates—even 500 years on—a victory over the Arbëreshë's erstwhile tormenters, the Ottoman Turks.

Arbëreshë Festivals

In the Arbëreshë villages, religious festivals have a quality all their own, thanks to Eastern and Greek Orthodox traditions. Carnival and Epiphany (January 6) are the inspiration for many ceremonies, notably the one at midday at **San Demetrio Corone,** which involves the symbolic release of a dove. In the same village, on the Saturday of Easter,

women take part in a ritual involving fire and water, whose pagan undertones hint at ancient roots. Among many other Easter festivals, the one in **Nocera Tirenese** stands out—a procession involving flagellants, whose spilled blood is deliberately splashed on the doors of houses to protect those within, and which must only be removed by rain.

Costa Ionica

The Costa Ionica, or Ionian Coast, runs along the arch of the Italian boot, about 320 miles (500 km) of lonely beaches, agricultural plains, small modern towns—often with their medieval forebears close by on inland hills—and a string of ancient Greek and Roman sites that were once some of the most powerful cities in the known world.

Ancient cave churches pockmark the deep ravine running through Massafra.

Costa Ionica
🗺 157 A4, B3, & B2
Visitor Information
✉ Piazza Giovanni XXIII, Metaponto
☎ 083 574 5606
🕐 Closed 1–3 p.m. & Oct.–May

**www.proloco
dimetaponto.it**

Massafra is just across Basilicata's border in Puglia, but it makes a convenient point from which to start an exploration of the Ionian Coast. One of the region's more unusual towns, it is strikingly similar to nearby Matera (see pp. 158–161). Massafra is cut by a ravine, the Gravina di San Marco, and honeycombed with ancient caves and cave churches dating from between the 9th and 14th centuries.

Unlike Matera, however, Massafra is barely on the visitor trail, and you'll need a local guide (*Via Vittorio Veneto 15, tel 099 880 4695*) or a sense of adventure to find many of the caves and their one hundred or more early Byzantine frescoes. The best and most easily accessed are **San Marco, La Candelora, San Lorenzo,** and **Madonna della Scala.** The last, in particular, is outstanding, a baroque church (1731) built around an earlier cave sanctuary with delicate 12th-century paintings and a primitive 8th-century crypt. Caves and cave art can also be found in the neighboring villages of **Mottala** (the church of San Nicola) and **Laterza,** another spectacular ravine-perched settlement with about 180 cave dwellings, some dating from 2000 B.C.

From Massafra, join the SS106, the road that follows the entire Ionian Coast to Reggio di Calabria. Almost immediately across Basilicata's border you come to **Metaponto,** close to the site of ancient Metapontum, founded by Greek settlers in the seventh century B.C. Like the sites farther along the coast, its ruins are patchy, and the only significant monument is the **Temple of Hera** (or Tavole Palatine), a Doric temple with 15 of it columns still standing. Excavations are in progress. Just outside the modern village is a small **antiquarium** (*Via Laferan, tel 083 574 5327, closed Mon. a.m., $*) with finds from the site.

Just 11 miles (18 km) south of Metaponto is modern **Policoro,** site of ancient Heracleia, founded in 433 or 434 B.C. Even less of this city has been found, but excavations continue, and some of the finds, along with those from Siris and other sites, are exhibited at the **Museo Nazionale della Siritide.**

Make the 5-mile (8 km) detour inland to see **Santa Maria d'Anglona,** a lovely 11th-century church on an isolated hilltop site that has been of religious significance since pagan times.

South of the agricultural plains around Policoro, the hills come hard against the coast until the tiny settlement of **Sibari.** This modest village is close to one of the most evocative of all ancient cities, Sybaris, whose 100,000 famously hedonistic citizens helped coin the word "sybaritic." The city's precise site remained unknown until recently. Its main rival, Kroton (see sidebar below), captured and razed it in 510 B.C., reputedly diverting the waters of the local Crati River to submerge the ruins. The site, 20 times larger than Pompeii, is now being studied, though little has been excavated. Much of what has been found comes from two later Roman colonies and is displayed at the **Museo della Sibaritide.**

The city's attackers came from a colony at **Crotone,** ancient Kroton, 36 miles (53 km) south, now an industrial center but in its day the most powerful colony in Magna Graecia. Founded in 710 B.C, it had dominion over much of Sicily and southern Italy. Most of the surviving stone was used to build the town's medieval castle, but artifacts from excavations fill the **Museo Archeologico,** the best of the coast's archaeological museums. ■

Museo Nazionale della Siritide
- ✉ Via Colombo 8
- ☎ 083 597 2154
- ⊕ Closed Tues. a.m.
- 💲 $

Museo della Sibaritide
- ✉ Strada Ionica 106
- ☎ 098 179 391
- ⊕ Closed Mon.
- 💲 $

Museo Archeologico
- ✉ Via Risorgimento
- ☎ 096 223 082
- ⊕ Closed Mon.
- 💲 $

Life of Luxury

Everything in ancient Sybaris was designed to contribute to a life of ease, the wealth accrued from the colony's fertile plain funding its citizens' indulgences. Their inventions are said to have included pasta, street lighting, and chamber pots, among others; their dress was notoriously lavish; cooks were prized and bought and sold by wealthy patrons; and the colony could boast 5,000 knights, four times as many as Athens. A famous tale tells how Sybarite horsemen, to amuse themselves, taught their horses to dance to the music of pipes. In battle against Kroton, it is said, the enemy won the day simply by playing their pipes, at which the Sybarites' horses stopped their charge in favor of dancing.

A Drive through the Sila Mountains

Richly varied landscapes make for an alluring drive through the Sila's remote backcountry anchored by Parco Nazionale della Calabria.

The varied landscape of Calabria's park

The Sila's scenery is a glorious mélange of meadows, granite plateaus, pastures, mixed forest (the Sila takes its name from *silva,* the Latin for "thick woods"), lakes, deep valleys, and high, often snowy peaks. This is empty country, the few roads high, winding, and slow, and the points of cultural, as opposed to scenic, interest few and far between.

If time is short, start from **Cosenza** and follow the SS107 east into the mountains to Camigliatello Silano (see below). If you can afford a more leisurely itinerary, begin to the north in the Sila Greca at **San Demetrio Corone ❶**, accessible from Sibari or the A3 expressway. The village is at the heart of the

NOT TO BE MISSED:

San Demetrio Corone • Strada delle Vette • Lago Arvo

South's distinctive Albanian, or Arbëreshë, culture (see pp. 162–163), whose presence in Italy dates from the Ottoman invasion of Arbëria (modern-day Albania).

Take the minor road south through the Arbëreshë village of **Acri** (a short detour west en route brings you to another, **Santa Sofia d'Epiro**), following the twisting road east from the junction below the village. From Acri, at 2,211 feet (674 m), this route climbs through typically varied countryside to 4,921 feet (1,250 m) below Monte Forgiari on the edge of the northernmost portion of **Parco Nazionale della Calabria.** Bear right on the SS177 to the junction of the SS282 at the eastern end of **Lago di Cecita ❷**, one of three large artificial lakes in the region.

Make a short detour left (east) on the SS282 to visit **La Fossita,** where park and forest authorities have a well-organized reserve of trails. Also here is a trailhead for the climb to the 5,518-foot (1,682 m) **Serra Ripollata,** maps for which are available in Camigliatello Silano and other local centers.

Return to the SS177 and drive to **Camigliatello Silano ❸**, a functional resort with summer hiking routes and a handful of winter ski trails. Then pick up the minor road toward Spezzano (*not* the SS107) and, after 6 miles (9.5 km), take the minor mountain road known as the **Strada delle Vette ❹** (Road of the Peaks) south toward Lorica and **Lago Arvo.**

This is one of the region's most spectacular roads, reaching higher than 6,000 feet (1,829 m) on the slopes of 6,325-foot (1,928 m) Monte Botte Donato, the Sila's highest point.

After 17 miles (27 km), turn right at the lakeshore to follow the SS108 bis west. A couple of miles beyond the lake's end, the SS178 offers the opportunity to rejoin the A3 (via Mangone). Otherwise, continue south,

turning left (east) on the SS108 at Bocca di Piazza then right on the SS179 signposted for Taverna. After 8 miles (13 km) you come to the **Villaggio Mancuso** ➎, a modern resort of wood-frame buildings and home to a national park visitor center. At Taverna the SS109 winds to **Catanzaro,** an unprepossessing provincial capital with fast onward road connections to the Ionian and Tyrrhenian coasts.

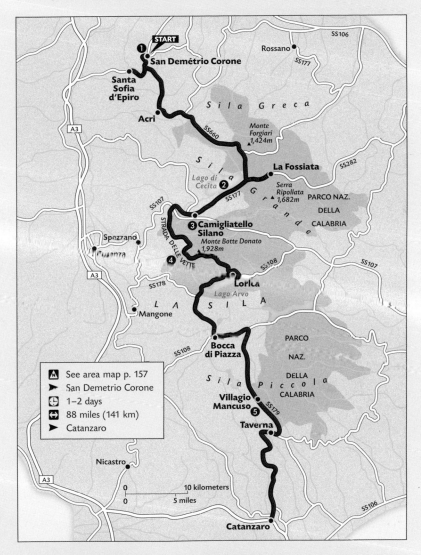

Parco Nazionale del Monte Pollino

The Parco Nazionale del Monte Pollino is the South's most compelling national park, a vast area of wilderness that embraces parts of Calabria and Basilicata and divides between the colossal massif of 7,368-foot (2,246 m) Monte Pollino to the north and the huge, intractable upland fastness of the Monti di Orsomarso to the south.

Tangy cheeses are made from the milk of sheep that graze in the Pollino uplands.

Parco Nazionale del Monte Pollino

Ⓜ 157 B4 & B5

Visitor Information

✉ Complessi Monumentali, Santa Maria della Consolazione, Rotonda

☎ 097 366 9311

🕐 Closed p.m. daily & Sat. & Sun.

www.parcopollino.it
www.parks.it

Much of the area is sparsely inhabited and is crossed by few roads, factors that helped preserve much of its pristine appearance before the establishment of the national park in 1993. Today, access is confined mostly to the A3 expressway, which bisects the region, the opening of which finally breached Pollino's mountainous wall, a barrier that had helped keep Calabria cut off from the rest of Italy for centuries.

Otherwise, in the north only a handful of roads such as the SS92 breaches Monte Pollino's flanks, often petering out in upland villages such as **Terranova di Pollino,** a good base (with Rotonda) for the northern part of the park. By contrast, in the **Monti di Orsomarso** (from *orso,* or bear, after the Apennine brown bears that once roamed here) not a single road penetrates one of Italy's ultimate wildernesses. Only the SS105, on the region's low, southern fringes, gives a hint of the landscapes to the north, empty but for secretive wolves, slow-wheeling birds of prey, and shepherds' huts that even the shepherds have abandoned.

Both regions support the rare Bosnian pine, or *pino loricato* *(Pinus leucodermis)*, a tree found only here and in the Balkans. (It is the park's symbol.) It is named for the *lorica*, the scaled shield of Roman legionaries, after its patterned bark. Pollino itself may take its name from the Latin, *Mon Apollineus*, Mountain of Apollo; or *Mons Pullinus*, the Mountain of the Young Animals, after the custom of driving young sheep and cattle to graze in high pasture. The Bosnian pine is confined to the driest, rockiest slopes, and only a thousand or so examples survive.

Other exotic flora in the region include the so-called burning bush *(Dictamnus albus)*, a strange plant that locals claim shines by night and does, in truth, sometimes have a luminous glow. There is also "manna," the Biblical food said to fall from the heavens, actually the sugary resin from the punctured barks of manna ash *(Fraxinus ornus)*, still occasionally used as a mild astringent.

Pollino's massifs present different faces to the visitor depending on whether you approach from north or south. The northern slopes that overlook the barren hills of Basilicata are gentle and green, and they contain some of the area's thickest forests, notably Magnano near San Severino and the Cugno dell'Acera and Duglia above Terranova di Pollino. The south-facing slopes are more Mediterranean, with a steeper and more spectacular mixture of sun-bleached rock and arid limestone

gorges. The most imposing of the latter is **Ranganello,** the South's grandest canyon, with trail access from the village of San Lorenzo Bellizzi, located due east of Pollino's summit.

To reach this summit, you can follow one of southern Italy's classic hikes, a five-hour round-trip starting from the 5,160-foot (1,573 m) **Colle dell'Impiso,** a pass a couple of miles northeast of the Rifugio de Gasperi *(tel 097 366 1080 or 097 366 4305)*, a mountain lodge with simple accommodations, maps, and trail information. Longer and more strenuous hikes include the climb from **Terranova del Pollino** via Lago della Duglia to the summit and from **Civita** to Pollino's slightly higher neighboring peak, 7,437-foot (2,267 m) Dolce-dorme. Views from both summits are stupendous, with three seas visible on good days: the Adriatic, Tyrrhenian, and Ionian. ∎

EXPERIENCE:
Hiking Tour of Pollino National Park

Southern Italy has the country for hiking, as well as numerous trails that follow old mule-tracks and ancient paths used by shepherds moving their flocks across the mountains. However, in the Pollino park and elsewhere, outdoor enthusiasts are hampered by the lack of good and up-to-date maps. One solution is to hire a local guide, who in the Pollino national park can be found by visiting www.parcopollino .it or www.parks.it; click on "Guide ufficiali." Both sites have pages in English and carry lists of official guides.

Maratea

Basilicata's share of Italy's western, Tyrrhenian coast is modest; just 18 miles (28 km) of high, rocky shoreline separate Campania's Cilento shoreline from the start of the Calabrian littoral to the south. At the heart of this small window on the sea, however, the region boasts one of southern Italy's most chic and sophisticated resorts—Maratea.

Boats old and new cluster along Maratea's waterfront.

The resort is not a single entity. It consists of several small linked communities, all good bases for exploring this part of the coast by boat, train, or car. The main Naples–to–Reggio di Calabria railroad runs along the coast, ducking in and out of tunnels, shadowed by the SS18, which plies a spectacular route between forested slopes and a craggy, cove- and cave-dotted coast. Fine, often undeveloped beaches of silvery gray sand are lapped by seas that gained a Blue Flag award in 2003, Western Europe's highest official recognition for the cleanliness of the water, among other swimming criteria.

Over the years, the area has become a favorite among Italians in the know, and it attracts a well-heeled clientele. Although it's not quite the secret it once was, its development has been largely responsible and restrained. There's little to see culturally, and little to do—though diving and other water sports are available—but this is one of the best places for many miles to spend two or three days on the beach.

The resort has two outstanding hotels: the long-established Locanda delle Donne Monache, a former convent overlooking Maratea's medieval town; and the Santavenere, southern Italy's most chic resort.

The area's heart is **Maratea Porto,** a tiny waterfront hamlet of pretty houses, yachts, and vividly painted fishing boats. It's reached by one of two minor roads from the SS18, the other one of which runs a short distance to the equally tiny **Fiumicello** to the north.

At the latter you'll find the visitor center and one of several good local beaches, most of which have *stabilimenti,* or private pay sections, where a modest fee buys you groomed sand, a sun chair and umbrella, plus restroom and refreshment facilities.

The original, ancient *borgo* (small town) of Maratea itself—also known as **Maratea Paese** or Maratea Inferiore—nestles in the foothills of Monte San Biagio, reached by another minor road off the SS18 a short distance south of the Maratea Porto junction. A place of eighth-century B.C. Greek foundation, the village is a warren of steep, tiny stone streets and alleys and ancient churches, notably the tenth-century **San Vito.**

The ancient ruins of **Maratea Antica** speckle the slopes behind and above town along the 3-mile

(5 km) road up Monte San Biagio. Dominating the 2,065-foot (624 m) peak, looking toward the mountainous interior, is the 66-foot (20 m) white marble statue of **Il Redentore,** or Christ, built here in 1963. From this lofty vantage you'll be dazzled by the sublime view of the coast's great northward sweep. Opposite the statue is the **Santuario di San Biagio,** a sanctuary built on the site of an ancient temple to Minerva in honor of San Biagio (St. Blaise), the town's patron saint. A procession bears a statue of the saint up the hill to the sanctuary on the second Sunday of May during the town's main *festa,* or festival.

INSIDER TIP:

The beaches at Maratea have become increasingly popular and are quite active in July and August. For a more peaceful experience, visit them in the winter months.

—PATRICIA DANIELS
National Geographic Books editor

Farther afield, **Marina di Maratea,** a more modern resort, lies 3 miles (5 km) south of the town on the SS18, while inland the little upland village of **Rivello,** reached on the scenic mountain road north of Maratea via Trecchina, makes a rewarding day trip. ∎

Maratea
🗺 157 A4
Visitor Information
✉ Piazza Gesù 40
☎ 097 387 6908
🕐 Closed daily p.m. (except Mon. & Thurs.) & Sat. & Sun. except July–Aug.
www.costadi maratea.it

Calabrian Riviera

Calabria's long Tyrrhenian coast is changing, finding fresh life in its new agricultural initiatives and the emergence of increasingly popular small resorts that make full use of the region's often beautiful beaches and spectacular scenery.

With sandy beaches and blue seas, Tropea is one of the Calabrian Riviera's most beautiful resorts.

Calabrian Riviera
 157 A4, B4, B3, B2, & B1

For a region with so long a coastline, and one so close to the ancient maritime cross-roads of the Mediterranean, Calabria has always had an uneasy relationship with the sea. The Greeks and Romans took advantage of the region's natural harbors and fertile coastal plains, but after the fall of the Roman Empire, the shores reverted to malarial swampland and the coastal towns fell prey to Saracen and other raiders. As a result, Calabrians retreated inland. Only recently has this changed, first in the 1950s, when DDT removed the threat of malaria, and lately with the resurgence of agriculture on the coastal plains and the advent of tourism in a string of resorts and villages loosely known as the Calabrian Riviera.

This riviera follows the region's Tyrrhenian coast, which stretches for about 150 miles (240 km) from Praia a Mare in the north to Reggio di Calabria in the south. Much of the area is a ravishing medley of cliffs, tawny beaches, rocky coves, granite outcrops, and hills and mountains covered in olives, figs, forest, or rough maquis scrub. For now, most remains unspoiled, but the spread of concrete is increasingly making itself felt in the region.

The main railroad from Naples and the SS18 road shadow most of the coast, joined by the A3 *autostrada* (expressway) in the southern reaches, making access easy. The north has its moments—Scalea, Diamante, and Paola are moderate, slightly disheveled resorts—but in this part of the region you are better off heading for **Maratea** (see pp. 170–171).

Calabria's finest stretch of coast begins much farther south, at **Pizzo,** just before the bulge of land known as the Promontorio del Poro, accessed by a scenic coastal road. The area's little provincial capital just inland from Pizzo, **Vibo Valentia,** is worth a visit for its churches and Norman castle, the latter home to an **archaeological museum** *(Via Castello, tel 096 343 350, $)* with Greek and Roman finds.

Most visitors, however, make straight for **Tropea,** far and away Calabria's best and most popular seaside resort, thanks largely to the long sandy beaches below the town and the picturesque cliff-top churches and Norman cathedral (1163). As elsewhere, new hotels are proliferating, but if you visit outside crowded August, the town retains considerable charm. The old quarter in particular is lovely to wander, with stores selling the organic products (fruit, vegetables, honey, jams, olive oils, and so forth) for which Calabrian agriculture is becoming renowned. The town and waterfront also have many restaurants, bars, and clubs.

Be sure to explore the rest of the Poro promontory, which has good beaches at **Zambrone, Parghelia, Joppolo,** and **Nicotera,** as well as some sublime coastal scenery. Some of the best landscapes are around **Capo Vaticano,** one of Calabria's least spoiled corners, but the whole promontory offers wonderful views of this so-called Costa Viola (Violet Coast), named after the color of the sea at sunset.

Farther south, past Gioia Tauro, **Palmi** is worth a stop for its cultural complex, home to a gallery of modern art and the **Museo Calabrese di Etnografia e Folklore Raffaele Corso** *(Casa della Cultura, Via F. Battaglia, tel 0966 262 250, closed Sat., Sun., & p.m. daily except Thurs., $),* one of Italy's best museums of rural and maritime life, past and present ∎

Vibo Valentia

🗺 157 B2

Visitor Information

✉ Piazza Diaz 11–12

☎ 096 345 300

🕐 Closed Sun. & 1–4 p.m.

Tropea

🗺 157 B2

Visitor Information

✉ Piazza Ercole

☎ 096 361 475

🕐 Closed Sun. & 1–4 p.m.

www.prolocotropea .eu

Scylla & Charybdis

Scylla and Charybdis were mythical creations, and they represented the unenviable choice that today might be described as being between a rock and hard place. Scylla was a monster who dwelt on a rock, Charybdis a whirlpool, or whirlpool-creating sea creature. The two lay either side of a channel less than an arrow's range apart, so that to avoid one was to move closer to danger from the other. Mariners—most famously Odysseus in Homer's epic poem, *The Odyssey*—had to chose the danger they preferred to face. The two were traditionally located in the Straits of Messina between Sicily and the Calabrian coast, where to this day there is a town called Scilla, though some scholars believe the myth may have its roots in Cape Skilla in northwest Greece.

EXPERIENCE: Olives & Olive Oil

Olive groves are found across much of Italy, but in the South, where you will find some of the country's oldest and largest trees, they are everywhere. The olive is part of the Oleaceae family (along with ash, lilac, and jasmine), and is drought-resistant, but susceptible to cold—temperatures below -10°F (-12°C) usually kill trees.

The International Olive Oil Council has declared Ravidà olive oil from Menfi, Sicily, one of Europe's finest. The oil can bought outside Italy, or visit the estate by appointment between March and November (*tel 39 0925 71 109, www .ravida.it*). Cooking classes can also be arranged by appointment and according to availability.

Should you be able to visit from late October to January, you will be able to see the harvest first hand. The timing is crucial: Pick too early and the oil's acidity will be low—a good thing—but so will the yields, and the taste will be bitter. Too late, and yields will be high, along with the acidity, rendering the oil rancid. Picking by hand is best, because farmers can select the best olives and return to individual trees, as olives on the same tree ripen at different times.

The traditional method of harvesting is to surround trees with nets and beat the branches with poles or, recently, to use mechanical claws which grasp the tree and vibrate in order to dislodge the fruit.

The olives are then washed and stored, ideally for no more than a day (or they may ferment). The olives, including the pits, are then crushed or chopped, traditionally between water- or mule-driven millstones, but now more often using metal grinders.

The resulting paste must then be pressed to extract the oil. Traditionally, this was achieved by spreading the paste on hemp mats and stacking them in a column, which was then compressed using weights or a wooden lever or screw press to squeeze out the oil. Today, fiber mats and a hydraulic press are used, usually in combination with centrifuge, which removes excess water.

More oil can be extracted from the paste if it is heated, if the paste is re-pressed, or if chemicals are used, but this affects flavor. As a result, the best oils come from the first "natural" pressing and are "cold pressed." European Union (EU) rules state that only oils extracted at temperatures below 27°C can be called "cold pressed."

Low acidity is important in olive oil. Extra-virgin oils should have acidity levels below 0.8 percent and virgin olive oil below 2 percent. However, acidity is not all, and low levels don't guarantee quality—tiny differences, in any case, will be imperceptible to most palates. Buy cold-pressed oils from small producers, and don't be taken in by deep green oils, which are not necessarily better than amber or light gold oils.

Southern Italy produces exceptional olive oils.

More Places to Visit in Calabria & Basilicata

Aspromonte

The Aspromonte (Bitter Mountain), last redoubt of the Apennines, is one of the wildest regions in Italy. Long a rural fastness, it has a history of lawlessness, and even today it still has a reputation as one of the strongholds of the 'Ndrangheta, the Calabrian mafia. But it is also a national park, a protected area that extends over a tortured series of ridges and upland plains centered on the summit of 6,413-foot (1,955 m) Montalto.

The main approach by car is on the SS183 (or SS112), which runs through the mountains' western reaches. In the south, near the coast, the area embraces fertile hinterlands known for their jasmine and bergamot orange, the latter used, among other things, to flavor Earl Grey tea. Pasture and areas of forest appear at higher elevations, remnants of the thick tree cover that once blanketed much of upland Calabria.

Side roads lead to atmospheric settlements, some little more than ghost towns. Of note is the SS183, which follows the coast 8 miles (12 km) east of Melito to **Roghudi** and **Roccaforte del Greco,** whose name hints at the region's strong Greek heritage. The dialect here, Grecanico, is said to be closer to the ancient language of Homer and Plato than to modern Greek; it is incomprehensible to most Calabrians, let alone Italians. To the south of the village is **Galliciano,** a hamlet still accessible only by foot or mule, and, beyond it, on a rough road (there is easier access from the SS106 coast road), the upland town of **Bova,** known for the Paleariza, an annual August fair of music and rural culture. Another scenic road (the SS184) climbs from **Reggio di Calabria,** passing the mountain resorts of **Santo Stefano** and **Gambarie,** both good hiking centers.

🗺 157 B1 ✉ **Visitor Information** Piazzale Mangeruca, Santo Stefano in the Aspromonte ☎ 096 574 3060, www.parcoaspromonte.it or www.parks.it 🕐 Closed p.m. daily & Sat. & Sun.

Locri–Gerace

The coastal resort of Locri in Calabria is 3 miles (5 km) north of the ancient Greek city of Locri Epizephyrii, founded in 710 B.C. or 683 B.C. The Greek writer Pindar commended the place as a model of good government, this being the first city in the Hellenic world to possess a written code of laws (drawn up in 664 B.C.). The city walls extended for 5 miles (8 km) and are still partly visible, along with other ruins, in the **archaeological park** (tel 096 442 0344, $), whose entrance is by the small **Museo Archeologico** (Contradà Marasa, tel 096 439 0023, closed Mon., $).

INSIDER TIP:

Reggio di Calabria is worth a visit for the Museo Nazionale della Magna Graecia, a recently renovated archaeological museum on Piazza de Nava.

—SUSAN STRAIGHT
National Geographic Books editor

When the Saracens destroyed what was left of the city in the seventh or ninth century A.D., the surviving citizens founded nearby **Gerace,** choosing a redoubtable crag-top site that would later also find favor with the Normans. The well-preserved medieval village is best known for its cathedral (1045), the largest in Calabria. Inside, 20 old granite columns dominate the pleasingly simple interior. There are also two fine apses and a venerable Byzantine crypt. Be sure to enjoy the superb views from the ruined castle and the two medieval churches of San Francesco and San Giovanello.

🗺 157 B1 & B2 ✉ **Visitor Information** Town Hall, Piazza del Tocco ☎ 096 435 6001

Rossano

Be sure to follow the winding road to Rossano, in Calabria south of Sibari, now little more than a village but between the 8th and 11th centuries one of southern Italy's main centers of Byzantine culture. The legacy of its heyday can be found in several fine early churches, notably tiny **San Marco,** the **Chiessetta di Panaghia,** and (out of town to the west, at the end of a lonely country road) the simple basilica of **Santa Maria del Patire,** with the yellow, black, and orange stone typical of the Armenian and Syrian churches from which it took its inspiration.

The city's key treasure, and one of the glories of Calabria, is the **Codex Purpureus Rossanensis,** an illuminated manuscript of the Gospels in Greek printed on 188 sheets of tissue-paper-thin parchment. Created in Palestine in the sixth century and brought here by monks fleeing the Muslim invasions, this is one of the oldest and most beautiful examples of the Gospels. It is kept in the **Museo Diocesano** next to the Angevin cathedral *(Palazzo Arcivescovile, tel 098 352 5263, closed Sun. & Mon. Oct.–June & 12–4 or 4:30 p.m. year-round; $).*
🅜 157 C4 ✉ **Visitor Information** Piazza Matteotti ☎ 098 352 0908, *www .prolocorossano.it*

Le Serre

Le Serre are the often overlooked mountains in Calabria between the more impressive Pollino and Aspromonte chains to the north and south. Easily seen from the Costa Ionica (on the scenic SS110 road) or Vibo Valentia (via the SS182) to the west, they are best known for their collection of churches. The most celebrated is **La Cattolica,** Italy's best-preserved Byzantine-style church. Built in the ninth or tenth century, the church and its distinctive five cupolas overlook the village of **Stilo.** Traces of fresco survive inside, along with four columns brought from the ancient Greek colony of Caulonia on the coast.

Close by, and reached on a mountain road

The Apennine Wolf

Wolves are virtually extinct in much of western Europe, but not in the Apennines, the spine of mountains that runs up the Italian peninsula. Here, and especially in Calabria and Basilicata's wild uplands, there survives *Canis lupus italicus,* or the Apennine wolf, Italy's national animal and a distinct subspecies. Although its numbers are increasing—with a total population of around 500 to 600 animals—interbreeding with feral dogs threatens the breed's purity. These are elusive creatures, however, and sightings are rare.

from Pazzano to the west, is **Bivongi,** home to the equally lovely Byzantine-Norman basilica of **San Giovanni Theristis,** while in Pazzano itself stands the cave church of **Santa Maria di Monte Stella.**

About 22 miles (36 km) northwest of Stilo is the larger village of **Serra San Bruno,** whose history is tied to the great Carthusian abbey of **Santi Stefano e Brunone,** set in pretty countryside just over a mile to the southwest. The abbey was begun in 1094 by St. Bruno of Cologne, the founder of the Carthusian religious order. This was the order's second abbey after its mother church at Chartreuse near Grenoble, France, the name of which was corrupted to charterhouse in English and *certosa* in Italian. Bruno himself lived and died at the little church of **Santa Maria del Bosco** beyond the main abbey, most of whose present complex dates from the 18th century, the original abbey having been destroyed by an earthquake. It is well worth visiting the small **museum** *(tel 096 370 608, www.museo.certosini.info, closed Mon., also a.m. Nov.–March, $$)* for the glimpses it affords into the abbey interior and of the life of the silent order of monks that still live, work, and pray here.
🅜 157 B2 & C2 ✉ **Visitor Information** *www.parks.it/parco.serre*

Sicily and Sardinia, islands whose cultures and histories are often separate from those of mainland Italy

Sicily & Sardinia

Detail from the cloister at Monreale, Palermo

Sicily & Sardinia

Sicily is an island separated from the rest of Italy not only by the sea but also by centuries of cultural experience. Yet it is a vital part of the country. In *Italian Journey* (1789), the German writer Johann Goethe observed that "to have seen Italy without seeing Sicily is not to have seen Italy at all, for Sicily is the clue to everything." He might have said much the same about Sardinia, as separate in its own way from mainstream Italy as Sicily.

The busy Corso Vittorio Emanuele II in Palermo, Sicily, scene of the city's evening stroll

Sicily was once at the hub of the European world. The largest island in the Mediterranean Sea (Sardinia is second), Sicily lay between the civilizations of Africa and Europe, providing a tempting prize for traders and invaders alike. Sardinia, too, held a pivotal position, which meant a stream of visitors, from Romans and Carthaginians to Pisans and Catalans.

Originally, Sicily was home to the Siculi, the Alimi, and the Sicani, ancient tribes from which it takes its present-day name. Between the 8th and 3rd centuries B.C., the Greeks ruled Sicily; in the 9th and 10th centuries A.D., it was under Arab control; and in the 11th century it was dominated by the Normans. Between times, the island also attracted Romans, Carthaginians,

Vandals, Spaniards, Byzantines, the French, Bourbons, and even the British.

Sicily's invaders bequeathed the island its extraordinarily rich heritage, the succession of cultures having molded every aspect of island life from art and architecture to language and cuisine. From the Greeks came the theaters at Syracuse and Taormina and the great temples at Agrigento, Selinunte, and Segesta. From the Romans came the magnificent mosaics at Piazza Armerina, while the Arabs brought Moorish-influenced architecture and much of Sicily's wonderfully eclectic cuisine.

In later centuries, the Normans introduced the majesty of Romanesque architecture, seen to best effect in the sublime cathedrals of Cefalù and Monreale. From the Spanish came the decorative exuberance of the baroque found in many churches and palaces.

All these artistic, cultural, and even culinary strands come together in Palermo, Sicily's capital. This teeming, decaying, and fascinating city provides a telling introduction to Sicily's magnificent past and its occasionally sordid present. Similar scenes exist on the Sicilian coastline, once one of Europe's loveliest. It is now best seen at places like Cefalù, Taormina, and offshore islands such as the Aeolian (Eolie) archipelago, known for the volcanic eruptions of Stromboli.

Inland, the landscapes are less ravaged: They range from the shimmering wheat fields of the

NOT TO BE MISSED:

Cappella Palatina in Palermo **182**

Cathedral and cloister at Monreale **182**

Norman cathedral at Cefalù **184–185**

Watching the volcanic eruptions of Stromboli from a boat **185–186**

Hiking Etna's upper slopes **187, 190**

Mosaics at the Villa Romana del Casale near Piazza Armerina **192**

Greek temples in the Valle dei Templi outside Agrigento **193–194**

A day on the beaches of the Costa Smeralda **196–198**

interior to the Madonie and Nebrodi mountains, whose wooded ridges run along much of the northern coast. Finally, there is Mount Etna, Europe's greatest active volcano, a smoldering peak of brooding majesty. ■

Rome

Naples

Sardinia, see map on p. 197

Area of map detail

3 ▷

San Vincenzo

I. Strómboli

I. Panarea

I. Filicudi

Isole Eólie (Lipari)

I. Alicudi

I. Salina

I. Lípari ● Lípari

● Porto Levante

I. Vulcano

Torre Faro

Milazzo ● A20 Messina

Golfo di Castellammare

PALERMO Baghería

● Cinisi

Monreale ◆

Cefalù

Barcellona

A19

Golfo di Termini Imerese

A20

N e b r o d i

Monti Peloritani

A18

Trápani Érice

Segesta Álcamo Partinico

Termini Imerese

SS120

Isole Égadi

Calatafimi

Corleone

M a d o n i e

Etna 3,315m ▲

Taormina Linguaglossa

2 ▷

Marsala

A29

Prizzi

SICILIA (SICILY)

Adrano

Rifugio Sapienza

Giarre

Nicolosi

SS121

Mazara del Vallo

Castelvetrano

Paternò

A18

Acireale

Selinunte

Sciacca

Caltanissetta

Enna

Misterbianco

A19

Catánia

Piazza Armerina

Pláfani

SS115

Agrigento

Villa Romana del Casale

Golfo di Catania

Augusta

Valle dei Templi

Gela

SS124

Golfo di Augusta

V a l d i A c a t e

N o t o

Siracusa (Syracuse)

1 ▷

0   60 kilometers

0   30 miles

Golfo di Gela

Ragusa

Módica

Golfo di Noto

Pantelleria

Isola di Pantelleria

△ B

Marina di Ragusa

△ C

Pachino

△ D

△ A

Sicily

Sicily's coastal sights range from the charming towns of Cefalù and Taormina to the mix of history and urban seediness that is Palermo. Inland, the landscapes are less ravaged: They range from the shimmering wheat fields of the interior to the Madonie and Nebrodi mountains, whose wooded ridges run along much of the northern coast. Finally, there is Mount Etna, Europe's greatest active volcano, a smoldering peak of brooding majesty.

The Moorish motifs of Palermo's 12th-century cathedral contrast with whimsical art of a later era.

Palermo

Palermo

🅰 179 B2 & opposite

Visitor Information

✉ Piazza Castelnuovo 34–35

☎ 091 605 8351

🕐 Closed Sat. & Sun.

✉ Aeroporto Falcone-Borsellino

☎ 091 591 698

🕐 Closed Sun.

www. palermotour ism.com

Big, battered, and bustling, Palermo is not a city for all tastes, its traffic, poverty, and decaying sense of baroque grandeur not for the fainthearted. At the same time, it is one of Italy's most vibrant and atmospheric cities, founded by the Phoenicians in the eighth century B.C. and still bearing the stamp of its later Arab, Norman, and Spanish rulers. Monuments to past glories rise amid the modern tenements and cramped backstreets, fighting for space in a city whose Arab bazaars, flourishing port, seedy dives, and teeming thoroughfares offer a dramatic contrast between past and present.

Central Palermo's sights are dispersed, so arm yourself with a map and be prepared for either a lot of walking or trips aboard the cabs or crowded buses that ply the city's three principal streets: Corso Vittorio Emanuele, Via Maqueda, and Via Roma. The most efficient approach to the key sights is to start at the western end of the first of these, Corso Vittorio Emanuele, working eastward to take in the clusters of attractions near its seaward conclusion and its intersection with Via Maqueda.

The **Palazzo dei Normanni,** or Palazzo Reale *(Piazza Indipendenza, tel 091 705 1111, www.ars.sicilia .it, www.ars.sicilia.it, closed Tues.– Thurs., & Sun. p.m., $$$; Cappella Palatina only, $$),* occupies the site

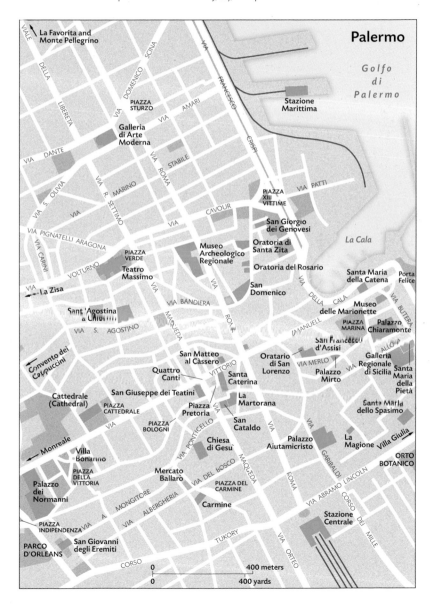

Palermo

Golfo di Palermo

La Favorita and Monte Pellegrino

VIALE DELLA

VIA DELLA LIBERTA

PIAZZA STURZO

Galleria di Arte Moderna

VIA DOMENICO SCINA

VIA FRANCESCO

VIA AMARI

Stazione Marittima

VIA DANTE

VIA STABILE

VIA ROMA

VIA R. MARINO

VIA SETTIMO

VIA S. OLIVIA

VIA PIGNATELLI ARAGONA

VIA CARINI

VIA CRISPI

PIAZZA XIII VITTIME

VIA PATTI

CAVOUR

San Giorgio dei Genovesi

Oratoria di Santa Zita

PIAZZA VERDE

VOLTURNO

Teatro Massimo

Museo Archeologico Regionale

Oratoria del Rosario

La Cala

Santa Maria della Catena

Porta Felice

La Zisa

VIA BANDIERA

San Domenico

VIA DELLA CALA

VIA BUTERA

Museo delle Marionette

PIAZZA MARINA

Palazzo Chiaramonte

Sant 'Agostina a Chiusa

VIA S. AGOSTINO

VIA MAQUEDA

VIA ROMA

MANUELI

San Francesco d'Assisi

ALLOIA

Convento dei Cappuccini

San Matteo al Càssero

Quattro Canti

VITTORIO

Santa Caterina

Oratorio di San Lorenzo

VIA MERLO

Palazzo Mirto

Galleria Regionale di Sicilia

Santa Maria della Pietà

Cattedrale (Cathedral)

San Giuseppe dei Teatini

PIAZZA CATTEDRALE

Piazza Pretoria

La Martorana

Santa Maria dello Spasimo

VIA

PIAZZA BOLOGNI

VIA PONTICELLO

San Cataldo

Monreale

Villa Bonanno

Chiesa di Gesù

Palazzo Aiutamicristo

VIA GARIBALDI

La Magione

Villa Giulia

ORTO BOTANICO

PIAZZA DELLA VITTORIA

Mercato Ballarò

VIA DEL BOSCO

MAQUEDA

PIAZZA DEL CARMINE

VIA ROMA

Palazzo dei Normanni

VIA A. MONGITORE

VIA ALBERGHERIA

Carmine

VIA ABRAMO LINCOLN

CORSO DEI MILLE

PIAZZA INDIPENDENZA

VIA

Stazione Centrale

PARCO D'ORLEANS

San Giovanni degli Eremiti

CORSO

TUKORY

VIA ORTEO

0   400 meters

0   400 yards

of the city's ninth-century Saracen fortress, a building enlarged by the Normans and transformed into a palace complex that became one of Europe's leading royal courts.

Guided tours conduct you around the 12th-century **Sala di Re Ruggero,** or Hall of Roger II, a chamber adorned with mosaics of hunting scenes. Roger, a Norman king, was also responsible for the magnificent **Cappella Palatina** *(tel 091 705 1111, closed Sun. p.m.),* built between 1132 and 1140, one of Palermo's highlights. This glittering private chapel encapsulates the composite architectural style that flourished in Sicily under the Normans. Ancient Roman columns support its predominantly Romanesque interior, which is overarched by a Moorish wooden ceiling and adorned with Byzantine mosaics, considered to be among Europe's finest. Also be sure—if they are open—to stroll around the palace's palm-fringed gardens, the **Villa Bonanno.**

Palermo had more than 200 mosques during its period of Arab rule (831–1072). Many were replaced by Christian buildings, including **San Giovanni degli Eremiti** *(Via dei Benedettini, tel 091 651 5019, closed Sun. p.m.),* a deconsecrated church, built between 1132 and 1148 to the south of the Palazzo dei Normanni. Its five bulging ocher domes bear witness to its Islamic predecessor. The cloister is as lovely as the church, the garden a scented enclave of palms, lemon trees, and subtropical plants.

Moving east along Corso Vittorio Emanuele, you come to Palermo's great honey-stone **Cattedrale,** or cathedral *(Piazza Cattedrale, Corso Vittorio Emanuele, tel 091 334 373, www.cattedrale .palermo.it),* begun in 1184, another monument to the city's Norman past. Its interior was much altered in the 18th century, but the exterior has retained its exotic blend of early architectural styles. Inside, the only surviving points of real interest are the royal tombs of Henry IV,

Monreale

Monreale, a town about 4 miles (7 km) from Palermo's center, has one of Europe's supreme cathedrals, the **Duomo di Monreale** *(Piazza Vittorio Emanuele, Monreale, tel 091 640 4413, cloister closed Sun. p.m., cloister $).* Founded in 1172 by the Norman king William II, it is a monument to the greatest traditions of Arab, Norman, and Byzantine art and architecture. A finely carved portal frames its main bronze doors (1186), which are adorned with 42 biblical scenes; a more Byzantine-influenced bronze door (1179) is on the cathedral's left (north)

side. Inside, the building resembles a giant casket of jewels, shimmering with gold leaf, paintings, and richly colored marbles, its nave and wooden ceiling supported by columns from earlier classical buildings. A glorious mosaic pavement (1182) mirrors the mosaics in the main body of the church. The royal tombs of kings William I and II lie in a chapel to the right of the apse. The celebrated Norman cloister is a bonus. Some 228 twin columns, most sinuously carved or inlaid with colored marbles, support the quadrangle's Arab-style arches.

Roger II, and the great Hohens-taufen emperor Frederick II and his wife, Constance of Aragon (located in two chapels in the south aisle).

Quattro Canti: The heart of Palermo is marked by Corso Vittorio Emanuele's intersection with Via Maqueda, known as the Quattro Canti, or Four Corners. Immediately to the south lies **Piazza Pretoria,** a ring of fine medieval and Renaissance build-ings centered on a 16th-century fountain known locally as the "Fountain of Shame" after its lascivious nude figures. Just to the south stands the church of **La Martorana** (Piazza Bellini, tel 091 616 1692, closed 1–3.30 p.m. & Sun. p.m.), also known as Santa Maria dell'Ammiraglio, because it was founded in 1142 by Roger II's admiral (ammiraglio). Baroque alterations spared the church's sensational Greek-crafted 12th-century dome mosaics.

Alongside La Martorana lies the 12th-century Norman church of **San Cataldo** (Piazza Bellini, tel 091 616 1692, closed 1–3:30 p.m. & Sun. p.m.), whose exterior bears Moorish influences and interior is a riot of baroque overelabora-tion. Another example of baroque exuberance is **San Giuseppe dei Teatini** (Piazza Pretoria, tel 091 331 239, closed 12–5:30 p.m.), built in 1612 on the Quattro Canti, whose plain-faced exterior conceals an interior of decorative splendor.

Piazza San Domenico & Around: Before continuing east on the Corso, head north on Via Roma, pausing to explore Palermo's vibrant market area in the streets around Piazza San Domenico. This colorful district is known as the Vucciria, from a phrase meaning "a place of noise and confusion."

INSIDER TIP:

Palermo's 12th-century La Zisa palace features a "Fountain Room" two stories high.

—RICCARDO STRANO
Director, Italian Government Tourist Board North America

While in the area, stop by **San Domenico,** the nearby **Oratorio del Rosario,** and the **Oratorio di Santa Zita** (or **Cita**). All three churches offer object lessons in the finer points of Sicilian baroque decoration.

Farther north, just off Via Roma, is Sicily's leading archaeological museum, the extensive **Museo Archeologico Regionale** (Piazza dell'Olivello 24, tel 091 611 6805, closed Sun. p.m. & Mon., $$). It is a repository for art and artifacts from the island's ancient sites.

Return to the Quattro Canti and head east to a cluster of sights grouped between the Corso and Via Alloro to the south. Chief among these is the **Galleria Regionale di Sicilia** (Via Alloro 4, tel 091 623 0011, closed 1:30–3:30, $$), an important collection of paintings and sculptures whose highlights are Antonello da Messi-na's painting of the "Annunciation"

San Domenico
- Piazza San Domenico
- ☎ 091 329 588
- Closed Mon.; Tues.–Fri. 11:30 a.m., Sat. & Sun. 11:30 a.m.–5 p.m.

www.domenicani-palermo.it

Oratorio del Rosario
- Via Bambinai 2
- Closed p.m. daily & Sun., but may open p.m. May–Sept. depending on staffing
- $$ (combined ticket with Oratorio di Santa Zita and 3 other local churches)

Oratorio di Santa Zita
- Via Valverde 3
- ☎ 091 332 779
- Closed p.m. daily & Sun., may open p.m. May–Sept. depending on staffing
- $$ (combined ticket with Oratorio del Rosario and 3 other local churches)

La Zisa
- Piazza Zisa
- ☎ 091 652 0269
- Closed 12–3 p.m. & Sun. p.m.
- $$

Cefalù
 179 C2

Visitor Information

✉ Corso Ruggiero 77

☎ 092 142 1050 or 092 142 2354 (for accommodations)

www.cefalu.it

(1473) and an exquisite 1471 bust of Eleonora of Aragon by Francesco Laurana.

Immediately north in Piazza Marina stands the **Palazzo Chiaramonte** (1307), a Gothic palace best known for its garden's magnolia fig trees. If gardens appeal, walk south to visit the **Villa Giulia** (Foro Umberto I, 21), laid out in 1778, and the 16th-century **Orto Botanico** (Botanical Garden) next door (Via Lincoln 2/A, tel 091 623 8234, www.ortobotanico.palermo .it, closed Sun. p.m. Nov.–Feb., $$).

For something more unusual, head to the eastern end of the Corso and the **Museo delle Marionette** (Piazzetta Niscemi 5, tel 091 328 060, closed 1–3:30 p.m. & Sat. & Sun., $$). The museum has a fine collection of puppets from Sicily and other parts of the world.

On the outskirts of the city (take a cab), be sure to visit the **Convento dei Cappuccini** (Via G. Mosca–Via Pindemonte, tel 091 652 4156, closed 12–3 p.m., Sun. a.m. & Mon., $), Palermo's most macabre sight. The convent's subterranean chambers contain numerous preserved corpses, dried using lime, arsenic, and the sun—a Capuchin tradition.

Cefalù

Cefalù has largely escaped the modern building that has done so much to spoil Sicily's once pristine coastline. Charming and compact, this likable town, built below an immense fortress-like crag, has several pleasant beaches, a charming main square, and a majestic Norman cathedral graced with one of the most sublime images of Christ in Western art.

Cefalù's main **Piazza del Duomo** is as satisfying a spot for a quiet drink or reflective half hour as you could wish for. Palm trees grow in each corner, overlooked by the amber-stoned facade of the

The twin towers of the Norman cathedral in Cefalù dominate the town's medieval skyline.

town's wondrous **Duomo** (1131–1240). Legend has it the building was raised to fulfill a vow by Roger II, Sicily's 12th-century Norman king, who pledged a church to the Madonna in gratitude for sparing his life in a shipwreck. The shrine was intended to be Sicily's most important religious building and a monument for Roger's Norman successors. Neither ambition was realized.

The church's interior is as restrained as its exterior; much has remained unchanged for more than 800 years. Note the wooden ceiling and Arab-influenced capitals, the latter perfect examples of the composite Sicilian-Norman Romanesque style. The celebrated **apse mosaic,** which depicts Christ Pantocrater—Christ in the act of blessing—dates from 1148, making it the earliest Sicilian example of a much repeated image.

A short distance from the cathedral lies the **Museo Mandralisca** (Via Mandralisca 13, tel 092 142 1547, www.museomandralisca .it, closed 1–3 p.m. Oct.–May, $$), a collection of coins, pottery, Greek and Roman artifacts, and an exceptional painting, "Portrait of an Unknown Man" (1472), by Sicily's eminent Renaissance artist, Antonello da Messina (1430–1479).

Isole Eolie

Sicily has many ravishing offshore islands—Ustica, Pantelleria, and the Egadi and Pelagie archipelagoes. None are as popular or as spectacular, however, as the Isole Eolie (Aeolian Islands), a coronet of seven volcanic islets. Visitors are drawn here by the

Getting to Isole Eolie

Ferries run to the islands from Naples (www.snav .it, May–Sept.), **Palermo, Reggio di Calabria, Cefalù, and Messina, but the most convenient access is from Milazzo. Reservations are generally only necessary if you take a car. Services are much less frequent October to April. Hydrofoils are twice as quick, but twice the price.** Alilauro (tel 081 497 2238, www.alilauro .it/eolie) **runs services from Milazzo, as do Ustica Lines** (092 387 3813, www .usticalines.it) **and Siremar** (www.siremar.it).

chance to witness raw volcanic activity and by the ethereal light, balmy climate, stark beauty, and aquamarine seas.

Walking and snorkeling are major attractions, as are the islands' volcanic black-sand beaches. The three big islands—Stromboli, Vulcano, and Lipari—are popular, so reserve accommodations in advance. Other islands, notably Salina, are quieter.

Stromboli is popular because its volcanic action is the most reliable—spectacular eruptions take place from its summit around four times an hour—but you can easily visit for the day from Lipari, Salina, or elsewhere. The port, most hotels, and other facilities are in **Stromboli Paese,** as is the island's main black-sand beach (north of Piscità). The main crater can be reached by foot (guides

Isole Eolie
🅰 179 C3

Visitor Information
✉ Corso Vittorio Emanuele II, 202, Lipari
☎ 090 988 0095
🕐 Closed 1:30–3:30 p.m., Sun., & Sat. p.m. Sept.–June

www.aasteolie.191.it

A café beckons at the foot of Taormina's stately church of San Giuseppe.

Taormina

 179 D2

Visitor Information

✉ Palazzo Corvaja,
Piazza Santa
Caterina

☎ 094 223 243

**www.gate2taormina
.com**

available), but it's a long climb to the 3,031-foot (924 m) summit. Allow about seven hours round-trip and take plenty of water. You can also admire the eruptions and lava flows at a distance from a boat (night trips are especially vivid).

Vulcano is the closest island to Milazzo. Its last major eruption was in 1980, though smoke holes smolder, mud baths bubble, and geysers spout. The island takes its name from the myth that this was where Vulcan, god of fire, kept his forge—the island subsequently lending its name to all things volcanic. Boats dock at **Porto Levante,** nestled beneath the Great Crater, whose summit offers fabulous views. The island's strange landscapes can also be enjoyed by boat from **Porto Ponente** (15-min. walk from Porto Levante), a place also known for its (busy) black-sand beach and therapeutic sulfurous mud baths.

Lipari is the largest and most scenically varied of the Aeolians, making up for its lack of volcanic activity with some beautiful landscapes. Boats dock at **Lipari** town, cradled between two bays: Marina Lunga, which has a beach, and **Marina Corta,** where you can pick up boats for excellent trips around the coast. The town has a pleasant old walled quarter and the superb **Museo Archeologico Regionale** *(Via del Castello, tel 090 988 0174, closed 1:30–3 p.m. & Sun. p.m., $$).*

Taormina

Taormina enjoys a fabled site, its beautiful location offering views across the blue expanse of the Ionian Sea on one side and the majestic profile of Mount Etna on the other. As well as enjoying some of Sicily's loveliest landscapes, the town boasts sandy beaches, chic designer stores, grand hotels, ancient monuments, and top-notch restaurants. All of these combine to make Taormina Sicily's most exclusive and visited resort.

The town is also blessed with a mild climate. Flowers fill the balconies of its medieval houses, most of which twist around steep streets and sun-dappled piazzas. Visitors enjoy the cafés on the

INSIDER TIP:

If you have time when visiting Etna, don't miss the town of Randazzo just north of the volcano, with its church built of lava and yellow pumice.

—TINO SORIANO
National Geographic photographer

panoramic main square, **Piazza IX Aprile,** or the establishments on Corso Umberto I, Taormina's main street.

More than most towns, this is a place to be enjoyed off-season, for its charms attract hordes of summer visitors, their numbers swollen by those attending the town's art and music festivals. Many the festivals take place in the town's premier sight, the sublimely situated **Teatro Greco** (tel 094 223 220, closed at dusk, $$). Writer Johann Goethe considered the theater's setting to be the "greatest work of art and nature."

Other sights are few and far between, but this is not a place you visit for art and architecture.

Try exploring the **Parco Duca di Cesarò** (Public Gardens) on Via Bagnoli Croce, or walk or drive the 2 miles (3 km) to the **Castello** on 1,279-foot (390 m) Monte Tauro. Built on the site of a Greek acropolis, the crumbling medieval fort offer tremendous views of the countryside.

Etna

Etna is Europe's highest volcano. Ancient mariners believed its snowy, smoldering summit—visible from far and wide—was the world's highest point. To the Arabs, it was simply the "Mountain of Mountains," while to the Greeks it was known as Aipho (meaning "I burn").

Etna is a youngster geologically. Formed about 60,000 years ago, it sprang from undersea eruptions on what is now the Plain of Catania. Unlike many volcanoes,

Etna
🏔 179 C2
Visitor Information
✉ Via del Convento, 45, Nicolosi
☎ 095 821 111
www.parcoetna.ct.it
www.parks.it

EXPERIENCE: Guided Tours of Mount Etna

Etna provides a wealth of hiking experiences, from gentle strolls through the pastoral scenery of its lower slopes to the high-mountain trails that wend through the almost lunar landscapes of its lava fields. **Etna Experience** (tel 095 723 2924, www.etnaexperience.com) offers well-picked tours, from the "Classic Experience" (9 a.m.–6:30 p.m., with hotel pickup, walking tour, and picnic) and "Etna & Wine Tour" to a day's more demanding hiking ("Solo Trekking Experience"). Tours are in English and Italian. **Etnatura** (www.etnatura.it) will also collect you from your hotel for a half-day minibus tour that takes in the volcano's high- and mid-level landscapes.

The Mafia

Everyone has heard of the Mafia. In 1866, Sicily's British consul reported to his superiors that *"maffie-elected juntas* share the earnings of the workmen, keep up intercourse with outcasts and take malefactors under their wing and protection." Both the word and the organization have ancient origins: The linguistic roots probably lie in an Arab word, *mu'afàh,* which means many things—protection, skill, beauty, ability, and safety.

The organizational roots are more elusive. Many scholars believe the seeds of this criminal group were sown as early as the 12th century, when secret societies were created to resist the imposition of rule by the Holy Roman Empire. Others point to the Bourbons, who used ex-brigands to police the remote Sicilian interior, a system that quickly led to the brigands taking bribes in exchange for turning a blind eye to the activities of their former criminal colleagues. Many also cite the rise of the *gabellotti,* middlemen who acted as rent collectors or mediators between peasants and landowners and quickly grew rich by intimidating the former and acting as agents for the latter. United by similar aims, the gabellotti quickly became a separate class, bound by codes of honor, behavior, and semiformal organization.

All theories are linked by a common thread: the centuries-old gulf between Sicilians and agents of authority, a gulf fostered by Sicily's long succession of exploitative foreign rulers.

Nowhere was the breach more keenly felt than by landless peasants forced to work on the island's *latifundia,* vast feudal estates owned by absentee landlords in Naples or Palermo. The system went back to Roman times and survived until well after World War II. Where conventional justice and authority were either lacking or despised, it was only a matter of time before the gap was filled by all manner of local arbitrators—the so-called *amici* (friends) or *uomini d'onore* (men of honor).

Traveler Patrick Brydone, writing in *A Tour through Sicily and Malta,* summarized the situation in 1773: "These banditti," he wrote, "are the most respectable of the island, and have the highest and most romantic notions of what they call their point of honour...with respect to one another, and to every person to whom they have once professed it, they have ever maintained the most unshaken fidelity. The magistrates have often been obliged to protect them, and even pay them court, as they are known to be extremely determined and desperate; and so extremely vindictive, that they will certainly put any person to death who has ever given them just cause of provocation." He might easily have been describing events two centuries later.

What many people do not know is that Italy once came within a whisker of overturning this state of affairs. Under Mussolini, the legendary police chief Cesare Mori used brutal and entirely illegal measures to combat the Mafia, and, but for World War II, might have crushed it entirely. Ironically, the intervention of the Americans foiled the venture. In preparing for the invasion of Sicily in 1943, the Allies had

Mafia Locations

Towns such as Prizzi and Corleone in the Sicilian interior receive a stream of curious visitors drawn by their appearance in Mario Puzo's Mafia novels. Fewer visit **Savoca,** a village northwest of Taormina seen in Francis Ford Coppola's classic movie, *The Godfather.* A visit here, and to other of the region's villages such as Forza d'Agrò and Casalvecchio Siculo, reveals landscapes and ways of life little changed in centuries.

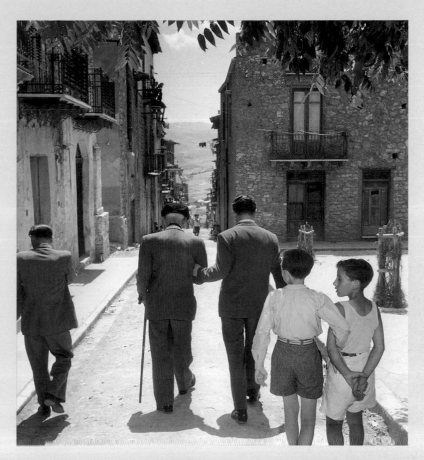

Children mimic the style of Sicilian-born gangster Charles "Lucky" Luciano (center), walking down a street in Sicily.

only one source of intelligence and logistical support—the Mafia—with whom it forged links by exploiting the contacts of Italian-American gangsters such as Lucky Luciano.

Once the Allies had taken the island, they further reinforced Mafia power by drafting its often highly placed members onto the new Allied Military Government—of 66 Sicilian towns, 62 were entrusted to men with criminal connections. Mafia power was further consolidated in Italy's postwar boom, when huge fortunes were made in construction. Money was then laundered into legitimate businesses

or funneled into narcotics, a trade that altered forever the nature of Mafia business.

Italian police have had some recent victories against the Mafia, notably with the arrest of longtime boss Bernardo Provenzano. Already convicted *in absentia* of more than a dozen murders, the 73-year-old Provenzano was found hiding in a Sicilian farmhouse in April 2006.

Despite some successes, the Mafia's dismemberment remains unlikely, largely because its tentacles are so tightly entwined in Italy's economy. Not for nothing do the Italians refer to the Mafia as *la piovra*—the octopus.

Catania
⛰ 179 C2

Visitor Information

✉ Via Cimarosa 10

☎ 095 730 6233 or 095 730 6211

www.apt.catania.it

Linguaglossa
⛰ 179 C2

Visitor Information

✉ Piazza Annunziata 5–7

☎ 095 643 094

www.proloco linguaglossa.it

Nicolosi
⛰ 179 C2

Visitor Information

✉ Via Vittorio Emanuele II, 45

☎ 095 914 488

www.aast-nicolosi.it

it tends to rupture rather than explode, creating huge lateral fissures instead of a single crater—some 350 have appeared to date. About 90 major and 135 minor eruptions have been documented, of which the most catastrophic occurred in 1669, when the pyrotechnics lasted for 122 days. Debris was thrown over 65 miles (104 km), and a mile-wide tongue of lava engulfed **Catania** more than 25 miles (40 km) away.

To experience Etna fully, you should visit the summit, at 10,876 feet (3,315 m), and explore its lower slopes. For the latter, take the private Circumetnea railroad (*www.circumetnea.it*), which circles the volcano, from Catania, or drive along a similar route; the approach from the village of **Linguaglossa** is superb. As well as mountain views, you see groves of orange, lemon, fig, and olive trees and other vegetation nurtured by the volcano's fertile soils.

Volcanic activity affects access to the summit and the areas you can safely approach (there was a major eruption in 2001). Guided tours are possible from Catania,

Taormina, **Nicolosi,** and elsewhere using minibuses and off-road vehicles. Or you can drive to the Rifugio Sapienza, a mountain refuge, and then take off-road SUV tours or walk (allow a full day) up the mountain. Wear tough boots.

Siracusa

Siracusa (Syracuse) was founded by the Greeks in 733 B.C. Between the third and fifth centuries B.C., it became Europe's most powerful city. For years, its only rivals were the Etruscans and Carthaginians, both of whom it defeated before succumbing to Rome in 214 B.C. Today, its old town, Ortigia, and the extensive archaeological zone (the Parco Archeologico), are essential stops on any Sicilian itinerary. Only the modern town, raised from the ruins of World War II bombing, is a disappointment.

Start your Syracusean odyssey either in the Parco Archeologico—a pleasant area ranged across the site of the ancient Greek city of Neapolis, above the sea and suburbs—or in Ortigia (or

EXPERIENCE: Cultural Tours of Sicily

You can experience Sicily's long history by land or by sea with cultural tours. **Amber Road Tours** *(tel 39 0743 224 946, www .amberroadtours.com),* based in Italy with American owners, provides a 12-day tour from Palermo to Etna, including archaeological tours and wine tastings. U.K. cultural tour operator **Martin Randall Travel** *(tel 44 [0] 20 8742 3355, www.martinrandall.com)* offers a 13-day

group tour of Sicily that takes in most of the island's key centers: Palermo, Monreale, Cefalù, Segesta, Selinunte, Agrigento, Taormina, and Noto, with an excursion to Reggio di Calabria. **Peter Sommer** *(tel 44 [0] 1600 888220, www. petersommer.com)* offers two Sicily tours—"Cruising by Etna" and "Sailing the Sicilian Coast"—that combine culture and cruising in traditional "gulet" boats.

Ortygia), which is squeezed onto a tiny island linked by a causeway to the modern town.

The entrance to the **Parco Archeologico** *(Largo Paradiso, tel 093 166 206, $$$)* is marked by a small visitor center and a sprawl of souvenir stands. Beyond these on the left lies the site's first major

left to perish in 413 B.C. Nearby is a grotto known as the **Orecchio di Dionisio** (Ear of Dionysius). Legend has it that the cave's acoustic properties allowed one of Syracuse's rulers to overhear conspirators talking, hence the name. Another nearby cave, the **Grotta dei Cordari,** was used by

Siracusa
Ⓜ 179 D1
Visitor Information
www.apt-siracusa.it
www.siracusa-sicilia.it

The imposing 18th-century baroque facade of the Duomo in Siracusa

ruin, the **Ara di Ierone II,** created as a vast sacrificial altar in the third century B.C.; as many as 450 bulls were slaughtered here in a single day. More survives of the fifth-century B.C. **Teatro Greco,** an amphitheater carved from the hillside's rock and, with 15,000 seats, one of the largest theaters in the Greek world.

Close to the theater lies the **Latomia del Paradiso,** site of a former quarry in which 7,000 Athenian prisoners were reputedly

Greek ropemakers, its humidity preventing hemp from breaking.

Before heading for Ortigia (buses and cabs run from outside the ruins), it makes sense to visit the **Museo Archeologico Regionale** *(Viale Teocrito 66, tel 093 146 4022, closed Sun. p.m. & Mon., $$$).* A museum of finds from the archaeological zone and elsewhere, it lies on the grounds of the Villa Landolina, about ten minutes' walk east of the Parco Archeologico.

Ortigia

Visitor Information

✉ Via Maestranza 33

☎ 093 165 201 or 093 146 4255

Piazza Armerina

🅰 179 C2

Visitor Information

✉ Viale Muscarà Generale 57

☎ 093 568 0201

www.piazza armerina.org

Ortigia formed the heart of ancient Syracuse for some 2,700 years, its easily defended island location and freshwater springs making it a natural fortress. It was here that the besieging Romans were held at bay for 13 years in the third century B.C. Today, much of the island has a pretty baroque and medieval appearance, largely the result of rebuilding that followed a calamitous earthquake in 1693. The Ponte Nuovo from the mainland leads into Piazza Pancali, home of the fragmentary **Tempio di Apollo** (565 B.C.), Sicily's oldest Doric temple.

Baroque Stars

The earthquake of January 11, 1693, in southeast Sicily, was one of the most destructive in the island's history, but it occurred during a period of prosperity, which meant that many of the region's towns were rebuilt along model lines in the majestic baroque style of the day. These towns can be explored from Siracusa, starting with honey-stoned Noto, a UNESCO World Heritage site, followed by Modica and Scicli, and ending with Ragusa, where the restored old center, Ragusa Ibla, is one of Sicily's loveliest old hill towns.

The town's most famous sight is the **Duomo** (Piazza Duomo), whose baroque facade conceals the Tempio di Atena, a fifth-century B.C. temple skillfully incorporated into the later Christian building. Also worth seeing are the **Fonte Aretusa,** Ortigia's precious original spring; the **Passeggio Adorno,** a scenic promenade; and the **Galleria Regionale** (Palazzo Bellomo, Via Capodieci 14,

tel 093 169 511, closed Sun. p.m. & Mon., $$$), a museum of paintings (including works by Caravaggio and Antonello da Messina) and other artwork.

Piazza Armerina

Piazza Armerina is a village lost in Sicily's central heartlands; it is a place of little note save for the **Villa Romana del Casale,** (tel 339 265 7640, www .villaromanadelcasale.it, $$) an isolated Roman villa 3 miles (5 km) to the southwest. Here are preserved some of Europe's most extensive and unspoiled Roman mosaics. This priceless treasure was buried by a landslide in the 12th century and thus protected from the elements until full-scale excavations between 1929 and 1960 brought its glories to light.

No one is sure to whom the Villa Casale belonged, but to judge from its opulence and huge extent—it contains more than 50 rooms—its owner must have been a figure of wealth and renown. The most persuasive theories suggest it was a hunting lodge and country retreat built for Emperor Maximianus Herculius, who reigned as co-emperor with the better known Emperor Diocletian between A.D. 286 and 305. Its role as a hunting lodge would seem to be borne out by the hunting scenes on many of its floor mosaics and by its rustic position.

While the villa's superstructure may have gone—skillfully fashioned modern walls and roofs suggest how it might once have appeared—the original mosaics survive in an almost pristine state. Their style resembles similar mosaics discovered in Roman villas across North Africa, suggesting their creators may have been Carthaginian.

This notion is evidenced by the villa's centerpiece, an African hunting scene some 200 feet (59 m) long. Woven into this scene's rippling narrative are vivid depictions of exotic animals such as tigers, ostriches, and elephants, many of them being captured for transportation to Rome for use in circuses and gladiatorial games.

Virtually every room features similarly fascinating mosaics, although the scene that attracts the most visitors is the one depicting ten female athletes in bikinis.

Agrigento

Modern Agrigento provides an ugly backdrop to Sicily's principal archaeological sight—the Valle dei Templi, or Valley of the Temples, site of the ancient Greek city of Akragas. Once this "loveliest of mortal cities," as the classical writer Pindar described it, was among the most important of Sicily's Greek colonies. Today, much of its former grandeur is still apparent in the valley's extensive ruins and its nine temples, the finest classical Greek remains outside Greece.

The city was founded in 580 or 582 B.C. by settlers from nearby Gela, itself founded by pioneers from the Greek island of Rhodes. Although earthquakes over the years laid much of the city low, the worst damage was inflicted by Christian settlers who vandalized the temples, sparing only the **Tempio della Concordia** (430 B.C.) because it was converted into a church in the sixth century.

This magnificent Doric temple is the finest in Sicily and the finest in the Greek world after the Thesion temple in Athens. Other only marginally less impressive temples lie close by along the Via Sacra.

The superb mosaics of the Villa Casale

Agrigento

  179 B1

Visitor Information

✉ Piazzale Aldo Moro 7

☎ 092 220 454

www.comune .agrigento.it

NOTE: A discounted joint ticket is available for the temples and Museo Archeologico.

Allow a morning to explore them, arriving early to avoid the crowds.

Among the temples are the 470 B.C. **Tempio di Giunone** (Juno) and the fifth-century B.C. **Tempio di Ercole** (Hercules). The site's western margins, reached by crossing the street known as the Via dei Templi, include the ruins of the half-finished **Tempio di Giove** (Jupiter). Had this temple been completed—work on it was interrupted by a Carthaginian raid in 406 B.C.—it would have been the largest temple in the Greek or Roman world.

To the north, at the end of the Via dei Templi, lies the **Quartiere Ellenistico-Romano,** the ruins of part of a later Greco-Roman town. Also here is the **Museo Archeologico Regionale** (*Contrada San Nicola, tel 092 240 1565, closed Sun. p.m. & Mon. p.m., $$*), a collection devoted to artifacts discovered in the valley. ∎

Each of the 34 columns is 22.5 feet (7 m) high.

Crepidoma, stepped base

Tempio della Concordia at Agrigento

Pediment

Cella, enclosed interior of temple

Stylobate, temple platform

Doric capital

The Tempio della Concordia rises in the Valle dei Templi, outside Agrigento. Built by the Greeks in 430 B.C., the temple is one of the best preserved in Europe. It owes its fine state of preservation to the fact that it was converted into a Christian basilica in the sixth century. Much of its sandstone would once have been brightly painted and covered in a stucco of white marble dust.

Sardinia

If Sicily is a world apart, then Sardinia—about 125 miles (200 km) from the African and Italian mainlands—seems more foreign still. It is the second largest island in the Mediterranean and, to all intents and purposes, a country in its own right, with its own language (Sardo), food, history, and powerful cultural traditions.

The beach at Romazzino on the Costa Smeralda

Its position accounts for much of its character, at once inaccessible but also at the maritime crossroads of Europe. In the earliest days of human habitation, 7,000 years ago, this meant the growth of an indigenous culture, the *nuraghi* civilization. Today, about 1,000 nuraghi, strange stone ruins, lie scattered across the island. In later years, its location meant a stream of foreign invaders.

For all its long history, however, the island remained mostly poor and undeveloped. As a result,

Sardinia has few of Sicily's set pieces, scenic or cultural. Instead, its principal attraction is a peerless coastline, with the Costa Smeralda and other resorts a magnet for those in search of golden sands and emerald seas; opportunities here for diving, sailing, and other water sports are unparalleled. In the interior, you find wonderfully varied scenery, from deep gorges to scrub-covered plains.

Costa Smeralda

Ask almost any Italian where he or she would most like to

spend an Italian beach vacation and chances are they will say Sardinia, and more specifically the Costa Smeralda, or Emerald Coast. Luxury resorts, built here beginning in the 1960s, have turned the area into one of Europe's most exclusive seaside retreats.

Those with time to spare will find a host of beautiful beaches, turquoise seas, and unspoiled resorts around the Sardinian

coast. Those with less time should make straight for the Costa Smeralda and any of its resorts—**Porto Rotondo, Portisco, Baia Sardinia,** and the granddaddy of them all, **Porto Cervo.** All are similarly chic and based mostly around upscale hotels or self-contained resort villages—but don't expect much by way of local color. Relatively undeveloped adjacent resorts include Santa Teresa Gallura, Palau, Cannigione, and the

Costa Smeralda

196 C3 & C4

Visitor Information

✉ Via Nanni 39, Olbia

☎ 078 955 7732

🕐 Closed p.m. daily & Sat.–Sun. Nov.–May

www.olbiaturismo.it

Alghero

⚠ 196 A3
Visitor Information
✉ Piazza Porta
Terra 9
☎ 079 979 054
www.algheroweb.it
**www.comune
.alghero.ss.it**

beaches at Punta Falcone, Capo Testa, and La Marmorata.

Some of the island's northern highlights are within a morning's drive. For example, from the SS199 east of Olbia, or from Castelsardo on the northern coast, you can visit a succession of Pisan-Romanesque churches. Take roads south and west toward Ozieri and Sassari and you pass half a dozen, including **Santissima Trinità di Saccargia,** Sardinia's loveliest religious building. This itinerary also gives you the chance to drive along the **Valle dei Nuraghi** (on the SS131), scattered with the nuraghi for which the island is celebrated (see sidebar opposite). It then leaves you well placed for visiting **Alghero,** one of northern Sardinia's most attractive towns.

Alghero

Sardinian towns are forgettable affairs on the whole, their medieval kernels blighted by modern buildings and uninspiring suburbs. Not so Alghero, a prettily situated port.

Gathered around a walled old quarter, this atmospheric town is popular with visitors, but its role as a busy fishing harbor means that it retains a role of its own.

Alghero owes much of its culture and appearance to the Spanish, and to the Catalans in particular, who ruled the town for some four centuries after landing here in 1354. The Catalan presence was so pervasive that the region acquired the nickname "Barcelonetta" or Little Barcelona. Catalan influence survives to this day, both in language—*plaça* and *iglesia* are used for square and church, for example—and in the decidedly Spanish look of the town's religious and domestic architecture.

Key sights in the old town's web of twisting cobbled lanes are the **Cattedrale** in Piazza del

The old quarter of Alghero has a distinctly Spanish appearance.

Nuraghi

Myth suggests the Sards are descended from Sardus, legendary son of Hercules. In truth, they could have come from almost anywhere in the Mediterranean. All that is known for certain is that an indigenous population existed before the arrival of the Phoenicians and Carthaginians in the first millennium B.C. Evidence of its presence lies scattered across the island, from the rock tombs—*domus de janas* (elves' dwellings)—of about 2000 to 1800 B.C. to the 7,000 or more mysterious nuraghi built by the tribes who inhabited Sardinia from around 1500 to 500 B.C.

Nuraghi were probably houses or fortified citadels. No two are the same, but most are conical, with circular vaulted interiors linked by passages to terraces and upper stories. They occur across Sardinia, but the three most famous are found at **Su Nuraxi,** outside Barumini; **Losa,** near Abbasanta; and **Sant'Antine,** between Macomer and Sassari. **Anghelu Ruiu,** 6 miles (10 km) north of Alghero, has the best concentration of ancient tombs.

INSIDER TIP:

For a journey through history, make a stop at Alghero, with its fortifications in the center of town, traditions, and crafts.

—GIOVANNI GUGLIELMOTTI
Associazione Salerno IdeAperta

Duomo (*off Via Roma*) and the church of **San Francesco** in Via Carlo Alberto. The former is a Catalan-Gothic building enlivened by an Aragonese portal, the latter a 14th-century Catalan-Gothic affair with Renaissance detailing and annexed to an exquisite cloister.

The town's best beaches lie to the north, as does the **Grotta di Nettuno** cave system (*tel 079 979 054, guided tours daily, $$$*), best reached by boat (*www.grottedinettuno.it*), although road access offers far-reaching views of the region's cliff-edged coastline. Arriving by car, however, means climbing down the 654-step **Escala del Cabriol** (Catalan for "goat's steps"). Allow ten minutes to clamber down.

Cala Gonone

Cala Gonone is a popular resort on Sardinia's east coast. It lies at the heart of the island's most spectacular coastal scenery, much of which is accessible by boat from the resort, or visible from above on the gloriously scenic road (SS125) that runs between the neighboring towns of Arbatax and Dorgali.

Ideally, aim to stay in Cala Gonone itself, a former fishing village gradually surrendering its former identity—but not its charm—to the march of modern hotels, restaurants, and other visitor facilities. If the accommodations are full, then **Dorgali,** just 6 miles (10 km) inland, makes a good alternative.

Approaching Cala Gonone from Arbatax and the south offers views of the **Gola su Gorruppu,** one of the island's

Cala Gonone

🅰 196 C3

Visitor Information

✉ Viale del Bue Marino 1/A

☎ 078 493 696

www.dorgali.it

Monti del Gennargentu

🏔 106 B2 & C2

Visitor Information
www.parks.it
www.parco
gennargentu.it

most breathtaking canyons. Views around Cala Gonone itself are best enjoyed from a boat, the most popular trips being to coves south of the village at **Cala di Luna** and **Cala Sisine.** Cliffs nearby tumble from the 3,000-foot (900 m) mountains that rear up along much of this stretch of coast. Boats *($$$$)* will also drop you for the day at secluded coves along the coast or provide access to the **Grotta del Bue Marino** *(tel 078 493 737, guided tours March/April–Oct.),* a spellbinding cave studded with stalactites and stalagmites.

Monti del Gennargentu

Sardinia's interior is one of western Europe's most traditional rural enclaves, an upland fastness where ancient customs, dress, and ceremonies are still preserved in remote, time-forgotten villages. No area is more starkly beautiful than the mountains of the Gennargentu.

Situated midway down the eastern half of the island, the Gennargentu rise to an elevation of 6,017 feet (1,834 m) in

INSIDER TIP:

Near the Gennargentu, stop by Orgosolo, where incredible graffitists have decorated the walls, some calling for revolution.

—TINO SORIANO
National Geographic photographer

a succession of mostly barren, rounded summits. The name means "silver gate," a reference to the snow that covers them in winter. Their heart is protected by the **Parco Nazionale del Gennargentu,** a national park that in truth is barely needed, for this wilderness is so remote that even the Romans did not fully penetrate its depths.

The Barbagia Mountains surround the main massif, while to the north lies the most primordial area of all, the limestone uplands of the Sopramonte—silent, sun-beaten, and the domain of wheeling griffon vultures. The Barbagia contain some striking scenery, notably the *tacchi* or *torroni,* high limestone

Malaria

Malaria today is largely considered a disease of the tropics, but for centuries it was also endemic in much of south, central, and northeast Italy. The word itself is Italian—*mal aria,* literally "bad air"—and the World Health Organization (WHO) declared Italy malaria-free only as recently as 1970 after intense postwar eradication programs.

The disease was especially prevalent in Sicily, Sardinia, and the coastal plains of Calabria, one reason for last area's still often-empty coastline and the preponderance of hill towns (built away from malarial areas).

A report for the WHO in 2001 warned that these areas still present the conditions necessary to support malaria. Although the disease has not reappeared, the increase of immigration from countries where malaria is still endemic, as well as changing environmental factors, could see the return of the disease to Italy.

tors such as Sadali, Si, and Ricci on Monte Arcueri and Monte Tonneri (near Seui) and the spectacular Piana Liana (4,242 feet/1,293 m), visible for miles around.

The only practical way of seeing the region is by car, following roads such as the SS125 from Arbatax to Dorgali, or the scenic drives from Aritzo, the main resort center, to Arcu Guddetorgiu, Seui, or Fonni, the highest of the island's villages at 3,300 feet (1,000 m).

Cagliari

Sardinia's capital looks a poor prospect on paper: It has a large port, and a surfeit of modern buildings. In the flesh, it is a surprisingly appealing place, blessed with a pleasant old center, a couple of major monuments, and easy access to beaches and flamingo-filled lagoons.

Head first for Sardinia's major museum, the **Museo Archeologico Nazionale** (*Piazza Arsenale, tel 070 684 000, closed Mon., $$*), perched on the northern flanks of the historic quarter, an area enclosed by 13th-century Pisan-built fortifications. The highlight of the museum's collection is a series of bronze statuettes, the artistic apex of the island's prehistoric nuraghic culture. In the same museum complex is a *pinacoteca*, or art gallery (*tel 070 684 000, closed Mon.*), devoted to Sardinian paintings from different eras.

South of the museum, in the old fortified Castello quarter, is the **Cattedrale** (*Piazza Palazzo*), or cathedral. The building dates from the 13th century, but the facade is a 20th-century addition, rendered

The cathedral and ramparts of the old quarter in Cagliari

in Pisan-Romanesque style. Inside, the highlights include a pair of stone pulpits, originally carved about 1160 for Pisa's cathedral. Also fascinating is the rock-hewn crypt, with sculptures by Sicilian artists of the saints whose remains were reputedly interred here.

Elsewhere in the old quarter, make for the **Bastione San Remy,** one of several terraces offering fine views. Farther afield, seek out the remains of the **Roman amphitheater** (*Viale Fra Ignazio*) and the churches of **Sant'Agostino** (*near Largo Carlo Felice*), fifth-century **San Saturno** (*Piazza San Cosimo*), and **Nostra Signora di Bonara** (*Viale Armando Diaz*) ■

Cagliari
📍 194 D1
Visitor Information
✉ Piazza Matteotti 9
☎ 070 669 255
http://visit-cagliari .it

More Places to Visit in Sicily & Sardinia

Erice, Sicily

The town of Erice appeals by virtue of its panoramic setting, hunched 2,461 feet (750 m) above the port of Trapani, and the charm and medievalism of its streets and squares (unusual in Sicily). The main sights are the mostly 16th-century church of **Santa Maria Assunta** and **Castello di Venere,** a 12th-century Norman castle on the site of the Eryx, a fortress and ancient shrine dating back to Greek and Phoenician times.

Ⓜ 179 A2 ✉ **Visitor Information** Viale Conte Pepoli 11 ☎ 092 386 9388, *www.prolocovalderice.it* ⊕ Closed p.m. daily & Sat. & Sun.

Segesta, Sicily

Sicily has many splendid Greek temples, but none occupy such dramatic surroundings as the tawny-stoned Segesta. The Doric temple (426–416 B.C.), in a shallow ravine, stands in majestic isolation at the heart of glorious countryside. The site probably dates back to the pre-Hellenic cultures of the 12th century B.C. A road from the site leads about a mile (2 km) toward the summit of **Monte Barbaro,** whose slopes offer glorious views and a dainty Greek theater (third century B.C.) still used for performances on summer evenings.

Ⓜ 179 B2 ✉ **Visitor Information** 25 miles (40 km) east of Trapani, just south of Calatafimi exit of A29 ☎ 092 495 2356 Ⓢ $$

Selinunte, Sicily

Selinunte was among Sicily's most powerful Greek colonies, but it fell into ruin after Carthaginian raids in 409 B.C. and 250 B.C. What survives places it second to Agrigento in archaeological terms, although only portions of its eight massive temples remain standing (much of the site is still being excavated). The best of its treasures have been removed to Palermo's Museo Archeologico Regionale (see p. 183), but a small on-site

museum displays some of the lesser artifacts. Like Segesta, the site has a pretty location, making the ruins pleasant to visit.

Ⓜ 179 B2 ☎ 092 446 251 Ⓢ $$

Barbagia, Sardinia

The Barbagia is one of the wildest regions on the island, which is to say one of the wildest in western Europe. It lies near the island's center, between Nuoro and the Monti del Gennargentu to the south. It is full of tiny, remote villages such as **Mamoida, Aritzo,** and **Fonni.** Older people still wear traditional dress, one of the few places in Sardinia where this is the case. Sheep farming provides virtually the only income. You can hike the remote hills, but you'll need a car to get the best from the area.

Ⓜ 196 B2 ✉ **Visitor Information** Piazza Italia 19, Nuoro ☎ 078 430 083 or 078 423 8878

Giara di Gesturi, Sardinia

A *giara* is a basalt outcrop, a geological feature found across Sardinia. The best is the Giara di Gesturi, a lofty plateau about 2,000 feet (600 m) high and 8 miles (13 km) across. Its summit is cloaked in lush vegetation and forests of cork oak, the latter a refuge for the intensely reclusive Sardinian pony. The plateau is good for walking and is also known for its birds and spring flora; the best access point is the village of **Gesturi,** 37 miles (60 km) north of Cagliari, via the SS197. While in the region you should also visit **Las Plassas,** a distinctive conical hill topped by a ruined 12th-century castle. Also be sure to visit 15th-century B.C. **Su Nuraxi,** the most important of the island's *nuraghi,* or prehistoric dwellings (see sidebar p. 199) just west of Barumini, a village 30 miles (50 km) north of Cagliari.

Ⓜ 196 B2 ✉ **Visitor Information** Piazza Matteotti 9, Cagliari ☎ 070 669 255

Travelwise

Above Positano

TRAVELWISE

PLANNING YOUR TRIP

When to Go

High summer (July–August) in southern Italy is hot. On the coast, islands, and in mountain resorts, it is also busy and expensive, with a shortage of rooms. The sea is warm as late as November, and in May, June, and September you can enjoy fine weather with fewer crowds.

Note that some island and coastal resorts close for all or part of the period from November to March. Many businesses, including bars and restaurants, may be shut in August.

Spring is delightful, especially if you wish to spend time in the countryside or on the coasts. Easter is busy, but an excellent time to visit if you are interested in festivals.

Websites

Websites for visitor centers are given where appropriate in the text. More general sites include:
www.beniculturali.it
www.bestofsicily.com
www.discoverbasilicata.com
www.enit.it
www.inaples.it
www.incampania.com
www.museionline.it
www.parks.it
www.regione.campania.it
www.regione.calabria.it
www.regione.sicilia.it/turismo
www.sardegnaturismo.it
www.siciliaonline.it
www.viaggiareinpuglia.it

Climate

As a general rule, southern Italy has mild winters and very hot, dry summers. Temperatures can be especially high (up to or over 104°F/40°C) in July and August.

Coasts often have a slightly cooling summer breeze, but they are still very hot. Upland areas are cooler and in winter can be very cold. Average daytime temperatures in Naples in January are a high of 54°F (12°C) and low of 39°F (4°C); 73/54°F (23/12°C) in May; 84/64°F (29/18°C) in July; and 71/54°F (23/12°C) in October.

What to Take

You should be able to buy everything you need in the larger towns and cities of southern Italy. You may have problems in smaller villages, especially in the mountains, where often you will find just one small general store.

You will need to dress up only for the grandest restaurants, but don't be too casual, as Italians generally dress fashionably. Always dress appropriately in churches—no bare shoulders or shorts. Dress codes are more conservative in the South than in central and northern Italy, especially in rural areas.

Bring a sweater, even in summer, for evenings can be cool. Bring good rain and cold-weather gear year-round if you intend to hike in the mountains. Hiking, camping, and other sports equipment can easily be bought or rented.

Electricity in southern Italy is 220V, 50 Hz, and plugs have two (sometimes three) round pins. You will need a plug adapter and possibly a transformer for U.S. appliances.

Don't forget your passport, driver's license, tickets, traveler's checks, and insurance documents.

Insurance

Make sure you have adequate travel and medical coverage, including repatriation and baggage and money loss. Keep all receipts for expenses. Report losses or thefts to the police and obtain a signed statement (denuncia) from police stations to help with insurance claims.

Further Reading

Among the books you may want to pack or read before your vacation is The Italians by Luigi Barzini (Simon & Schuster, 1996). It was first published in 1964, but no writer, before or since, has produced a more penetrating or better-written analysis of Italy.

Other works include Naples '44 and The Honoured Society, both by Norman Lewis; Christ Stopped at Eboli by Carlo Levi; and Old Calabria, Siren Land, and South Wind by Norman Douglas.

HOW TO GET TO SOUTHERN ITALY

Passports

U.S. and Canadian citizens must have passports to enter Italy for stays of up to 90 days. No visas are required. U.K. citizens require passports, but can remain as long as they wish.

By Airplane

All major North American airlines have flights to Rome's Leonardo da Vinci airport (also known as Fiumicino) and Milan's Malpensa, with connecting Alitalia and Meridiana flights to Naples, Palermo, Catania, and other regional airports. Rome is the closer and more convenient hub.

Meridiana-Eurofly (tel 866 387 6359, www.meridiana.it) flies from New York's JFK to Naples and Palermo one to two times weekly June–September.

Several scheduled, charter, and low-cost airlines offer direct flights to Naples, Palermo, Bari, Brindisi, and a variety of other regional airports in southern Italy and Sardinia from the U.K. and other European cities.

You will arrive in Naples at Capodichino airport *(tel 081 789 6259 or 848 888 777 toll-free in Italy, www.gesac.it)*, 5 miles (8 km) from the city center. To reach the center (Piazza Garibaldi), take an Alibus *(tel 800 639 525, www.anm .it)* express shuttle, leaving every 30 minutes *(6:30 a.m.–11:50 p.m.)*, or the public transit bus 3S. A cab should cost around $25.

Smaller airports in southern Italy include Bari, Brindisi, and Lamezia. Major airports on Sardinia include Cagliari, Olbia, and Alghero. Sicilian airports include Trapani and the islands of Pantelleria and Lampedusa. There are many flights between these airports, plus connections from hubs at Rome, Naples, Palermo, and other major Italian cities.

Useful Numbers
In Italy
Rome airports, tel 06 65 951; www.adr.it
Milan airports, tel 02 7485 2200; www.sea-aeroportimilano.it
Alitalia, tel 06 65 631 or 06 65 644; www.alitalia.it
Meridiana, tel 892 928 in Italy, or +39 078 952 682 from abroad; www.meridiana.it

In the U.S. & Canada
Alitalia (U.S.) tel 800/223-5730; www.alitaliausa.com
Alltalia (Canada), tel 800/223 5730
American Airlines, tel 800/433-7300; www.aa.com
Continental, tel 800/525-0280; www.continental.com
Delta, tel 800/221-1212; www.delta.com
United, tel 800/241-6522; www.ual.com

GETTING AROUND
Getting around Towns & Cities
Most historic town and city centers are small enough to explore on foot. Only one or two outlying sights in Palermo, Siracusa, and Agrigento require cabs or public transport. Bicycles and motor scooters are available for rent in several towns.

By Bus & Metro
Buy your ticket for town and city buses beforehand, usually from designated bars (look for bus company logos or tobacconists, *tabacchi,* with a white "T" on a blue background). Validate it by stamping it in a small machine on the bus. Board buses at the rear and leave through the central doors. Inspectors board buses at random; passengers without valid tickets are fined.

Buses in Naples are run by ANM *(tel 800 639 525, www .anm.it)*. There is no central depot. Traffic often makes service slow. Tickets are valid for 90 minutes.

Bus tickets are also valid for Naples's metro (subway) system. Stations are indicated by a red "M" sign.

By Cab
Cabs are difficult to hail on the street. Most congregate at taxi stands on main piazzas or outside railroad stations. It is legal for drivers to charge extra for luggage placed in the trunk, for rides early or late in the day, on Sundays and public holidays, or for trips to airports or outside city limits. Always check that the meter is switched on and reset at the start of journeys.

Only take cabs with license numbers. In case of dispute, note the cab number. You may wish to negotiate a non-metered price

for longer journeys. Cabs can be reserved by phone for an extra fee. The dispatcher will give you the number and call sign of your cab. Round to the nearest euro, or tip about 10 percent.

Reliable firms include Consortaxi *(tel 081 552 5252, www .consortaxi.it)* and Partenope *(tel 081 551 5151, www.radiotaxipartenope.it)*.

Getting around the Region
By Airplane
It is worth traveling by plane only if you are going from Naples to Palermo or Sardinia in a hurry. You may also need to fly to some of Sicily's more distant offshore islands such as Pantelleria or Lampedusa. Alitalia has many connections. Smaller airlines include Blu-Express *(tel 199 419 777, www.blue-express.com)* and Airitaly *(tel 895 589 5589, www .airitaly.com)*.

By Bus
Buses (*pullman* or *autobus*) are an efficient means of traveling around much of southern Italy, especially in rural areas. Fast services also run on highways between all major towns. Although buses generally look alike (they're usually blue), they are operated by a number of different companies.

In Naples, SITA *(tel 081 386 6711, www.sitabus.it)* runs most services from Piazza Garibaldi (long-distance services) or Piazzale dell'Immacolata (Naples-area services).

Buses usually depart from a town's main square, outside a railroad station, or from a bus depot *(autostazione)*. In general, you must buy your ticket, usually from the depot or the nearest bar or station kiosk, before boarding the bus. Inquire at local visitor centers for details.

By Car

City centers tend to be congested, but in rural areas you will often have the road to yourself. Routes are generally well marked, from the ordinary thoroughfare—*nazionale* (N) or *statale/strada statale* (S or SS)—to a fast four- or six-lane toll expressway—*autostrada*.

If you have to travel a long distance, take an expressway; other roads tend to be slow.

Driving Information: If you break down, turn on the emergency lights and place a warning triangle behind the car. Call the Automobile Club d'Italia (ACI) emergency number *(tel 803 116, www.aci.it)*. The car will be towed to the nearest ACI-approved garage. Car rental firms often have their own arrangements for breakdowns and accidents.

See p. 209 for what to do in a traffic accident.

Peak traffic in towns and cities occurs weekdays and Saturdays 10 a.m.–1 p.m. and 4–9 p.m., particularly on Friday and Sunday evenings. Expect heavy traffic before and after major public holidays, and the first and last weekends of August.

Gas *(benzina)* is expensive and priced by the liter (0.26 U.S. gallon). Gas stations along autostradas are open 24 hours and generally accept credit cards. Other gas stations usually close 1–4 p.m., after 7 p.m., and all day Sunday, and many accept only cash. Some stations have machines that accept large-denomination euro notes and dispense gas automatically during closed periods.

Parking is often difficult in towns, cities, and villages. It is better to visit Naples without a car. Areas in many old centers are closed to traffic at busy times. If in doubt, park in an outlying lot and walk to the center.

Car theft and theft from cars can be a problem in some areas. Leave your car in a supervised lot and never leave valuables inside.

U.S. and Canadian drivers in Italy must hold a national driver's license *(patente)*. They are also required to carry a translation of the license or an international driver's license. You must wear a seat belt and have license, insurance, and other documents with you at all times.

Penalties for drunken driving are severe.

The speed limit is 50 kph (31 mph) in built-up areas and 110 kph (68 mph) outside them, unless marked otherwise. Limits on the autostrada are 130 kph (80 mph), 150 kph (93 mph) on designated stretches, and 110 kph (68 mph) for vehicles with engine capacity under 1100cc.

Renting a Car: It is easy to rent a car in large towns, cities, and at major airports. Costs are high by U.S. standards; it may be worthwhile to arrange car rental before leaving home. Drivers must be over 21 and hold a full license in order to rent a car.

By Ferry

Car and passenger ferries *(traghetti)* and/or hydrofoils *(aliscafi)* operate on numerous routes in southern Italy, Sicily, and Sardinia. Hydrofoils are generally twice as fast and twice as expensive as ferries.

Daily schedules and links can be found in *Il Mattino*, Naples's main newspaper, and online at www.acam-campania.it. Services are reduced or suspended October–April. Hydrofoils may be canceled in poor weather.

The main operators are Alilauro *(tel 081 497 2238, www.alilauro.it)* and Caremar *(tel 892 123, www.caremar.it)* for ferry and/or hydrofoil services from Naples to Sorrento, Capri, Ischia, Procida, and the Amalfi Coast.

Other services along that coast include SNAV *(tel 081 428 5555, www.snav.it)*; Metrò del Mare *(tel 199 600 700, www.metrodelmare.com)*; Sant'Andrea *(tel 081 873 190, www.coopsantandrea.it)*; Navigazione Libera del Golfo *(tel 081 552 0763, www.navlib.it)*; and Medmar *(tel 081 333 4411, www.medmargroup.it)*.

Tirrenia *(tel 081 251 4711 or 829 123, www.tirrenia.it)* goes to Palermo, Sardinia, and the Aeolian Islands. TTT Lines *(tel 081 580 2744 or 800 915 365 toll-free in Italy, www.tttlines.it)* sails to Catania (in Sicily).

By Train

All of southern Italy's main centers are connected by rail, but rural and inland services can be slow and infrequent. Between cities the express Inter-City (IC) train services (at additional expense) or Eurostar (ES) services (which require extra fees plus reservations) are faster. Both services run between big towns and cities on the mainland's east and west coasts, and between Palermo and Messina. New superfast Frecciarossa services connect Rome to Naples, Bari, and Reggio di Calabria as well as Milan to Lecce and Bari.

There are small private lines in Sicily *(Circumetnea, tel 095 541 250, www.circumetnea.it)* and around Naples, where the Ferrovia Circumvesuviana *(tel 081 772 2111, www.vesuviana.it)* serves Pompeii, Sorrento, and Herculaneum.

Before traveling, tickets must be validated in the yellow or gold machines located on train platforms and in station ticket halls. Travel with a nonvalidated ticket risks a heavy fine.

If you intend to do much of your traveling by train, then buy the *Pozzorario*, a cheap biennial schedule available at station kiosks, or visit the website of the state network, Trenitalia (www.trenitalia.it).

PRACTICAL ADVICE
Communications
Post Offices
You can buy stamps (francobolli) from a post office (ufficio postale) or most tabacchi.

The Italian postal system (www.poste.it) can be slow. Allow 15 days for letters between Italy and North America (longer for postcards). Priority post (posta prioritaria) costs more, but delivery is guaranteed—within three days to the U.S. and next day in Europe. Use email or fax for hotel and other reservations.

The main Naples post office is at Piazza Matteotti 2 (tel 081 552 0502).

Telephones
Telecom Italia (TI) phone booths are found on streets and in bars, restaurants, and TI offices in larger towns. Look for red or yellow signs showing a telephone receiver and dial. Most phones take coins and cards (schede telefoniche), which can be purchased at tabacchi and newspaper stands. Cards have a small perforated corner that must be removed before use.

Telephone numbers have between four and eleven digits. Call 12 for information, 176 for assistance in English, 170 for the intercontinental operator (15 for Europe), and 172 1011 for collect calls.

Calling rates are lowest on Sundays and 10 p.m.–8 a.m. weekdays. Hotels add a significant surcharge to calls made from rooms.

Cell phone coverage is good in most of southern Italy.

To call any number within Italy, dial the full number, including the town or city code (for example, 081 in Naples or 091 in Palermo).

To call Italy from abroad, dial the international code (011 from the U.S. and Canada, 00 from the U.K.), then the code for Italy (39), followed by the area code (including the initial 0) and number.

Etiquette &
Local Customs
On the whole, southern Italians are more reserved and conservative than northern Italians. They are also generally polite and considerate in social situations (except in lines).

Upon meeting someone, or entering or leaving, use a simple buon giorno (good day) or buona sera (good afternoon/evening). Do not use the informal ciao (hi or goodbye) with strangers.

"Please" is per favore, "thank you" is grazie, and prego means "you're welcome."

Before a meal, say buon appetito (enjoy your meal), to which the reply is grazie, altrettanto (thank you, and the same to you). Before a drink, the toast is salute or cin cin.

Say permesso when you wish to pass people, and mi scusi if you wish to apologize, excuse yourself, or stop someone to ask for help. A woman is addressed as signora, a young woman as signorina, and a man as signore.

Kissing on both cheeks is a common form of greeting among men and women who know each other well.

Visitors to churches and cathedrals are welcome to explore the interiors and grounds—but only if dressed appropriately and not while services are in progress.

When Italians form a line at all, they are very assertive. In stores, banks, and other offices, you should not expect for people to wait their turn.

Smoking in bars, restaurants, and other enclosed public places is prohibited, but smoking elsewhere is common in Italy.

Holidays
Stores, banks, offices, and schools close on these holidays:

Jan. 1	New Year's Day
Jan. 6	Epiphany
Spring	Easter Sunday
Spring	Easter Monday
April 25	Liberation Day
May 1	Labor Day
June 2	Republic Day
Aug. 15	Ferragosto or Assumption
Nov. 1	All Saints' Day
Dec. 8	Immaculate Conception
Dec. 25	Christmas Day
Dec. 26	Santo Stefano

Hours of operation may be disrupted the day after or before a holiday if it falls on a Thursday or Tuesday.

Media
Most Italian newspapers are sold from newsstands (edicola), which in larger towns or resorts also stock foreign-language newspapers and periodicals.

Among national papers, Corriere della Sera (www.corriere.it) and La Repubblica (www.repubblica.it) are popular.

Southern Italy has strong regional papers, notably Naples's Il Mattino (www.ilmattino.it), the Palermo-based Il Giornale di Sicilia, and Messina's La Gazzetta del Sud. These offer information on local events, museum hours, etc.

Money Matters
The euro (€) is the official currency of Italy. Euro notes are issued in denominations of 5, 10, 20, 50, 100, 200, and 500 euros. Coins come in 1 and 2 euros, and 1, 2, 5, 10, 20, and 50 cents.

Most major banks, airports, railroad stations, and tourist areas have automated teller machines (*Bancomat*).

Currency and traveler's checks—best bought in euros before you leave—can be exchanged in most banks and exchange offices (*cambio*), but lines are often slow.

In rural areas, small towns, and much of the South, ATMs and cambio facilities are rare.

Credit cards are accepted in hotels and restaurants in most major towns and cities. Look for credit card symbols or the *Carta Sì* (literally, "yes to cards") sign. Many businesses still prefer cash, and smaller establishments, especially in rural areas, may not take cards. Always ask before ordering or reserving a room.

Opening Times
Hours of operation can present a problem. For the most part, there are no firm schedules. Opening times of museums and churches in particular can change with little or no notice.

Some institutions in big cities are shifting to northern European hours (with no lunch or afternoon closing, indicated by the phrase *orario continuato*). Generally, businesses in Naples and much of the South still close 1–4:30 p.m., especially in summer.

Use the following schedule as a general guide only:

Banks are open Monday–Friday 8:30 a.m.–1:30 p.m. Major banks may open for an hour in the afternoon and on Saturday morning.

Churches are usually open 8 or 9 a.m.–12 p.m. and 3 or 4 p.m.–6 or 8 p.m. Many churches close on Sunday afternoon.

Gas stations are open 24 hours a day on *autostradas*. Elsewhere they tend to follow store hours.

State-operated museums usually close Sunday afternoon and Monday. Many close for lunch 1–3

or 4 p.m. Archaeological sites usually open daily 9 a.m.–dusk or one hour before sunset.

Post offices are open Monday–Saturday 8 or 9 a.m.–2 p.m. Major locations remain open until 6 or 8 p.m.

Many restaurants close on Sunday evening and on Monday or another weekday. Many establishments close in July and August and in January. Some may close November–February, or longer.

Store hours are generally 8:30 or 9 a.m.–1 p.m. and 3:30 or 4–8 p.m. Monday–Saturday. Many stores close on Monday morning and another half day during the week. Some major city stores may be open seven days a week 9 a.m.–7:30/8 p.m.

Restrooms
Few public buildings have restrooms. Generally you will have to resort to facilities in bars, railroad stations, and gas stations, where standards are generally low. Ask for *il bagno* (pronounced eel BAHN-yo), take a few tissues, and don't confuse *Signori* (Men) with *Signore* (Women). Tip any attendant 25 or 30 cents.

Time Difference
Southern Italy runs to CET (Central European Time), one hour ahead of Greenwich Mean Time and six hours ahead of Eastern Standard Time. Noon in Italy is 6 a.m. in New York.

Tipping
In restaurants where a service charge (*servizio*) is not included, leave 10–15 percent; even if the charge is included, you may want to leave 5–10 percent. In bars, tip a few cents for drinks if you're at the bar and 50 cents–2 euros for waiter service. In hotel bars, be slightly more generous.

Tip chambermaids and doormen about 50 cents–1 euro, the bellhop 1–3 euros for carrying your bags, and the concierge or porter 4–8 euros if he or she has been helpful. Double these figures in the most expensive establishments.

Tip restroom and checkroom attendants 25 to 50 cents. Tip porters up to 2 euros at your discretion. Cab drivers will expect around 10 percent.

Travelers with Disabilities
Southern Italy is a difficult place for travelers with disabilities. Busy streets with badly parked cars present obvious problems, and uneven, steep streets in rural villages are unwelcoming to wheelchairs.

Businesses will always try to accommodate, but only the larger museums and higher-category hotels will be equipped to deal with wheelchairs.

Consult an Italian embassy or consulate for details of the special procedures required to bring a guide dog into Italy.

Useful contacts in North America include Access-Able (*www.access-able.com*), which specializes in online advice; SATH (*tel 212/447-7284, www.sath.org*); and Mobility International (*tel 541/343-1284, www.miusa.org*).

Visitor Information
Italian State Tourist Offices
www.italiantourism.com or www.enit.it

United States
630 Fifth Ave., Ste. 1565
New York, NY 10111
Tel 212/245-5618
Fax 212/586-9249

500 N. Michigan Ave., Ste. 2240

Chicago, IL 60611
Tel 312/644-0990
or 312/644-0996
Fax 312/644-3109

12400 Wilshire Blvd., Ste. 550
Los Angeles, CA 90025
Tel 310/820-1898
or 310/820-9807
Fax 310/820-6357

Canada
175 Bloor St. E, Ste. 907
South Tower
Toronto, ON M4W 3R8
Tel 416/925-4882
Fax 416/925-4799

United Kingdom
1 Princes St.
London W1R 8AY
Tel 020 7408 1254
Fax 020 7399 3567

EMERGENCIES
Embassies &
Consulates in Italy
U.S. Embassy
Mailing address:
Via Vittorio Veneto 120, Rome
Tel 06 4674 2420/1
http://rome.usembassy.gov

U.S. Consulate
Piazza della Repubblica 2, Naples
Tel 081 583 8111
http://naples.usconsulate.gov

Canadian Embassy
Visa, immigration, consular:
Via Zara 30, Rome
Tel 06 854441
www.canada.it
www.canadainternational.gc.ca/
italy

Canadian Consulate
Viale Carducci 29, Naples
Tel 081 401 338
www.canada.it
www.canadainternational.gc.ca/
italy

U.K. Embassy
Via XX Settembre 80/A, Rome
Tel 06 4220 0001
http://ukinitaly.fco.gov.uk
www.canadainternational.gc.ca/
italy

U.K. Consulate
Via dei Mille 40, Naples
Tel 081 423 8911
http://ukinitaly.fco.gov.uk

Emergency Phone Numbers
Police, tel 112
Emergency services, tel 113
Fire services, tel 115
Car breakdown, tel 803 116
Ambulance, tel 118

For legal assistance in an emergency, contact your embassy or consulate (see above) for a list of English-speaking lawyers.

Health
Check that your health insurance covers you while in Italy and that any travel insurance includes sufficient medical coverage.

For minor complaints, first visit a drugstore or pharmacy (una farmacia), indicated by a green cross outside the store. Staff is well trained and can offer advice or help find a doctor (un medico).

Bring an ample supply of any prescription drugs (medicina) you require. Should you need to refill a prescription, pharmacies will direct you to a doctor.

Visit a hospital (un ospedale) for serious complaints. Italian hospitals often look run-down, but treatment is generally good.

Before leaving home, consider joining (free) the International Association for Medical Assistance to Travelers (tel 716/754-4883 in U.S. or 519/836-0102 in Canada, www.iamat.org). Members receive a directory of English-speaking IAMAT doctors on call 24 hours a day and are entitled to receive

medical services at set rates.

Tap water is generally safe, but do not drink water marked acqua non potabile, and never drink from streams in the mountains or elsewhere. Milk is pasteurized and safe.

Hospitals in Naples
Cardarelli
Via Antonio Cardarelli 9
Tel 081 747 1111 or 800
019 774 220
www.ospedalecardarelli.it

Santobono
Via M. Fiore 6
Tel 081 220 5111
www.santobono.na.it

Lost Property
If you lose property, go first to the local visitor center for help. Bus, tram, train, ferry, and metro systems in cities usually have lost property offices, but they can be hard to find and are usually open only a few hours a day. Hotels should also be able to help.

To report a more serious loss or theft, go to the police station or questura In Naples, the main questura is at Via Medina 75 (tel 081 794 1111, questure.poliziadistato.it/Napoli). Many city police stations have English-speaking staff. You'll be asked to complete and sign a form (denuncia) reporting any crime. Keep your copy for insurance claims.

What to Do in a Traffic Accident
Put on hazard lights and place a warning triangle 165 feet (50 m) behind the car. Call the police (tel 112 or 113). Ask witnesses to remain, make a police statement, and exchange insurance and other relevant details with the other driver(s). Call the car rental agency, if necessary, to inform the staff of the incident.

Hotels & Restaurants

Southern Italy offers a variety of accommodations to suit all tastes and budgets. It does not have the sheer number of hotels of northern and central Italy, but you can still choose from a fine selection of hotels in centuries-old buildings and family-run establishments, sumptuous island resorts and some of Europe's most celebrated luxury resorts. Restaurants are equally varied, from humble Neapolitan pizzerias to venerable Amalfi Coast classics, the pleasures of the South's immensely varied food and wine as much a part of your visit as museums and galleries.

HOTELS

Accommodations in the best central locations are recommended. When possible, quiet, out-of-town alternatives are provided as well. Hotels have also been selected for their character, charm, or historical associations.

Note that even in the finest hotels, bathrooms may have only a shower (doccia) and no tub (vasca). Rooms are often small by U.S. standards. Always ask to see a selection of rooms before you register.

Star Rating System

Hotels are officially graded from one star (most basic) to five stars (luxury). In a three-star establishment and above, all rooms should have a private bath-shower, telephone, and television. Most two-star hotels also have private bathrooms.

Reservations

Book in advance, especially in tourist areas and in high season (July–Aug.). If the hotel doesn't have a website or an email address (most do), reserve by phone and confirm by fax. Reconfirm a few days before arrival.

Hoteliers are obliged to register every guest, so when checking in, you will be asked for your passport. Checkout times range from around 10 a.m.–12 p.m., but you should be able to leave luggage at the hotel reception.

Prices

All prices are officially set, and room rates must be displayed by law at reception and in each room. Prices for different rooms can vary within a hotel, but all taxes and service fees should be included in the rate.

Price categories given in the entries are the most expensive rates for double (matrimoniale) or twin (doppia) rooms and are for guidance only. Seasonal variations often apply, especially in coastal resorts, where high-season (summer) rates may demand that you take full- or half-board packages. Half board (mezza pensione) includes breakfast and lunch, while full board (pensione completa) includes all meals. Such packages are always priced on a per-person basis.

At busy times, hotels may also insist on a minimum two- or three-day stay policy.

Credit Cards

Most hotels and restaurants accept major credit cards. The smallest and simplest trattorias may not. Abbreviations used in the text are AE (American Express), DC (Diners Club), MC (Mastercard), and V (Visa). Look for card symbols or the Italian Carta Sì sign outside. As a general rule, AE and DC are less widely accepted than V and MC.

RESTAURANTS

The following selection of restaurants reflects the best of southern Italy's regional cooking, with a mix of upscale restaurants and more humble Old World trattorias. Don't be afraid to experiment, especially in rural areas. If in doubt, note where the locals eat and follow their lead.

Dining Hours

Breakfast (colazione) usually consists of a cappuccino and bread roll or sweet pastry (brioche) taken standing in a bar 7–9 a.m. Larger and more expensive hotels increasingly offer buffet breakfasts.

Lunch (pranzo) is usually 12:30–2 p.m.; the infamous long lunch is increasingly a thing of the past in urban areas, except on Sundays. Siestas, however, are widely taken across the South, especially in summer.

Dinner (cena) begins about 8 p.m., with last orders taken about 10 p.m. (later in cities). Dinner hours may be earlier in rural areas and small towns.

Paying

The check (il conto) must be presented by law as a formal receipt. A price scrawled on a piece of paper is illegal and you are within your rights to demand an itemized ricevuta.

Bills may include a cover charge (coperto), a practice the authorities are trying to ban. Many restaurants get around the law by charging for bread brought to your table whether you want it or not. Check that your card is acceptable before ordering.

Meals

Meals traditionally begin with appetizers (antipasto—literally

---

🏨 Hotel   🍴 Restaurant   ⓘ No. of guest rooms   💺 No. of Seats   🅿 Parking   🕐 Closed   ⊟ Elevator "before the meal"), a first course (*il primo*) of soup, pasta, or rice, and a main course (*il secondo*) of meat or fish. Vegetables (*contorni*) or salads (*insalata*) are often served separately with or after il secondo.

Desserts (*dolci*) may include or be followed by fruit (*frutta*) and cheese (*formaggio*). Italians often round off a meal with an espresso (*never* a cappuccino or latte) and brandy, *grappa* (a clear, brandylike spirit), or an *amaro* (a bitter digestif).

You don't need to order every course—a primo and salad are acceptable in all but the grandest restaurants. Many Italians choose to go to an ice-cream parlor (*gelateria*) as part of an after-dinner stroll.

Set Menus
The menu in Italian is *il menù* or *la lista*. Fixed-price menus are available in many restaurants in tourist areas, but the quality is invariably poor. Of better value in more upscale restaurants is the *menu gastronomico,* where you pay a fixed price to sample a selection of the special dishes.

Bars, Cafés, & Snacks
Bars and cafés are perfect for breakfast and often provide snacks such as filled rolls (*panini*) or sandwiches (*tramezzini*). A few may offer a light meal at lunch. It always costs less to stand at the bar. You pay a premium to sit down and for the mandatory waiter service. Street food is also a feature of cities such as Naples and Palermo. Stands or small stores selling slices of pizza (*pizza al taglio*) are common.

Tipping & Dress
Tip between 10 and 15 percent where service has been good and where a service charge (*servizio*) is not included.

As a rule, Italians dress well but informally to eat out, especially in better restaurants. A relaxed casual style is a good rule of thumb. Jacket and tie for men are rarely necessary, but often the better dressed you are, the better you will be received.

Smoking
Smoking is banned in bars, cafés, and restaurants.

Listings
The hotels and restaurants listed here have been grouped first by region or town and city as presented in the main guide, then listed in descending order of price, with hotels preceding restaurants, then alphabetically. For disabled access, check with the establishments.

L = lunch D = dinner

■ NAPLES

Hotels

🏨 GRAND ALBERGO
🍴 VESUVIO
$$$$$ ★★★★
VIA PARTENOPE 45
TEL 081 764 0044
FAX 081 764 4483
www.vesuvio.it
Built in 1882, this fine hotel has welcomed the likes of Humphrey Bogart and Errol Flynn. The rooftop **Caruso** restaurant, has superb views.
🛈 161 🅿 ⮂ Ⓢ Ⓐ ⛱ 🍸
Ⓐ All major cards

🏨 GRAND HOTEL
🍴 PARKER'S
$$$$$ ★★★★★
CORSO VITTORIO EMANUELE II 135
TEL 081 761 2474
FAX 081 663 527
www.grandhotelparkers.com
Its position west of the center between the Spanish Quarter

and Vomero hill affords wonderful views of the Bay of Naples. The **George** restaurant rates highly on its own account. Wi-Fi available.
🛈 82 🛏 19 🅿 ⮂ Ⓢ 🍸
Ⓢ Ⓐ All major cards

🏨 PALAZZO ALABARDIERI
$$$$$ ★★★★
VIA ALABARDIERI 38
TEL 081 415 278
FAX 081 1972 2010
www.palazzoalabardieri.it
Situated close to Piazza dei Martiri, this elegant hotel forms part of a restored palazzo built in 1870. It opened as a hotel in 2004, its style combining the old and modern. Wi-Fi available.
🛈 33 🅿 ⮂ Ⓢ Ⓐ 🍸
Ⓐ All major cards

🏨 SAN FRANCESCO AL
🍴 MONTE
$$$$$ ★★★★
CORSO VITTORIO EMANUELE II, 328
TEL 081 423 9111
FAX 081 251 2485
www.hotelsanfrancesco.it
Opened in 2002, this hotel forms part of a restored 16th-century convent. The superb rooms are converted monks' cells and all enjoy superb views of the bay. There are two restaurants, one of which is in the lovely panoramic garden. A regular, free shuttle bus provides service to the city center.
🛈 45 🅿 ⮂ Ⓢ Ⓐ ⛱
Ⓐ All major cards

🏨 CARAVAGGIO
$$$$ ★★★★
PIAZZA CARDINALE SISTO RIARIO SFORZA 157
TEL 081 211 0066
FAX 081 442 1578
www.caravaggiohotel.it
Like Constantinopoli 104, one of few hotels at the heart of Naples's *centro storico*. Opened

in 2001, it lies just behind the Duomo and forms part of a converted 17th-century palazzo. Rooms are modern.
[I] 18 P ⊟ Ⓢ Ⓢ
🅢 All major cards

CONSTANTINOPOLI 104
$$$$ ★★★★
VIA SANTA MARIA DI CONSTANTINOPOLI 104
TEL 081 557 1035
FAX 081 557 1051
www.constantinopoli104.it
Although located close to Naples's busy historic heart, this peaceful gem has been converted from a 19th-century neoclassical palazzo. Comfortable rooms have small private terraces or overlook the pool and garden. Wi-Fi available.
[I] 19 P ⊟ Ⓢ Ⓢ ▣
🅢 All major cards

MERCURE ANGIOINO NAPOLI CENTRO
$$$$ ★★★★
VIA A DE PRETIS 123
TEL 081 552 9500
FAX 081 552 9509
www.mercure.com
A comfortable hotel with a location close to the *centro storico* and port area. Rooms are spacious and modern. One floor is nonsmoking.
[I] 85 P ⊟ Ⓢ Ⓢ 🅢 All major cards

PALAZZO TURCHINI
$$$$ ★★★★
VIA MEDINA 21–22
TEL 081 551 0606
FAX 081 552 1473
www.palazzoturchini.it
Part of a renovated 17th-century palace that opened as a hotel in 2004. It's centrally located, convenient to the sights of Via Toledo, Royal Naples, and the *centro storico*. Soundproofed rooms are spacious.
[I] 27 P ⊟ Ⓢ Ⓢ
🅢 All major cards

CHIAJA HOTEL DE CHARME
$$$ ★★★★
VIA CHIAIA 216
TEL 081 415 555
FAX 081 422 344
www.hotelchiaia.it
Stay in part of the home of Marchesa Lecaldano for a touch of Old World aristocratic style. Wi-Fi available.
[I] 33 P ⊟ Ⓢ Ⓢ 🅢 All major cards

IL CONVENTO
$$$ ★★★
VIA SPERANZELLA 137/A
TEL 081 403 977
FAX 081 400 332
www.hotelilconvento.com
This family-run hotel has the distinction of being (barely) in the Quartieri Spagnoli, just a block from the southern end of busy Via Toledo. Wooden beams, pastel walls, and stone floors recall the 17th-century convent from which the hotel was converted. Rooms and bathrooms are modern.
[I] 14 P ⊟ Ⓢ Ⓢ 🅢 All major cards

DECUMANI HOTEL DE CHARME
$$$ ★★★
VIA SAN GIOVANNI MAGGIORE PIGNATELLI 15
TEL 081 551 8188
FAX 081 551 8188
www.decumani.it
This central hotel opened in 2009 and is ideally placed for exploring both Spaccanapoli and the Via Toledo shopping area. It forms part of fine palace, with a dazzling ballroom, that was once home to the last bishop of Bourbon Naples.
[I] 22 P ⊟ Ⓢ 🅢 All major cards

HOTEL DES ARTISTES
$$ ★★★
VIA DEL DUOMO 61
TEL 081 446155

PRICES
HOTELS
An indication of the cost of a double room in the high season is given by $ signs.

$$$$$	Over $280
$$$$	$160–$280
$$$	$100–$160
$$	$40–$100
$	Under $40

RESTAURANTS
An indication of the cost of a three-course meal without drinks is given by $ signs.

$$$$$	Over $80
$$$$	$50–$80
$$$	$35–$50
$$	$20–$35
$	Under $20

FAX 081 211 0403
www.hoteldesartistesnaples.it
This pleasantly old-fashioned budget option is just moments from the Duomo, occupying one floor of a historic palazzo and opening onto a peaceful courtyard.
[I] 11 P ⊟ Ⓢ 🅢 All major cards

Restaurants

LA CANTINELLA
$$$$$
VIA CUMA 42 (CORNER OF VIA N. SAURO)
TEL 081 764 8684
www.lacantinella.it
The food in this most-praised of Naples restaurants is more sophisticated than you'll find in the city's more typical neighborhood trattorias. The atmosphere in the busy dining rooms resembles a nightclub. The wine list is exceptional.
🕮 90 🕐 Closed Sun. from

June–Oct. & 2 weeks in Aug.
🚫 ❄ All major cards

🍴 CIRO A SANTA BRIGIDA
$$$$$
VIA SANTA BRIGIDA 71–73
TEL 081 552 4072
www.cirosantabrigida.it
Like La Cantinella, Ciro, as it is usually known, is considered a touchstone for refined Neapolitan cuisine. Fish and seafood are generally better bets than meat-based dishes. Service is charming and the setting below the Castel dell'Ovo lovely. 🍴 130 🕐 Closed Sun. except Dec. & 2 weeks in Aug. 🚫 ❄ All major cards

🍴 GIUSEPPONE A MARE
$$$$$
VIA FERDINANDO RUSSO 13
TEL 081 769 1384
www.giuseppone.com
Another classic Neapolitan restaurant of long-standing reputation. It is west of the city center in Posillipo (you'll need a cab), but the views of the bay and fine seafood merit the trip. 🍴 160 🕐 Closed Sun., Mon., & 2 weeks in Aug. 🚫 ❄ All major cards

🍴 PALAZZO PETRUCCI
$$$$–$$$$$
PIAZZA SAN DOMENICO MAGGIORE 4
TEL 081 552 4068
www.palazzopetrucci.it
Refined, one-Michelin star cooking in a minimalist dining room in a period palace on one of the historic center's most attractive squares. 🍴 55 🕐 Closed D Sun., L Mon., L Sun. in July & Aug., & 3 weeks in Aug. 🚫 ❄ All major cards

🍴 LA BERSAGLIERA
$$$$
BORGO MARINARI 10–11
TEL 081 764 6016
www.labersagliera.it
This waterfront restaurant can

be busy with vacationers, but its atmosphere and long history make this a fun place to visit at least once. 🍴 200 🕐 Closed Tues. & part of Jan. 🚫 ❄ All major cards

🍴 DA ETTORE
$$$
VIA SANTA LUCIA 56
TEL 081 764 0498
www.ristoranteettore.it
An unpretentious neighborhood restaurant, it specializes in fish and seafood, but many come here for the pizzas and pagniotielli (pizza-dough wraps with fillings). House wine is poor—go for a bottle. Book or arrive early. 🍴 50 🕐 Closed Sun. & Aug. 🚫 ❄ No cards

🍴 MIMÌ ALLA FERROVIA
$$$
VIA ALFONSO D'ARAGONA 21
TEL 081 553 8525
Mimì has been drawing visitors and wealthier locals alike for decades. Lively, cordial atmosphere, an elegant interior, and faultlessly prepared Neapolitan dishes. 🍴 180 🕐 Closed Sun. & 1 week in Aug. 🚫 ❄ All major cards

🍴 OSTERIA LA CHITARRA
$$$
RAMPE SAN GIOVANNI MAGGIORE 1/B
TEL 081 552 9103
www.osterialachitarra.it
A great trattoria run by two courteous brothers. Lunch is simple, with a choice of just three or four dishes. Dinner allows more options. 🍴 32 🕐 Closed Sun., Mon., & Aug. 🚫 ❄ All major cards

🍴 ANTICA OSTERIA PISANO
$$–$$$
PIAZZETTA CROCELLE AI

MANNESI, 1
TEL 081 554 8325
A location with lots of passing trade on the corner of Via del Duomo and Spaccanapoli, plus inexpensive Neapolitan food, make this tiny trattoria a popular place for lunch. 🍴 35 🕐 Closed Sun. & 2 weeks in Aug. 🚫 ❄ No cards

🍴 HOSTERIA TOLEDO
$$–$$$
VICO GIARDINETTI A TOLEDO 78/A (OFF VIA TOLEDO)
TEL 081 421 257
This restaurant in a Quartieri Spagnoli tenement from the 17th century serves simple but perfect Neapolitan food such as pasta alle cozze e vongole (pasta with clams and mussels). Ask for a table on the upper floor. 🍴 70 🕐 Closed D Tues. & usually 2 weeks in Aug. 🚫 ❄ All major cards

🍴 VECCHIA CANTINA
$$–$$$
VICO SAN NICOLA ALLA CARITÀ 13–14
TEL 081 552 0226
Proximity to the Pignasecca market ensures the freshest produce at this tiny restaurant on the northern fringes of the Quartieri Spagnoli. This is the sort of Old World trattoria that is fast disappearing in northern and central Italy. 🍴 50 🕐 Closed 1 week in Aug. 🚫 ❄ All major cards

■ EXCURSIONS FROM NAPLES

HERCULANEUM

🍴 VIVA LO RE
$$$
CORSO RESINA 261 ERCOLANO
TEL 081 739 0207
www.vivolore.it
Good dining options are rare near the archaeological site. Take a cab to this restaurant

on the outskirts of the town. Pleasantly rustic in style, it offers simple, well-prepared Campanian dishes such as *zuppa di verdure* (vegetable soup).

🍴 55 🕐 Closed D Sun., Mon., & Aug. 🔵 🅰 All major cards

POMPEII

🏨 **AMLETO**
$$-$$$ ★★★★
VIA BARTOLO LONGO 10
TEL 081 863 1004
FAX 081 863 5585
www.hotelamleto.it
A comfortable and recently opened hotel with "themed" historic rooms. The best place to stay if you want to be near the ruins—they are barely 100 yards (90 m) away.

ℹ 26 🅿 🖥 🔵 🔵 🅰 All major cards

🍴 **PRESIDENT**
$$$$$
PIAZZA SCHETTINI 12–13
TEL 081 850 7245
www.ristorantepresident.it
An elegant restaurant, popular with locals, that offers creative Campanian meat and fish dishes.

🍴 55/25 🕐 Closed D Sun. & Mon. Dec.–Feb. 🔵 🅰 All major cards

🍴 **IL PRINCIPE**
$$$$$
PIAZZA BARTOLO LONGO 1
TEL 081 850 5566
www.ilprincipe.com
Il Principe's dining room aims to re-create the splendor of ancient Pompeii. Dishes combine modern cooking with ancient foods such as *garum*, a Roman sauce.

🍴 70 🕐 Closed Mon. 🔵 🅰 All major cards

PAESTUM

🏨 **HOTEL BEACH SAVOY**
🍴 **$$$$-$$$$$ ★★★★**
VIA POSEIDONIA 84063
TEL 082 872 0100
FAX 082 872 0807
www.hotelsavoybeach.it
This grand and elegant hotel sits just 200 yards from the beach and about a mile from the ruins. Its upscale restaurant is frequented by locals both for its food and outdoor patio.

ℹ 42 🅿 🖥 🔵 🔵 🅰 🅰 🖥 🅰 All major cards

🍴 **LE TRABE**
$$$$
VIA CAPODIFIUME 1
TEL 082 872 4165
Le Trabe's pretty rural setting (in gardens by a stream and an old mill) is its main strength, but the regularly changing menu and creative seafood offerings (plus pizzas) are above average.

🍴 90 🕐 Closed D Sun., Mon. Oct.–March 🔵 🅰 All major cards

🍴 **DA NONNA SCEPPA**
$$-$$$
VIA LAURA 45
TEL 082 885 1064
www.nonnasceppa.com
Family-run Da Nonna Sceppa and its pleasant pine-wood setting stands out, despite its size. Pizzas, homemade pastas, and seafood are always good.

🍴 180 🕐 Closed Thurs. Oct.–April & part of Oct. 🔵 🅰 All major cards

■ AMALFI COAST

AMALFI

🏨 **SANTA CATERINA**
🍴 **$$$$$ ★★★★★**
VIA NAZIONALE 9
TEL 089 871 012
FAX 089 871 351
www.hotelsantacaterina.it
Like most hotels on this coast, Amalfi's leading hotel retains something of the feel of the 1970s—pleasantly dated or old-fashioned, depending on your point of view. Service is charming, as are the views. Standard rooms are plain.

ℹ 62 + 9 suites 🅿 🕐 Closed Nov. & Jan.–Feb. 🖥 🖥 🖥 🅰 All major cards

🏨 **AMALFI**
🍴 **$$$ ★★★**
VIA DEI PASTAI 3
TEL 089 872 440
FAX 089 872 250
www.hamalfi.it
A perfect location near the Duomo if you want a simple, comfortable, and inexpensive base in town. Friendly service and a pretty garden.

ℹ 40 🅿 🖥 🔵 🅰 All major cards

🍴 **LA CARAVELLA**
$$$$$
VIA MATTEO CAMERA 12
TEL 089 871 029
www.ristorantelacaravella.it
The location near the main road into town may not be the best, but the food here has won a Michelin star.

🍴 30 🕐 Closed Tues. & part of Nov. & Dec., as well as Jan.–mid-Feb. 🔵 🅰 AE, MC, V

🍴 **DA GEMMA**
$$$
VIA FRÀ GERARDO SASSO 9
TEL 089 871 345
www.trattoriadagemma.com
Charming old-fashioned trattoria with the odd modern decorative and culinary flourish. Fair prices, first-rate food, and a warm welcome.

🍴 30 🕐 Closed Wed. & early Jan.–early March 🔵 🅰 All major cards

RAVELLO

🏨 **CARUSO**
🍴 **$$$$$ ★★★★★**
PIAZZA SAN GIOVANNI DEL TORO 2
TEL 089 858 801

FAX 089 858 806
www.hotelcaruso.com
The Caruso is the most recently
upgraded of Ravello's luxury
hotels. This historic lodging
has one of the village's
best locations. There is little
difference between this and
the Palazzo Sasso, though the
latter is a little less expensive.
Wi-Fi available.
(1) 42 + 6 suites **P** **○**
Closed early Nov.–late
March/early April **⊟** **⑤**
⑤ **≈** **♥** **⑤** All major cards

🏨 PALAZZO SASSO
🍴 $$$$$ *****
VIA SAN GIOVANNI DEL TORO 28
TEL 089 818 181
FAX 089 858 900
www.palazzosasso.com
This is the best place to stay
on the Amalfi Coast, partly
because of the breathtaking
views (request a room facing
the coast) and partly because
the converted medieval palace
has been given a tasteful modern veneer. The **Rossellinis**
restaurant is exceptional–it has
two Michelin stars–but rather
formal. If possible, dine outside
on the terrace.
(1) 31 + 8 suites **P**
○ Closed Nov./Dec.–Feb.
⊟ **⑤** **⑤** **≈** **♥** **⑤** All
major cards

🏨 VILLA CIMBRONE
🍴 $$$$$ ****
VIA SANTA CHIARA 26
TEL 089 857 459
FAX 089 857 777
www.villacimbrone.com
Greta Garbo vacationed at this
lovely villa set among gardens
before it was converted into a
hotel. It is less showy and more
intimate than the Caruso and
Palazzo Sasso but a steep walk
from the rest of the village.
(1) 19 + 2 suites **P** **○** Hotel
closed Nov.–March, restaurant
closed L **⊟** **⑤** **⑤** **≈** **♥**
⑤ All major cards

🏨 GRAAL
🍴 $$$$ ****
VIA DELLA REPUBBLICA 8
TEL 089 857 222
FAX 089 857 551
www.hotelgraal.eu
Although a little faded in places,
the Graal has a great location,
bright rooms with terraces
and sea views, reasonable
prices for this expensive village,
and a decent restaurant.
Wi-Fi available
(1) 36 **P** **⊟** **⑤** **⑤** **≈**
⑤ All major cards

🏨 BONADIES
🍴 $$$ ****
PIAZZA FONTANA MORESCA 5
TEL 089 857 918
FAX 089 857 370
www.hotelbonadies.it
Opened in 1880 and still run
by the founder's descendants,
the Hotel Bonadies is popular
with Italians and has a pool
with fine views. Rooms feature a mixture of period and
modern decor.
(1) 36 **P** **⊟** **⑤** **⑤** **≈**
⑤ All major cards

🍴 CUMPÀ COSIMO
$$$$
VIA ROMA 48
TEL 089 857 156
A simple pizzeria-restaurant in
the middle of the village that
has been run by the same family for more than 70 years.
▥ 50 **○** Closed some Mon.
⑤ **⑤** All major cards

🍴 DA SALVATORE
🏨 $$$$
VIA DELLA REPUBBLICA, 2
TEL 089 857 227
www.salvatoreravello.com
A modest-looking and relaxed
restaurant with delicious food
and stupendous views from
both the dining room and
summer terrace. Six moderately
priced rooms.
▥ 90/50 **○** Closed Mon.
Nov.–March **⑤** **⑤** AE, DC, V

POSITANO

🏨 SAN PIETRO
🍴 $$$$$ *****
VIA LAURITO 2
TEL 089 875 455
FAX 089 811 449
www.ilsanpietro.it
Positano has two of Italy's most
celebrated five-star hotels, the
San Pietro and La Sirenuse.
San Pietro is most loved for its
breathtaking view (of Positano
tumbling to the sea). All rooms
have sea views, thanks to their
dramatic arrangement on
numerous rock-hewn terraces
Wi-Fi available.
(1) 55 + 7 suites **P** **○** Closed
Nov.–March **⊟** **⑤** **≈** **⑤** **♥**
⑤ All major cards

🏨 LA SIRENUSE
🍴 $$$$$ *****
VIA CRISTOFORO COLOMBO 30
TEL 089 875 066
FAX 089 811 798
www.sirenuse.it
Stay in this historic hotel, a
former 18th-century villa, if you
wish to be close to Positano.
All rooms have private terraces,
but ask for one with a sea view.
Wi-Fi available.
(1) 61 + 2 suites
P Closed Dec.–Feb.
⊟ **⑤** **⑤** **≈** **♥** **⑤** All
major cards

🏨 CASA ALBERTINA
🍴 $$$$ ***
VIA DELLA TAVOLOZZA 3
TEL 089 875 143
FAX 089 811 540
www.casalbertina.it
Located in a quiet location just
outside the village. Rooms have
the slightly dated feel common
to many hotels on the Amalfi
Coast, but are cool in summer
and enjoy good views. The
hotel is relaxed and well run;
you may be required to take
half or full pension in high
season. Wi-Fi available.

⑤ Nonsmoking **⑤** Air-conditioning **≈** Indoor Pool **≈** Outdoor Pool **♥** Health Club **⑤** Credit Cards

Ⓘ 20 P ⊜ ⊗ ⬚
⬚ All major cards

🍴 DONNA ROSA
$$$$$

VIA MONTEPERTUSO 97–99
TEL 089 811 806
Just outside the village, so
quieter than restaurants in
Positano. The fish and seafood
are superb, and the panoramic
terrace lovely. Be sure to
make reservations.
⬚ 40 ⬚ Closed early Jan.–
mid-March & Tues. Oct.–early
Jan. & mid-March–May; also
closed L Mon. & Tues. June–
Sept. & L all of Aug. ⬚ ⬚ All
major cards

🍴 IL CAPITANO
$$$

HOTEL MONTEMARE, VIA
PASITEA 119
TEL 089 811 351
www.hotelmontemare.it
Virtually everything here,
from breadsticks to pasta , is
homemade. Fish and seafood
are excellent, especially the
seafood antipasti. In summer,
book a table on the terrace,
overlooking the sea.
⬚ 35 ⬚ Closed Nov.–March
& L Wed. ⬚ All major cards

🍴 IL RITROVO
$$$

VIA MONTEPERTUSO 77
TEL 089 812 005
www.ilritrovo.com
Escape Positano's summer heat,
high prices, and summer crowds
high above the village. More
rustic than the Donna Rosa, it
offers of old Amalfitan dishes
such as *spaghetti con pomorodini*
(spaghetti with cherry tomatoes)
and simple chicken and rabbit
stews. One- and seven-day
cooking courses are available.
⬚ 65 ⬚ Closed Jan.–early
Feb. & Wed. except Easter–Oct.
⬚ ⬚ All major cards

AMALFI COAST DRIVE

🏨 GRAND HOTEL
🍴 EXCELSIOR VITTORIA
$$$$$

PIAZZA TASSO 34, SORRENTO
TEL 081 877 7111
FAX 081 877 1206
www.exvitt.it
Since it opened in 1834,
Sorrento's grandest hotel has
welcomed guests such as Lord
Byron and European royalty.
It has been run by the same
family for its history and many
of the antiques are original.
Ⓘ 82 + 16 suites P ⬚
Check with hotel for winter
closings ⊜ ⊗ ⬚ ⬚ All
major cards

🏨 HOTEL BOTANICO
🍴 SAN LAZZARO
$$$$ *****

VIA LAZZARO 25, MAIORI
TEL 089 877 750
FAX 089 877 490
www.botanicosanlazzaro.it
This family-run hotel affords
some of the most spectacular
views of the Amalfi Coastline.
Once a quarantine hospital, the
elegant building has just undergone a four-year renovation.
The hotel is currently accessible
only by a long, winding staircase; porters carry your bags.
Ⓘ 18 P ⊜ ⊗ ⬚ ⬚ All
major cards

🍴 LA ANTICA TRATTORIA
$$$$$

VIA PADRE R. GIULIANI 33,
SORRENTO
TEL 081 807 1082
www.lanticatrattoria.com
A lovely restaurant with a
pergola and tables arranged
around six small dining salons. It
has been in business over 200
years, offering local specialities
such as *pezzogna* (fish in a spicy
tomato and shellfish sauce).
⬚ 50 ⬚ Closed Feb. & Mon.
Nov. & Dec. ⬚ ⬚ All
major cards

PRICES

HOTELS
An indication of the cost of
a double room in the high
season is given by $ signs.

$$$$$	Over $280
$$$$	$160–$280
$$$	$100–$160
$$	$40–$100
$	Under $40

RESTAURANTS
An indication of the cost of
a three-course meal without
drinks is given by $ signs.

$$$$$	Over $80
$$$$	$50–$80
$$$	$35–$50
$$	$20–$35
$	Under $20

🍴 LA CAMBUSA
$$$$

PIAZZA VESPUCCI 4,
POSITANO
TEL 089 875 432
www.lacambusapositano
.com
La Cambusa, close to the beach,
has been a fixture of Positano
since 1970, serving a large variety
of fish and seafood prepared every which way, from pastas and
carpaccios to soups and salads.
⬚ 60 ⬚ Closed Nov.–Dec.
⬚ ⬚ All major cards

SOMETHING SPECIAL

🍴 DON ALFONSO 1890
🏨 $$$$$

CORSO SANT'AGATA 11,
SANT'AGATA SUI DUE GOLFI
TEL 081 878 0026
www.donalfonso1890.com
Many claim that this is the
best restaurant in southern
Italy (Michelin has awarded it
two stars). The setting, with

🏨 Hotel 🍴 Restaurant Ⓘ No. of guest rooms ⬚ No. of Seats P Parking ⬚ Closed ⬚ Elevator views over two gulfs, is superb, and the dining rooms and service are elegant without being too formal. Most of the produce comes from the owners' organic farm. There are five apartments to rent (*$$$$$*) if you wish to stay overnight. In the same village but at the other extreme, **Fattoria Terranova** (*Via Pontone 10, tel 081 533 0234, closed Nov.–early March*) offers good, simple local cooking.

🏠 4 ⚡ 50 🕐 Closed Nov.–Feb.; Mon. & Tues. March–mid-June & mid-Sept.–Oct.; Mon. mid-June–mid-Sept. ❄️
💳 All major cards

🍴 TAVERNA DEL 🏨 CAPITANO
$$$$
PIAZZA DELLE SIRENE 10–11, MASSA LUBRENSE, LOCALITÀ MARINA DEL CANTONE
TEL 081 808 1028
www.tavernadelcapitano.it
A fine restaurant with two Michelin stars and a simple 15-room hotel (*$$$*) by a private beach make this an excellent place to stop for lunch or spend a few days. The airy rooms have sea views.

🏠 10 ⚡ 103 🕐 Closed Jan.–Feb., restaurant closed Mon., & Tues. Oct.–May ❄️ 💳 All major cards

🍴 BRACE
$$$
VIA CAPRIGLIONE 146, LOCALITÀ VETTICA MAGGIORE, 0.5 MILE (1 KM) FROM PRAIANO
TEL 089 874 226
A nice setting, wholesome home cooking (including pizzas), and prices that are reasonable by the standards of the area make this restaurant popular for lunch or dinner.

⚡ 85 🕐 Closed Feb. & Wed. mid-Oct.–mid-March ❄️ 💳 All major cards

🍴 HOSTERIA DI BACCO 🏨 $$$
VIA G B LAMA 9, FURORE
TEL 089 830 360
www.baccofurore.it
This restaurant and three-star, 20-room hotel (*$$*) in the hills away from the coast has been run by the same family since 1930. All rooms have terraces overlooking vineyards, source of the good house wine.

🏠 20 ⚡ 103 🕐 Closed part of Nov., restaurant also closed Fri. Dec.–mid-March ❄️
💳 All major cards

🍴 SAN PIETRO
$$$–$$$$
PIAZZA SAN FRANCESCO 2, CETARA
TEL 089 261 091
www.sanpietroristorante.it
Known for its low prices, fine ingredients, and the courtesy of owner Franco Tammaro. Try the restaurant's own smoked fish (*pesce affumicato*). In the same village you might also want to visit the slightly more expensive **Acqua Pazza** (*Corso Garibaldi 38, tel 089 261 606, www.acquapazza.it, closed Mon.*).

⚡ 50 🕐 Closed Tues. & mid-Jan.–mid-Feb. 💳 All major cards

ISCHIA

🏨 MEZZATORRE RESORT 🍴 & SPA
$$$$$ ★★★★★
VIA MEZZATORRE 23, SAN MONTANO, FORIO
TEL 081 986 111
FAX 081 986 015
www.mezzatorre.it
Smaller and more exclusive than the Regina Isabella, the Mezzatorre is situated in a lovely part of the island and offers spa and other facilities.

🏠 47 + 10 suites 🕐 Closed Nov.–mid-March/early April
💳 ❄️ All major cards

🏨 REGINA ISABELLA 🍴 $$$$$ ★★★★★
PIAZZA SANTA RESTITUTA 1, LACCO AMENO
TEL 081 994 322
FAX 089 190 0190
www.reginaisabella.it
Ischia's finest resort hotel is set on beautiful grounds and offers one of the country's most modern and well-equipped thermal spas.

🏠 125 + 3 suites 🅿️
🕐 Closed Nov.–Easter
💳 ❄️ All major cards

🍴 IL MELOGRANO
$$$$$
VIA GIOVANNI MAZZELLA 110, FORIO
TEL 081 998 450
www.ilmelogranoischia.it
The island's best restaurant is a tiny place in a beautiful setting. Everything here is presented with care, and the food has a delicate touch.

⚡ 36 🕐 Closed early Jan.–mid-March, Mon. Oct. ❄️ 💳 All major cards

CAPRI (CAPRI TOWN)

🏨 GRAND HOTEL 🍴 QUISISANA
$$$$$ ★★★★★
VIA CAMERELLE 2
TEL 081 837 0788
FAX 081 837 6080
www.quisiana.com
The grandest of Capri town's hotels. The hotel's restaurant, **Quisi**, is the island's best. Come for a drink in one of the stylish bars, even if you are not staying.

🏠 148 + 13 suites 🕐 Closed Nov. March., restaurant closed L, & D Sun. except mid-June–mid-Sept. 💳 ❄️ All major cards

🏨 PUNTA TRAGARA 🍴 $$$$$ ★★★★★
VIA TRAGARA 57
TEL 081 837 0844
FAX 081 837 7790

www.hoteltragara.com
Perched on a clifftop that
affords tremendous views. Le
Corbusier designed this villa in
the 1920s before it became a
hotel. While rooms have ter-
rific terraces, the interiors are
relatively uninspiring. The hotel
bar is a great place to watch
the sunset.
🛈 40 + 4 suites 🕒 Closed
Nov.–March ⊜ Ⓢ Ⓒ Ⓐ All
major cards

🏨 **LA MINERVA**
🍴 **$$$$** ★★★★
VIA OCCHIO MARINO 8
TEL 081 837 0374
FAX 081 837 5221
www.laminervacapri.com
A gem of a hotel in a tranquil
area a little removed from the
town center. Intimate rooms
and flower-decked terraces.
🛈 18 🕒 Closed Nov.–Feb.
⊜ Ⓢ Ⓒ Ⓐ All major cards

🏨 **VILLA SARAH**
$$$$ ★★★
VIA TIBERIO 3/A
TEL 081 837 7817
FAX 081 837 7215
www.villasarah.it
A welcoming family-run hotel
with a pretty garden, about ten
minutes' walk from the center
of Capri town. Only upper
rooms have sea views. Reserve
well in advance.
🛈 19 🕒 Closed Nov.–Easter
⊜ Ⓢ Ⓒ Ⓐ All major cards

🍴 **LA CAPANNINA**
$$$$
VIA DELLE BOTTEGHE 12BIS/14
TEL 081 837 0732
www.capinnina-capri.com
A glamorous but unstuffy and
consistently good restaurant
just off the Piazzetta. Mostly
classic fish creations with some
meat dishes.
🍽 120 🕒 Closed mid-Nov.–
mid-March, Wed. March
Ⓒ Ⓐ All major cards

🍴 **DA TONINO**
$$$$$
VIA DENTECALA 12–14
TEL 081 837 6718
Tonino Aprea and his son,
Gennaro, run this charming
restaurant away from the
town's visitor-filled streets.
Innovative meat and fish dishes,
and in summer you can dine
alfresco. The 800-strong wine
list is stellar.
🍽 45 🕒 Closed Wed. &
mid-Jan.–Easter Ⓒ Ⓐ All
major cards

🍴 **DA GEMMA**
$$$$
VIA MADRE SERAFINA 6
TEL 081 837 0461
www.dagemma.it
This was writer Graham
Greene's favorite restaurant
when he lived on the island.
The typical Caprese food is
rarely more than reliable, but
this is a place to come for history as much as gastronomy.
🍽 60 🕒 Closed Mon. & Jan.–
Feb. Ⓒ Ⓐ All major cards

CAPRI (ANACAPRI)

🏨 **CAPRI PALACE HOTEL**
🍴 **$$$$$** ★★★★★
VIA CAPODIMONTE 14
TEL 081 978 0111
FAX 081 837 3191
www.capripalace.com
The island's best hotel is situated among flower-covered
terraces. Luxurious without
being pretentious. **L'Olivo**
restaurant is outstanding in
its own right, and the roof
terrace offers views as far as
Vesuvius. Service is faultless.
Wi-Fi available.
🛈 67 + 11 suites Ⓟ 🕒 Closed
Nov.–March ⊜ Ⓢ Ⓩ Ⓐ Ⓥ
Ⓐ All major cards

🏨 **VILLA LE SCALE**
🍴 **$$$$$**
VIA CAPODIMONTE 64
TEL 081 838 2190

FAX 081 838 2796
www.villalescale.com
This is a *residenza d'epoca*, or
historic lodging, and so does
not have an official star rating,
but it is easily as good as many
of the island's top luxury hotels.
Wi-Fi available.
🛈 6 + 1 suite Ⓟ 🕒 Closed Nov.–
Easter ⊜ Ⓢ Ⓒ Ⓩ Ⓐ All
major cards

🏨 **BIANCAMARIA**
$$$$ ★★★
VIA ORLANDI 54
TEL 081 837 1000
FAX 081 837 2060
www.hotelbiancamaria.com
An unassuming but comfortable and informal hotel at the
heart of the village's pedestrian-
only zone.
🛈 25 Ⓟ 🕒 Closed Oct.–
March ⊜ Ⓢ Ⓒ Ⓐ All
major cards

🍴 **GELSOMINA ALLA**
🏨 **MIGLIARA**
$$$–$$$$
VIA MIGLIARA 72
TEL 081 837 1499
www.dagelsomina.com
Offers very good value and
sweeping sea views from its
glorious hilltop location in the
countryside a short drive from
the village. The restaurant
offers local meat and fish clas-
sics. Five rooms for rent.
🛈 5 🍽 100 🕒 Closed
Jan.–Feb., Tues. Oct.–Dec., &
March–April Ⓒ Ⓐ All major
cards

■ **PUGLIA**

IL GARGANO

🏨 **PALACE HOTEL**
🍴 **SAN MICHELE**
$$ ★★★★
VIA MADONNA DEGLI ANGELI,
MONTE SANT'ANGELO
TEL 088 456 5653
FAX 088 456 5737
www.palacesanmichele.it

This former convent has been beautifully converted into a hotel. The rooms are large and airy. The restaurant, **L'Arcangelo**, combines Puglian and classic Italian cuisine.

🛈 55 +7 suites 🛏 30/100
🅿 All major cards

🍴 MEDIOEVO
$$–$$$
VIA CASTELLO 21, MONTE SANT'ANGELO
TEL 088 456 5356
www.ristorantemedioevo.it
Good value and a warm welcome from patron Pasquale Mazzone are key features of this restaurant in the town's historic center (which you can reach only on foot). It has a charming medieval dining area and fine Gargano cuisine.

🍽 60 Closed 2 weeks in Nov. & Mon. except Aug.
All major cards

BARI

🏨 DOMINA HOTEL AND
🍴 CONFERENCE BARI-PALACE
$$$$ ****
VIA LOMBARDI 13
TEL 080 521 6551
FAX 080 521 1499
www.dominahotels.com
The venerable Palace Hotel is the classic place to stay in Bari. It is more conveniently located than most other large hotels. The **Murat** restaurant is good in its own right.

🛈 190 + 6 suites 🛏 80/30
Restaurant closed Sun. & Aug. All major cards

🍴 ALBEROSOLE
$$$$
CORSO VITTORIO EMANUELE II, 13
TEL 080 523 5446
www.alberosole.com
A beautiful old dining room that forms part of a

13th-century palace on the street that divides the old and new towns. Offers pan-Mediterranean cuisine, with an emphasis on seafood.

🍽 40 Closed Mon., 1 week in Jan., & 3–4 weeks July–Aug.
All major cards

🍴 LA PIGNATA
$$$$
CORSO VITTORIO EMANUELE II, 173
TEL 080 523 2481
www.ristorantelapignatabari.com
La Pignata is the best and most expensive of Bari's many fish and seafood restaurants. On one of the modern city's busiest main streets, its single dining room provides a calm and elegant retreat.

🍽 90 Closed Aug.
All major cards

🍴 AL SORSO PREFERITO
$$$
VIA VITO NICOLA DE NICOLÒ 40
TEL 080 523 5747
www.sorso-preferito.com
A popular and busy fish and seafood restaurant with reasonable prices.

🍽 130 Closed Sun. p.m.
All major cards

🍴 OSTERIA DELLE TRAVI
$–$$
LARGO CHIURLIA 12
TEL 339 157 8848
A family-run trattoria with a warm welcome, low prices, and old-fashioned Puglian home cooking, including a wonderful buffet of antipasti.

🍽 95 Closed Sun. p.m., Mon., & 2 weeks in Aug.
No cards

ROMANESQUE PUGLIA DRIVE

🏨 TENUTA COCEVOLA
🍴 $$$$ ****
CONTRADA COCEVOLA,

NEAR ANDRIA
TEL 088 356 6945
FAX 088 356 9706
www.tenutacocevola.com
An intimate countryside retreat off the SS170 road between Andria and Castel del Monte. The property has recently been converted and rooms are fresh and elegant. An excellent base and a perfect place to relax.

🛈 24 Restaurant closed D Sun. & Mon. All major cards

🏨 SAN PAOLO AL CONVENTO
$$$–$$$$ ****
VIA STATUTI MARITTIMI 111, TRANI
TEL 088 348 2949
FAX 088 348 7096
http://sanpaoloconvento.it
A converted convent and historic monument dating from the 15th century. Most rooms overlook the cloister, the seafront, or the town's public gardens. There is no restaurant, but a buffet breakfast is served in the former chapel.

🛈 33 All major cards

🍴 TORRENTE ANTICO
$$$$$
VIA FUSCO 3, TRANI
TEL 088 348 7911
Traditional dishes are given a modern edge at this intimate restaurant in Trani's old quarter. Try risotto con zucchine e gamberi (risotto with zucchini and shrimp) and the rum babà with a Chantilly cream.

🍽 30 Closed Sun. p.m., Mon., & part of Jan. & July
All major cards

🍴 BACCOSTERIA
$$$–$$$$
VIA SAN GIORGIO 5, BARLETTA
TEL 088 353 4000
Reservations are essential here, thanks to the limited seats and the restaurant's good reputation. The wine list is excellent.

If the restaurant is booked, **Antica Cucina** *(Via Milano 73, tel 088 352 1718, www .anticucina1983.it., closed Mon. & part of July, $$$)* makes an excellent alternative.
🍴 25 🕐 Closed Sun. p.m., Mon., Tues, & 2–3 weeks in Aug. 💳 🚫 All major cards

🍴 U.P.E.P.I.D.D.E
$$$
VICOLO SANT'AGNESE 2 AT CORNER OF CORSO CAVOUR, RUVO DI PUGLIA
TEL 080 361 3879
www.upepidde.it
The name is slang for something small but pleasing. This restaurant is anything but pretentious. It offers traditional seasonal cooking, including excellent grilled meats.
🍴 60 🕐 Closed Mon. & 3–4 weeks in July–Aug. 💳 🚫 All major cards

TRULLI COUNTRY

SOMETHING SPECIAL

🏨 MASSERIA SAN
🍴 DOMENICO
$$$$$ ****
VIA LITORANEA 379, SAVELLETRI DI FASANO
TEL 080 482 7769
FAX 080 482 7978
www.imasseri.com
One of the first of Puglia's *masserie*, or fortified farm and manor houses, to be converted into a luxury hotel, the 15th-century Masseria San Domenico is still one of the best, a glorious collection of historic buildings set amid olive groves. The spa is exceptional, and so, too, is the large outdoor pool. Service is first-rate. The hotel has a private beach. This is a superb base for exploration of the area.
🛏 44 + 6 suites
🅿 🛗 🚫 💳 🚫 (seawater) 🚫 All major cards

🏨 RELAIS VILLA SAN
🍴 MARTINO
$$$$$ *****
VIA TARANTO 59, MARTINA FRANCA
TEL 080 485 7719
FAX 080 480 1026
www.relaisvillasanmartino.com
This converted 19th-century *masseria* stands in ravishing gardens. Its spa, peaceful surroundings, and attractive rooms and public areas make this an excellent place to spend several relaxing days. Wi-Fi available.
🛏 15 + 6 suites
🅿 🛗 🚫 💳 🚫 🚫
🚫 All major cards

🏨 MASSERIA I MONTI
$$$$ ****
STRADA PROVINCIAL NOCI-BARSENTO, NEAR PUTIGNANO
TEL 080 497 3235
FAX 080 496 1922
www.barsentum.it
More intimate than some other *trulli* hotels, it is also more exotic, with touches of old Indian and Moroccan decor.
🛏 10 🅿 🚫 💳 🚫 All major cards

🏨 MASSERIA IL
🍴 FRANTOIO
$$$$
RESIDENZA D'EPOCA
SS16, 3 MILES (5 KM) NW OF OSTUNI
TEL 083 133 0276
www.masseriailfrantoio.it
This wonderfully converted 16th-century historic *masseria* is classed as *residenza d'epoca*, so it has no official star rating (though it is the equivalent of a four- or five-star hotel).
🛏 9 🅿 🕐 Restaurant closed L in summer 🛗 🚫 💳
🚫 MC, V

🍴 FORNELLO DA RICCI
$$$$$
CONTRADÀ MONTEVICOLI, CEGLIE MESSAPICA

TEL 083 137 7104
The village of Ceglie Messapica is worth the detour to eat at one of the region's most highly regarded restaurants (it has a Michelin star).
🍴 70 🕐 Closed Sun. & D Mon., Tues. in summer, last 2 weeks of Sept. & Feb. or March 💳 🚫 All major cards

🍴 OSTERIA GIÀ SOTTO
L'ARCO
$$$$$
CORSO VITTORIO EMANUELE II 71, CAROVIGNO
TEL 083 199 6286
www.giasottolarco.it
As with Fornello da Ricci, it is well worth making a slight detour to eat at this exquisite little restaurant on the second floor of a small palazzo. The good food is precisely prepared and has earned a Michelin star.
🍴 35 🕐 Closed Sun. & Mon. Nov.–May & part of Nov. 💳 🚫 All major cards

---

🏨 Hotel 🍴 Restaurant 🛏 No. of guest rooms 🍴 No. of Seats 🅿 Parking 🕐 Closed 🛗 Elevator

IL POETA CONTADINO
$$$$$
VIA INDIPENDENZA 21,
ALBEROBELLO
TEL 080 432 1917
www.ilpoetacontadino.it
An elegant, central restaurant, with one of Italy's best wine cellars and delightful cooking, including an appetizer of warm salad with *caposante* (scallops) and wild porcini.
🍴 50 🕐 Closed 3 weeks in Jan. & Mon. Oct.–June 🅢 🅢 All major cards

OSTERIA CANTONE
$$$$
CONTRADA FANTESE
TEL 080 444 6902
www.masseriacantone.it
A stately *masseria* and its attractive garden. The dining room resembles a private home, and the Puglian cuisine uses many local ingredients.
🍴 60 🕐 Closed L Sat. & D. Sun. Nov.–June 🅢 🅢 All major cards

OSTERIA DEL TEMPO PERSO
$$$$
VIA TANZARELLA VITALE 47, OSTUNI
TEL 083 130 4819
www.osteriadeltempoperso.com
A traditional trattoria at the heart of the old quarter, this has been a reliable source of typical Puglian cooking.
🍴 70 🕐 Closed Mon. Sept.–June 🅢 🅢 All major cards

LA CANTINA
$$$
VICO LIPPOLIS 8, ALBEROBELLO
TEL 080 432 3473
www.ilristorantelacantina.it
Four small steps take you from the crowded streets of central Alberobello into a tiny restaurant that has been run by the Lippolis family for over 50 years. The traditional food includes Puglian classics.
🍴 32 🕐 Closed Tues. & part of Feb. & June 🅢 🅢 All major cards

LECCE

🏨 PATRIA PALACE
🍴 $$$$$ *****
PIAZZETTA RICCARDI 13
TEL 083 224 5111
FAX 083 222 45002
www.patriapalacelecce.com
This is the best place to stay in Lecce. It is located a few seconds' walk away from Santa Croce, the city's architectural masterpiece.
🛏 63 P 🖨 🅢 🅢 🅢 All major cards

🏨 RISORGIMENTO
🍴 RESORT
$$$$$ *****
VIA IMPERATORE AUGUSTO 19
TEL 083 224 6311
FAX 083224 5976
www.risorgimentoresort.it
Lecce's second luxury-class hotel opened in 2007 in a beautifully restored palazzo close to the central Piazza Sant' Oronzo. Interiors are airy, clean-lined, and contemporary. There are two restaurants, **Le Quattro Spezerie** *(closed L Mon.)* and less formal **Dogana Vecchia**. Wi-Fi available.
🛏 45 + 2 suites P 🖨 📺 🅢 🅢 All major cards

🍴 ALLE DUE CORTI
$$$
CORTE DEI GIUGNI 1
TEL 083 224 2223
www.alleduecorti.com
Menus change often according to season. Conveniently located in the old center. All the pasta here is homemade, as are the *spumoni lucchesi* (Lucchese ice creams).
🍴 65 🕐 Closed Sun. 🅢 🅢 All major cards

🍴 OSTERIA DEGLI SPIRITI
$$$
VIA CESARE BATTISTI 4
TEL 083 224 6274
www.osteriadeglispiriti.it
An attractive vaulted dining room in the former stables of a palazzo near the Villa Comunale. Excellent local food and good wines from the Salentine Peninsula.
🍴 55 🕐 Closed D Sun. & L Mon. in winter; L Sun. & Mon. in summer, & 2 weeks in Sept. 🅢 🅢 All major cards

🍴 CASARECCIA LE ZIE
$$
VIA COLONELLO COSTADURA 19
TEL 083 224 5178
A wonderful family-run trattoria that offers definitive versions of many simple, classic, southern Puglian dishes.
🍴 50 🕐 Closed D Sun., Mon., part of Aug., & Easter 🅢 🅢 All major cards

IL SALENTO

🏨 PALAZZO BALDI
🍴 $$$$ ****
CORTE BALDI 2, GALATINA
TEL 083 656 8345
FAX 083 656 4835
www.hotelpalazzobaldi.com
Galatina is at the heart of the Salento region, and this converted bishop's palace makes a good base for exploration.
🛏 11 + 3 suites P 🕐 Restaurant closed Sun. 🅢 🅢 🅢 🅢 All major cards

🍴 DA SERGIO
$$$
CORSO GARIBALDI 9, OTRANTO
TEL 083 680 1408
Da Sergio has been serving perfectly prepared seafood since time immemorial. It is so small and popular that you will very likely have to wait in line, especially in summer.
🍴 35 🕐 Closed Wed. except July & Aug., & part of Feb. & Nov. 🅢 🅢 All major cards

CALABRIA & BASILICATA

MATERA

LE GROTTE DELLA CIVITA
$$$$$ ★★★★
VIA CIVITA 28
TEL 083 533 2744
FAX 083 533 7331
www.sassidimatera.com
This wonderfully evocative hotel opened in 2009, converted entirely from ancient sassi. Rooms and public areas are caves, but comfortable, romantic, candle-lit caves, with crackling fires in winter and discreet modern comforts. Breakfast is served, but there is no formal restaurant.
🏨 18 💳 All major cards

SAN DOMENICO AL PIANO
$$$ ★★★★
VIA ROMA 15
TEL 083 525 6309
FAX 083 525 6309
www.hotelsandomenico.it
Partly aimed at the business traveler, the hotel's excellent facilities and central location make it a comfortable base. Wi-Fi available.
🏨 72 P 🛗 💳 All major cards

SANT'ANGELO
$$ ★★★★
PIAZZA SAN PIETRO CEVEOSO
TEL 083 531 4010
FAX 083 531 4735
www.hotelsantangelosassi.it
As in Le Grotte (above), the rooms here are caves, albeit four-star ones—restored sassi excavated from soft stone.
🏨 16 P 🛗 💳 All major cards

SASSI
$ ★★★
VIA SAN GIOVANNI VECCHIO 89
TEL 083 533 1009
FAX 083 533 3733
www.hotelsassi.it
Another hotel at the heart of the sassi district in a structure from the 18th century.
🏨 32 + 3 P 🛗 💳 All major cards

BACCANTI
$$$$
VIA SANT'ANGELO 58–61
TEL 083 533 3704
www.baccantiristorante.com
Not only is this currently the best restaurant in town, but it is located in the heart of the sassi district. The dining rooms are partly excavated from tuff. Traditional dishes are given a modern twist.
🍴 110 Closed Sun. D & Mon. 💳 All major cards

LE BOTTEGHE
$$$
PIAZZA SAN PIETRO BARISANO 22
TEL 083 534 4072
www.lebotteghemt.it
The four striking dining rooms here were used for centuries as workshops (botteghe). The food served is honest regional fare—fave (broad beans), tagliatelle e ceci (noodles and chickpeas), agnello alle brace (grilled lamb).
🍴 60 Closed D Sun., D Tues.–Fri. Oct.–March, & part of Jan. 💳 All major cards

LUCANERIE
$$$
VIA SANTO STEFANO 61
TEL 083 533 2133
Lucanerie offers wholesome local cooking that uses many ingredients from the owners' farm. This is a real local favorite.
🍴 45 Closed Aug., D Sun. & Mon. 💳 All major cards

COSTA IONICA

LA CASA DI GIANNA
$$$ ★★★★
VIA PAOLO FRASCÀ 4, GERACE
TEL 096 435 5024
FAX 096 435 5081
www.lacasadigianna.it
La Casa di Gianna occupies a historic building from the 17th century. Elegant rooms and tasteful restaurant. If the hotel is full, the four-star, 14-room La Casa nel Borgo (Via Nazionale, tel 096 435 5150, www.lacasanelborgo.it, closed Nov.) is almost as charming.
🏨 9 P 🛗 💳 All major cards

SCIGLIANO
$$ ★★★
VIALE MARGHERITA 257, ROSSANO STAZIONE
TEL 098 351 1846
FAX 098 351 1848
www.hotelscigliano.it
This modern, five-story, family-run hotel offers a warm welcome and professional service. In the newer, lower town.
🏨 36 P 🛗 💳 All major cards

LA STREGA
$$$$$
VIA FRATELLI BANDIERA 61, PALAGIANELLO
TEL 099 844 4678
It is worth the detour to this restaurant if you are en route to the Ionian Coast from Matera. One of the best places to eat in southern Italy, its single dining room forms part of an old mill. The food features innovative variations on classic Puglian dishes.
🍴 103 Closed Mon., L Tues., & 2 weeks in July 💳 All major cards

PARCO NAZIONALE DEL MONTE POLLINO

PICCHIO NERO
$$ ★★★
VIA MULINO 1, TERRANOVA DI POLLINO
TEL/FAX 097 393 170

www.picchionero.com
A pleasant family-run hotel made all the more appealing by its restaurant, with excellent Basilicatan mountain cooking.
🛈 25 🅿 🕒 Closed part of Nov. or Dec. 🌀 Ⓢ Ⓢ
Ⓢ All major cards

🍴 DA PEPPE
$$–$$$
CORSO GARIBALDI 13, ROTONDA
TEL 097 366 1251
Da Peppe's two dining rooms are part of a historic palazzo. Try the *tagliolini al tartufo* (fine pasta strands with truffle) or *bocconcini di coniglio alle erbe* (tender rabbit with herbs).
🍴 70 🕒 Closed D Sun. & Mon. Ⓢ Ⓢ All major cards

🍴 LUNA ROSSA
$$
VIA MARCONI 18, TERRANOVA DI POLLINO
TEL 097 393 254
www.federicovalicenti.it
The simplicity of this two-room restaurant in an old house at the center of town belies the zest (and value) of the cooking.
🍴 60 🕒 Closed Wed. & part of Sept. Ⓢ Ⓢ All major cards

MARATEA

🏨 LA LOCANDA DELLE
🍴 DONNE MONACHE
$$$$$ ****
VIA CARLO MAZZEI 4
TEL 097 387 7487
FAX 097 387 7687
www.locandemonache.com
This historic, celebrated hotel is a converted 18th-century convent. Less expensive than the Santavenere, the better rooms have large terraces.
🛈 22 + 5 suites 🅿
🕒 Closed mid-Oct.–Easter
🌀 Ⓢ Ⓢ ⚊ Ⓢ All major cards

🏨 SANTAVENERE
🍴 $$$$$ *****
LOCALITÀ FIUMICELLO, 3 MILES

(5 KM) FROM MARATEA
TEL 011 818 5270
FAX 011 818 5221
www.hotelsantavenere.it
The second of Maratea's historic hotels is the most chic resort in southern Italy. There are glorious grounds, a dazzling private beach, tennis courts, and spa cures.
🛈 30 + 7 suites 🅿 🕒 Closed Nov.–March 🌀 Ⓢ Ⓢ ⚊ 🎽
Ⓢ All major cards

🏨 VILLA DEL MARE
🍴 $$$$ ****
LOCALITÀ ACQUAFREDDA, 7.5 MILES (12 KM) FROM MARATEA
TEL 097 387 8007
FAX 097 387 8102
www.hotelvilladelmare.com
Broad panoramas over garden and coastline. Most rooms have balconies, and there is a spa.
🛈 73 🅿 🕒 Closed Nov.–March 🌀 Ⓢ Ⓢ ⚊ Ⓢ All major cards

🍴 ZÀ MARIUCCIA
$$$$$
VIA GROTTE 2, LOCALITÀ FIUMICELLO
TEL 097 387 6163
This rustic-elegant restaurant has a lovely location with a sea terrace. Its signature dish is the meat- and cheese-based *ravioli di ricotta dolci in ragù d'agnello* (sweet ricotta cheese ravioli with a lamb sauce). Reservations are a must.
🍴 24 🕒 Closed Nov.–Feb., Thurs. except Aug., & L June–Aug. Ⓢ Ⓢ All major cards

🍴 TAVERNA ROVITA
$$$$
VIA ROVITA 13
TEL 097 387 6588
Two rustic rooms provide the setting for the serving of regional specialties such as *fusilli vecchia Maratea* (pasta with sausages and basil).
🍴 50 🕒 Closed Nov.–Feb. & Wed. except June–Aug. Ⓢ Ⓢ All major cards

🍴 IL GIARDINO DI EPICURO
$$$–$$$$
CONTRADA MASSA PIANO
TEL 097 387 0130
A family-run trattoria. Pasta is homemade and the menu has plenty of meat options in an area that otherwise serves mostly fish and seafood.
🍴 30 🕒 Closed Nov. & Tues. Sept.–May Ⓢ Ⓢ All major cards

CALABRIAN RIVIERA

🏨 PORTO PIRGOS
🍴 $$$$$ *****
MARINA DI BORDILA, 2 MILES (4 KM) FROM PARGHELIA
TEL 096 360 0351
FAX 096 360 0690
www.portopirgos.com
A superb and intimate resort hotel on a promontory over a private bay. The views some of the best on this coast.
🛈 18 🅿 🕒 Closed mid-Oct. or Nov.–April
🌀 Ⓢ Ⓢ ⚊ Ⓢ All major cards

🏨 LOCANDA DAFFINÀ
🍴 PALAZZO D'ALCONTRES
$$$ ****
CORSO UMBERTO I 160, VIBO VALENTINA
TEL 096 347 2669
FAX 096 354 1025
www.lalocandadaffina.it
An elegant hotel and restaurant in a noble palace at the heart of the town, with a handful of beautifully appointed rooms.
🛈 9 🅿 🕒 Restaurant closed Sun. 🌀 Ⓢ Ⓢ
Ⓢ All major cards

🏨 LA PINETA
🍴 $$ ***
VIA MARINA 150, TROPEA
TEL 096 361 700
FAX 096 362 265
www.albergolapineta.net
La Pineta has a dated 1970s look, but it offers reasonable

prices and a good location on the edge of a *pineta* (pine woods).
(i) 60 P (C) Restaurant closed Sun. D 🔁 🕃 🕃 🕭 All major cards

🍴 DE GUSTIBUS
$$$
VIALE DELLE RIMEMBRANZE 58–60, PALMI
TEL 096 625 069
A small and pleasing restaurant. The menu reworks old Calabrian dishes with care and precision.
🪑 35 (C) Closed Sun.–Mon. except July–mid-Aug., L mid-July–Aug., 1 week in July, & 2 weeks in Sept. 🕃 🕭 All major cards

🍴 OSTERIA DEL PESCATORE
$$
VIA DEL MONTE 7, TROPEA
TEL 096 360 3018
An old-fashioned trattoria, with a simple interior, fair prices, and first-rate food. Try some *'nduja*, the classic Calabrian sausage.
🪑 36 (C) Closed Wed. & late Oct.–late March 🕃 🕭 No cards

PARCO NAZIONALE DELLA SILA

🏨 CAMIGLIATELLO
🍴 $$$ ★★★★
VIA FEDERICI, CAMIGLIATELLO SILANO
TEL 098 457 8496
FAX 098 457 8268
www.hotelcamigliatello.it
A comfortable base in a region with few hotels. In winter, the bar with its fireplace is a snug retreat, and in summer, the restaurant is a good spot from which to admire the scenery.
(i) 40 P 🔁 🕃 🕃 🕭 All major cards

🏨 AQUILA & EDELWEISS
🍴 $ ★★★
VIALE STAZIONE 11, CAMIGLIATELLO SILANO
TEL 098 457 8044
FAX 098 457 8753
www.hotelaquilaedelweiss.com
This central, family-run hotel is adequate, but it is the restaurant that makes it memorable, albeit at relatively high prices.
(i) 48 P (C) Restaurant closed Tues. except July–Aug. 🔁 🕃 🕃 🕭 All major cards

🍴 LA TAVERNETTA
$$$$
CAMPO SAN LORENZO 14, 3 MILES (5 KM) NE OF CAMIGLIATELLO
TEL 098 457 9026
www.latavernetta.info
Having refurbished his restaurant, Pietro Lecce has turned his attention to wine, with a tasting room that allows you to choose from over 1,000 vintages.
🪑 80 (C) Closed 2 weeks in Nov., Mon. except June–Sept. 🕃 🕭 All major cards

■ SICILY & SARDINIA

SICILY

PALERMO

🏨 CENTRALE PALACE
🍴 HOTEL
$$$$$ ★★★★
CORSO VITTORIO EMANUELE II, 327
TEL 091 336 666
FAX 091 334 881
www.centralepalacehotel.it
Palermo's best hotel occupies a 19th-century building two blocks west of the Quattro Canti, a busy but central location. The service is excellent and there is a lovely roof-garden restaurant.
(i) 101 + 3 suites P 🔁 🕃 3 🕃 🕭 All major cards

🏨 LETIZIA
$$ ★★★
VIA DEI BOTTAI 30
TEL 091 589 110
FAX 091 589 110
www.hotelletizia.com
Centrally located near Piazza Maffei, the Letizia has well-renovated rooms, some of which have internal patios.
(i) 13 P 🔁 🕃 🕭 All major cards

🏨 POSTA
$$ ★★
VIA ANTONELLO GAGINI 77
TEL 091 587 338
FAX 091 587 347
www.hotelpostapalermo.it
A city institution close to San Domenico, the Posta offers good-size rooms and excellent value given its central location.
(i) 30 P 🔁 🕃 🕭 All major cards

🍴 OSTERIA DEI VESPRI
$$$$$
PIAZZA CROCE DEI VESPRI 6
TEL 091 617 1631

---

www.osteriadeivespri.it
This single-room restaurant was once used to store the carriages of the Palazzo Gangi above. Today it offers some of Palermo's most accomplished cooking. Good wine list.
🚹 35 🕐 Closed Sun. & part of Feb. & Aug. 💳 💳 All major cards

🍴 SANT'ANDREA
$$$$
PIAZZA SANT'ANDREA 4
TEL 091 334 999
Close to the Vuccíria market and San Domenico, Sant'Andrea is a delightful restaurant with a long-standing good reputation.
🚹 80 🕐 Closed Sun. & L 💳 💳 All major cards

🍴 DAL MAESTRO DEL BRODO
$$$
VIA PANNIERI 7
TEL 091 329 523
Market-fresh ingredients from the Vuccíria market go into traditional dishes such as *pasta con le sarde* (pasta with sardines) and *pesce spada e menta* (swordfish with mint) at this welcoming trattoria.
🚹 100 🕐 Closed Mon. Sept.– mid-June, Sun. mid-June–Aug., & 2 weeks in Aug. 💳 💳 All major cards

🍴 ANTICA FOCACCERIA
$
VIA ALESSANDRO PATERNOSTRO 58
TEL 091 320 264
www.afsf.it
An atmospheric, family-run tavern founded in 1834. It offers a handful of hot dishes and traditional snacks such as *panelle* (chickpea fritters) and *meusa* (grilled beef spleen). More conventional snacks and sandwiches are also available.
🚹 200 🕐 Closed Tues. 💳 💳 All major cards

CEFALÙ

🏨 KALURA
🍴 $$ ★★★
VIA V CAVALLARO 13, CALDURA
TEL 092 142 1354
FAX 092 142 3122
www.hotel-kalura.com
This hotel occupies a superb location above the sea (with its own beach) and offers gracious rooms (those on the grounds are best), tennis, and other sports facilities.
🛏 75 P 💳 💳 💳 🏊 💳 All major cards

🍴 LA BRACE
$$$
VIA XXV NOVEMBRE 10
TEL 092 142 3570
www.ristorantelabrace.com
Classic Sicilian cooking has been honed here for over 20 years. Try the *bruschette di pesce* (toast with fish), *spaghetti all'aglio* (pasta with garlic and chili), and cannoli for dessert.
🚹 50 🕐 Closed Mon., L Tues., & mid-Dec.–mid-Jan. 💳 💳 All major cards

ISOLE EOLIE

🏨 A' PINNATA
🍴 $$$$$ ★★★★
BAIA PIGNATARO, LIPARI
TEL 090 981 1697
FAX 090 981 4782
www.pinnata.it
Room terraces in this smart, intimate, and new hotel offer views along much of Lipari's eastern coast.
🛏 12 P 🕐 Closed mid-Oct.– March 💳 💳 💳 All major cards

🏨 VILLA AUGUSTUS
$$$$ ★★★
VICO AUSONIA 16, LIPARI
TEL 090 981 1232
FAX 090 981 2233
www.villaaugustus.it
Family-run since the 1950s, this converted patrician villa

is a good central hotel with gardens, panoramic balconies, and spacious rooms.
🛏 34 P 🕐 Closed Nov.–Feb. 💳 💳 💳 All major cards

🍴 E' PULERA
$$$$
VIA ISABELLA CONTI VAINICHER, LIPARI
TEL 090 981 1158
www.pulera.it
E' Pulera offers often exceptional Aeolian cooking. The same owners run the larger but similarly priced **Filippino** *(Piazza Municipio, tel 090 981 1002, closed Mon. in low season),* a well-known, informal establishment where the cooking is almost as good.
🚹 80 🕐 Closed L & Feb.–April 💳 💳 DC, MC, V

🍴 LA NASSA
$$$$
VIA G FRANZA 36, LIPARI
TEL 090 981 1319
www.lanassa.it
An outstanding restaurant, also known for Aeolian specialties, with a fine terrace for alfresco dining.
🚹 45 🕐 Closed mid-Nov.– mid-March & L except July– Aug. 💳 💳 All major cards

TAORMINA

🏨 GRAND HOTEL TIMEO
🍴 & VILLA FLORA
$$$$$ ★★★★★
VIA TEATRO GRECO 59
TEL 094 223 801
FAX 094 262 8501
www.grandhoteltimeo.com
Better value—and arguably a better hotel—than the more famous San Domenico, the Timeo has a superb terrace setting close to the Greek theater. Rooms are spacious and bright, and all have balconies. The hotel's chic **Il Dito e la Luna** restaurant has its own good reputation. Wi-Fi available.

---

(1) 72 P ⊖ ⚫ ≋ ▼ ⚫ All major cards

🏨 SAN DOMENICO
🍴 PALACE
$$$$$ ***
PIAZZA SAN DOMENICO 5
TEL 094 261 3111
FAX 094 262 5506
www.hotelsandomenico
taormina.it
The famous and infamous have all stayed at the San Domenico, a converted 15th-century monastery and one of Italy's most celebrated hotels. Its reputation is perhaps overstated, but the vast public spaces, gardens, and wonderful rooms are beyond reproach. Wi-Fi available.
(1) 105 P ⊖ ⚫ ≋ ▼
⚫ All major cards

🏨 VILLA SCHULER
$$ **
PIAZZETTA BASTIONE–VIA
ROMA
TEL 094 223 481
FAX 094 223 522
www.hotelvillaschuler.com
First choice among the less expensive hotels, this is a small, family-run gem of a place to stay. Fine service and comfortable rooms. Wi-Fi available.
(1) 26 P 🕐 Closed mid-Nov.–
Feb. ⊖ ⚫ ⚫ All major cards

🍴 AL DUOMO
$$$$
VICO EBREI 11
TEL 094 262 5656
www.ristorantealduomo.it
Al Duomo is an excellent, lively restaurant with homey atmosphere, good service, and well-prepared local food.
➕ 40 🕐 Closed Feb. & Mon.
Nov.–March ⚫ ⚫ All
major cards

🍴 'A ZAMMÀRA
$$$$
VIA FRATELLI BANDIERA 15
TEL 094 224 408
www.zammara.it

In summer, dine in a lovely garden of orange trees. Sicilian cuisine and a good wine list.
➕ 75 🕐 Closed Wed. except
Aug. ⚫ ⚫ DC, MC, V

ETNA

🏨 BIANCANEVE
🍴 $$ ***
VIA ETNEA 163, NICOLOSI
TEL 095 911 176
FAX 095 911 194
www.hotel-biancaneve.com
A large, modern hotel with a pool, sports facilities, and views of Mount Etna.
 (1) 83 P ⊖ ⚫ ≋ ⚫ All
major cards

🏨 SCRIVANO
🍴 $ ***
VIA BONAVENTURA 2,
RANDAZZO
TEL 095 921 126
FAX 095 921 433
www.hotelscrivano.com
This hotel-restaurant has spacious rooms and modern fittings; an excellent, if rather austere retaurant.
(1) 30 P ⊖ ⚫ 4 ⚫
⚫ All major cards

SIRACUSA

🏨 DES ETRANGERS ET
MIRAMARE
$$$$ ***
PASSEGGIO ADORNO 10–12
TEL 093 131 9100
FAX 093 131 9000
www.desetrangers.it
Syracuse's highest-rated hotel is a recently converted 19th-century palace at the heart of the old town on Ortygia. There is access to a private beach, health club, and sauna.
(1) 80 P ⚫ ≋ ▼ ⚫ All
major cards

🏨 GRAN BRETAGNA
$$ *
VIA SAVOIA 21
TEL/FAX 093 168 765

www.hotelgranbretagna.it
A welcoming and well-run hotel that has been an Ortygia fixture for years. Some of the spacious rooms in the 18th-century building preserve frescoed ceilings.
(1) 17 P ⚫ ⚫ All
major cards

🍴 DON CAMILLO
$$$$$
VIA MAESTRANZA 92–100
TEL 093 167 133
www.ristorantedoncamillo
siracusa.it
This lovely restaurant in a converted 15th-century palazzo on the eastern side of Ortygia is the top choice in Syracuse.
➕ 100 🕐 Closed Sun., Nov.,
& 10 days in July ⚫ ⚫ All
major cards

🍴 ARCHIMEDE
$$$
VIA GEMMELLARO 8
TEL 093 169 701
www.trattoriaarchimede.it
A Syracusan fixture. Its three large dining rooms are adorned with historic photographs of the town. There is a particularly good antipasti buffet.
➕ 150 🕐 Closed Sun. but
might open Sun. in summer
⚫ ⚫ All major cards

AGRIGENTO

🏨 BAGLIO DELLA LUNA
🍴 $$$$$ ****
CONTRADA MADDALUSA
TEL 092 251 1061
FAX 092 259 8802
www.bagliodellaluna.com
This beautifully restored 13th- and 15th-century castle/country house 4 miles (7 km) from the town center is ringed by gardens and has elegant rooms. In **Il Dèhor** (closed L Mon.), it boasts the region's best restaurant. Wi-Fi available.
(1) 24 ➕ 100 P ⊖ ⚫
⚫ All major cards

🏨 VILLA ATHENA
🍽 $$$$$ ★★★★
VIA PASSEGGIATA
ARCHEOLOGICA 33
TEL 092 259 6288
FAX 092 240 2180
www.villaathena.it
Agrigento's finest hotel is a
converted 18th-century villa
that has recently been updated
and is the place to stay in the
Valle dei Templi. It has a pool, an
above-average restaurant, and
great views of the Tempio della
Concordia. Wi-Fi available.
🛏 40 🅿 🟦 🟦 🗠 All
major cards

🍽 DEI TEMPLI
$$$
VIA PANORAMICA DEI TEMPLI 15
TEL 092 240 3110
www.trattoriadeitempli.it
Vaulted ceilings, stone arches,
and terra-cotta floors provide
a rustic atmosphere in a busy
but friendly restaurant near the
temples. The menu is mainly
fish- and seafood-based.
🪑 100 🕐 Closed Sun. July–
Aug. & Fri. Sept.–June, early
July 🟦 🗠 All major cards

🍽 LEON D'ORO
$$$
VIALE EMPORIUM 102
TEL 092 241 4400
A well-run restaurant whose
menu mixes traditional and
more innovative fish and
seafood dishes. There is a
large garden for outdoor dining
and one of the dining rooms
is nonsmoking.
🪑 120 🅿 🕐 Closed Mon.
🟦 🗠 All major cards

PIAZZA ARMERINA

🏨 PARK HOTEL PARADISO
$$$ ★★★★
CONTRADA RAMALDO
TEL 093 568 0841
FAX 093 568 3391
www.parkhotelparadiso.it
A comfortable, if unremark-

able, hotel with many facilities
(including sauna and tennis
courts). Convenient for Villa del
Casale (which has few lodgings).
🛏 95 🟦 🟦 🟦 🗠 All
major cards

🍽 AL FOGHER
$$$$
CONTRADA BELLIA 1
TEL 093 568 4123
www.alfogher.net
Two intimate rooms in a
former railway building set the
stage for a mixture of regional
cooking infused with inventive
touches. The wine list is excellent and there is a garden for
summer meals alfresco.
🪑 55 🅿 🕐 Closed D Sun.,
Mon., & part of Jan. 🗠 All
major cards

SARDINIA

COSTA SMERALDA

🏨 CALA DI VOLPE
$$$$$ ★★★★★
CALA DI VOLPE, PORTO CERVO
TEL 078 997 6111
FAX 078 997 6617
www.starwood.com/luxury
The Emerald Coast's leading
hotel is an elegant re-creation
of a traditional Sardinian village.
Tennis courts and access to a
nine-hole golf course. Wi-Fi
available.
🛏 97 + 17 suites 🅿 🟦 🟦
🟦 🗠 All major cards

ALGHERO

🏨 VILLA LAS TRONAS
$$$ ★★★★★
LUNGOMARE VALENCIA 1
TEL 079 981 818
FAX 079 981 044
www.hotelvillalastronas.com
An art nouveau villa on a
promontory overlooking the
sea. The town is close by, but
the hotel's gardens and beach
provide peace and privacy.
Wi-Fi available.

🛏 22 + 3 suites 🅿 🟦
🟦 🟦 🟦 🗠 All major cards

🍽 AL TUGURI
$$–$$$
VIA MAIORCA 113
TEL 079 976 772
www.altuguri.it
A tiny place whose cuisine
combines Sardinian and
Catalan traditions.
🪑 50 🕐 Closed mid-Dec.–
Jan. & Sun. except summer
🟦 🗠 All major cards

CALA GONONE

🏨 COSTA DORADA
$$$$ ★★★★
LUNGOMARE PALMASERA 45,
CALA GONONE (NUORO)
TEL 078 493 332
FAX 078 493 445
www.hotelcostadorada.it
A comfortable hotel in a pleas-
ant coastal setting.
🛏 27 + 1 suite 🕐 Closed
Nov.–Easter 🟦 🗠 All
major cards

CAGLIARI

🏨 REGINA MARGHERITA
$$$$ ★★★★
VIALE REGINA MARGHERITA 44
TEL 070 670 342
FAX 070 668 325
www.hotelreginamargherita
.com
The best of the hotels close to
Cagliari's old quarter.
🛏 99 🅿 🟦 🗠 All
major cards

🍽 DAL CORSARO
$$$$
VIALE REGINA MARGHERITA 28
TEL 070 664 318
www.dalcorsaro.com
Impeccable, creative cooking in
an elegant two-room restaurant.
Reservations a must.
🪑 80 🕐 Closed Sun., L Sat., &
Aug. 🟦 🗠 All major cards

Shopping in Naples & Southern Italy

Apart from Naples, the towns and cities of southern Italy cannot compare with their central and northern Italian counterparts as shopping destinations. Where the region does offer good retail opportunities, however, is in the areas of food, wine, and arts and crafts.

Stores

Many southern Italian stores are small, family-run affairs, even in cities. Most neighborhoods have their own baker (panificio), fruit seller (fruttivendolo), butcher (macellaio), and food shop (alimentari).

Pastry and home-made candy stores (pasticceria) are particular features of southern towns. Department stores and supermarkets are found only in the largest centers.

Markets

Most towns and cities have at least one street market (un mercato), usually open every day except Sunday from early morning to early afternoon. Smaller towns may have a one-day market that operates on a similar schedule.

What to Buy

Many regions and towns have outstanding local wines and foods, notably cheeses, oils, dried or candied fruits, cakes, sun-dried tomatoes, capers, and artichokes. Check import restrictions in North America if you plan to take meat and other produce home.

Ceramics are often the main craft products, while larger cities have antique shops full of treasures large and small. Coral and turquoise jewelry are good buys on the coast.

In general, the more fashionable shopping districts of cities and resorts offer the high-quality clothes, lingerie, fabrics, linens, jewelry, kitchenware, design objects, and other items for which Italy is renowned. Do not expect any bargains, however.

Opening Hours

Most small stores are open from around 9 a.m.–1 p.m. and 3:30–8 p.m. Shops in city centers and tourist areas may stay open all day (orario continuato). Virtually all stores are closed on Sunday and most have a closing day (giorno di riposo or chiusura settimanale). Some may also close for a half day, usually Monday morning or, in the case of many food stores, Wednesday or Thursday afternoon.

Payments

Supermarkets and department stores usually accept credit cards and traveler's checks, as do larger clothes and shoe stores. Cash is required, however, for virtually all transactions in small groceries and other stores.

Exports

Many Italian products include a value-added goods and services tax known as IVA. Non-European Union residents can claim an IVA refund for purchases over €150 made in any one store.

Shop with your passport and ask for invoices to be made out clearly, showing individual articles and tax components of prices.

Keep all receipts and invoices and have them stamped at the customs office at your airport of departure, or the last exit from EU territory. You then have 90 days to mail the invoice to the store, though it is easier to make the claim at the Tax Free Office in the last EU airport of your trip.

Forms, receipts—and sometimes the goods—must all be produced. Refunds are provided on the spot

as cash or as credits to your credit card account.

Some stores are members of the Tax-Free Shopping System and issue a time-saving "tax-free check" for the amount of the rebate, which can be cashed directly at the Tax Free Office.

■ NAPLES

Shopping—or at least joining the jostling throng of Neapolitan shoppers—is an essential part of the Naples experience. You may not buy anything, but it is still great fun to wander the many markets, window-shop along Via Toledo, or marvel at the bald-faced cheek of the many street vendors selling counterfeit goods.

Off the main streets, you will find a range of tiny specialist stores of a type that has vanished in many other northern Italian and northern European towns. Shops here still have character and individuality, even if the items they are selling—dusty mandolins or cheap household goods—are unlikely to find their way into your luggage.

There are some good buys, however. Naples is filled with antique and jewelry shops, its food is tremendous, shoes and leather goods are inexpensive, and there are items here—such as the city's famous Christmas crèche (presepio) figures—that you won't find anywhere else.

As a rough guide, the most upscale shopping area is on and around Via Chiaia, plus Piazza Vanvitelli and Via Scarlatti, while for shopping on a budget, head to Via Toledo, Corso Umberto I, or the streets in the centro storico.

Key tips are to keep a close watch on your wallet and

handbags—ideally, don't carry them—and keep in mind limited opening hours (see opposite).

Antiques

Antique shops are found throughout the city, though some are little more than junk stores. Some of the best are found in and around Piazza dei Martiri in the Chiaia district and Via Constantinopoli in the *centro storico*. The city's most respected store is **Bowinkel** *(Piazza dei Martiri 24, tel 081 764 4344, www .bowinkelernesto.com)*, full of precious prints and paintings. **Affaitati** *(Via Benedetto Croce 21, tel 081 444 427)* has been in business since 1885; **Arte Antica** *(Via Domenico Morelli 45, tel 081 764 6897)* has an excellent selection of prints and watercolors.

Books

Dealers in secondhand and antique books are common, but most titles are in Italian. The best place for English-language titles, including maps and guides, is **Feltrinelli** *(Via Santa Caterina a Chiaia 23, off Piazza dei Martiri, tel 081 240 5411, www.lafeltrinelli.it,)* the city's largest bookstore.

Cakes & Pastries

The *pasticceria* (pastry shop) is a feature of every Neapolitan neighborhood. The best are the 200-year-old **Scaturchio** *(Piazza San Domenico Maggiore 19, tel 081 551 7031, www.scaturchio.it)* and **Moccia** *(Via San Pasquale a Chiaia 21–22, tel 081 411 348)*, founded in 1920.

Ceramics

If you are not going to the towns in question, the distinctive painted ware of Vietri on the Amalfi Coast and other parts of southern Italy can be found in stores across the city. These ceramics are usually inexpensive, unlike the hand-painted Capodimonte porcelain for which Naples has long been famous.

Chocolate

Many *pasticcerie* also sell chocolate, especially **Scaturchio** (see above), but the standout shop is **Gay-Odin** *(Via Toledo 214, tel 081 417 7843, www.gay-odin.it; also at Via Benedetto Croce 61, tel 081 551 0794)*, followed by **Perzechella** *(Vico Pallonetto a Santa Chiara 36, tel 081 551 0025)* and **Gennaro Bottone** *(Via Chiaia 35, tel 081 764 2832)*.

Department Stores

For the convenience of one-stop shopping, visit **Coin** *(Via Scarlatti 88–100, tel 081 578 0111, www .coin.it)*, which sells upscale goods, including clothes, perfumes, and homeware.

Designer Stores

All the big names of Italian and international fashion cluster on and around Piazza dei Martiri on the eastern edge of the Chiaia district. Tiny Via Calabritto is the epicenter of chic, with Armani, Gucci, Versace, and others, along with Via Filangieri a couple of blocks north of Piazza dei Martiri, where you'll find Max Mara and Valentino, among others.

Food

Visit the Pignasecca market (off Via Toledo: see pp. 57–60) or other street markets to see where most Neapolitans do their food shopping. All neighborhoods will have one or more delicatessens. All are good—they have to be to survive—but **Augustus** *(Via Toledo 147, tel 081 551 3540)* is a perfect example of the combination of food store, bar, and pasticceria found across the city. **Antica Delizie** *(Via Pasquale Scura 14,* *tel 081 551 3088)* has excellent mozzarella, among many other gastronomic treats.

Handicrafts

The centro storico is full of workshops making all manner of craft items. The best known are the Christmas crèche figurines made and sold in many stores on Via San Gregorio Armeno. Also visit the venerable **Talarico** *(Vico Due Porto a Toledo 4/B, tel 081 401 979)*, which has been producing various handicrafts for over a century; it is especially known for its superb silk umbrellas.

Homeware

For top-quality sheets, towels, and other linens, visit **Frette** *(Via del Mille 2, tel 081 418 728, www.frette.com)*.

Ice Cream

The Monacelli family has been making ice cream at **Gelateria della Scimmia** *(Piazza Carità 4, tel 081 552 0272)* for three generations since 1933. Also excellent are **Scaturchio** (see Cakes & Pastries above), **Otranto** *(Via Scarletti 78, tel 081 558 7498)*, **Chalet Ciro** *(Via Francesco Caracciolo, tel 081 669 928, www.chaletciro .it)*, and **Bilancione** *(Via Posillipo 238/B, tel 081 769 1923)*. The last two require a special journey west of the old center, but as two of the city's classic ice-cream parlors, they're well worth the trip.

Jewelry

Naples is renowned for its cameos and gold jewelry. The **Borgo degli Orefici** (Town of the Goldsmiths) district in the historic center (bounded by Via del Duomo, Corso Umberto I, Via Marina, and Via Porta di Massa) is one of the oldest goldworking quarters in Europe. It is also one of the largest, with an estimated

200 craftspeople and 100 stores in a half-square-mile (1.3 sq km) area. **Caruso** *(Piazzetta Orefici, 7 off Via Capoci, tel 081 554 4922, www.gioiellicaruso.it)* is one of the key shops. For the best cameos and coral jewelry, visit **Ascione** *(Galleria Umberto I, Piazzetta Matilde Serao 19, tel 081 421 111, www.ascione.it)*, which has been in business for over 150 years.

Perfumes & Cosmetics

Its roots are in Florence, but the Naples outlet of the **Officina Profumo** *(Via Santa Caterina a Chiaia 20, tel 081 407 176)* is well worth a visit for a range of products based on recipes concocted centuries ago by the monks of Florence's Santa Maria Novella monastery.

Shoes & Leather

Most of the shoes of all qualities sold as "Made in Italy" across the globe are produced in and around the city. Most residents of Naples buy their footwear in the Pignasecca and other markets, also good sources of bags and other leather products. For superior local leatherware, visit **Parlato** *(Via San Pasquale a Chiaia 27, tel 081 406 677)* and **Tramontano** *(Via Chiaia 142–143, tel 081 414 837, www.tramontano.it)*.

Stationery

You'll never be short of a pen and paper in Naples; there are stationery shops *(cartoleria)* everywhere. **Gambardella** *(Largo Corpo di Napoli 3, tel 081 552 1333)* in the historic center is the most fun, crammed with more than 500 different paper creations, most of them handmade.

■ AMALFI COAST & THE ISLANDS

Capri and Ischia offer a wealth of clothes boutiques and designer names, but prices are high. Capri is famous for its chic sandals and for the much sought-after perfumes of **Carthusia** *(Via Camerelle 10)*.

Positano was known for its indigenous fashions in the 1960s, but today most shops sell bland mass-produced items. Ceramics, though, are good buys up and down the coast, particularly in Vietri. So, too, are food and drink, whether the fine local cheeses of Agerola and other mountain villages or the ubiquitous *limoncello* (a lemon-based liqueur).

Traditional paper can be found in Amalfi, and the olive oil from around Sorrento is prized. Sorrento also offers lace, wood, and embroidery handicrafts, but sadly all three traditions are dying out.

■ PUGLIA

Wine is the best buy in Puglia, this being one of the areas of southern Italy (with Sicily) where new producers are most enthusiastically embracing innovative methods and new blends. See pages 22–23 for the names of the best producers and a selection of recommended wines.

Olive groves, many hundreds—perhaps thousands—of years old, are another feature of the region, and the oil they produce is some of the best in Italy. Food stores in most towns will have a reasonable choice, or you can buy at the source from the many farms *(azienda agricola)* you will pass while exploring the countryside.

Bari and Brindisi are the only places that offer shops in any great numbers, including a handful selling local art, artifacts, and handicrafts.

■ CALABRIA & BASILICATA

Reggio di Calabria is the only town in either region of any real retail stature, but even here pickings are slim. Food, though, especially organic produce, is an emerging feature of the area, and you will be able to buy products resort towns such as Tropea or on farms advertising honey, olive oil, and other goods that are *produzione propria* (own production).

Handicrafts are a feature of the mountains, such as the wood and wrought-iron work around Melfi and the terra-cotta and papiermâché products from Matera.

■ SICILY & SARDINIA

Sicily has some of the best new wines in Italy, with Planeta one of the outstanding producers. Food, again, is another good buy, especially cheeses, oils, capers, candied fruits, and the almond-paste "fruit" *(frutta alla Martorana)* of Palermo. Coral jewelry is common, but of widely varying quality, and traditional lace and embroidery can still be found in some rural centers. Rugs are a specialty of Erice, a town in the west of the island, and cane goods are made in Monreale just outside Palermo.

In Palermo itself, Via Bara all'Olivella is the street for arts and crafts, along with Via Calderai. Designer and other fashionable names line Via della Libertà and nearby streets such as Via Enrico Parisi.

Via Roma, Via Maqueda, Via Ruggero Settimo, and the pedestrian-only Via Principe di Belmonte are also major shopping streets.

In Sardinia, cheese is a good buy, and in more remote villages you may also find lace, embroidery, and other handicrafts.

Festivals & Other Events

Naples and southern Italy have numerous fascinating and colorful festivals, religious ceremonies, historic pageants, fairs, markets, and local events. Christmas and Holy Week celebrations, in particular, are some of the most striking in Europe, and there are several arts and cultural festivals of international renown. Many celebrations, though, are small, local affairs, restricted to a town or village and often held in honor of a saint, a historic event, or a local product of note.

If you plan your trip around a major event, be sure to reserve accommodations and make travel arrangements well in advance, or you may find that everything is booked.

There's a good chance, especially if you visit at Easter time or in the summer, that you'll stumble across a *festa*, or small festival. Most follow a similar pattern, with processions in which participants, often in traditional costume, accompany a float with an image of a saint. These are followed by church services, traditional songs and dances, the village marching band, fireworks, and much eating and drinking.

Watch for flyers advertising a festa or *sagra* (a food or wine fair). You can also consult visitor information centers or their websites for details of upcoming events.

Religious Festivals

Easter, Christmas, and Carnival are the three major periods during which you will find religious festivals. Holy Week celebrations across the South are extraordinary, especially in Sicily and rural Calabria and Basilicata. Most towns and villages hold dramatic processions and *misteri* (scenes from Christ's Passion), often with robed and hooded penitents and confraternities in torchlit parade. The most famous and striking are at Sorrento and Procida in Campania; at Enna, Erice, Messina, and Ragusa in Sicily; and at Taranto, Lecce, Bari, and Ruvo di Puglia in Puglia. Most take place on Good Friday.

Carnival celebrations (*usually in Feb.*) are colorful across most towns and cities. Naples is especially known for its displays of *presepi*, or Christmas crèches.

Arts & Music

Many religious and saints' festivals also include cultural events, especially music. In late spring and summer these are augmented by a wide range of dedicated music, drama, dance, and other cultural festivals, especially in Naples, on Sicily, and in the towns of the Amalfi Coast. Many are staged in spectacular settings, such as the events at Taormina and Syracuse, which are held in the towns' ancient Greek amphitheaters. Increasingly, events go on for several weeks or months, as does the opera season at Naples's celebrated opera house, San Carlo.

Calendar of Events

Where contact details are not given, visitor centers and their websites can provide further information.

January

Epiphany (*Jan. 5–6*) Celebrations across the South to celebrate the feast of the Epiphany, especially in Naples, which holds a fair devoted to La Befana (The Witch) in Piazza del Plebiscito.

Festa d'o'Cippo di Sant'Antonio (*Jan. 17*) Naples. A procession held in honor of St. Anthony Abbot, the protector of animals.

Opera The opera season at Naples's San Carlo opera house

runs most of the year, with the exception of July and August. Tickets, though, are always at a premium (*www.teatrosancarlo.it*).

February

Carnevale (*10 days leading up to Ash Wednesday*) Processions and entertainments across southern Italy. Capua and Paestum (Campania) plus Manfredonia (Puglia) have particularly vibrant festivities.

Galassia Gutenberg (*dates vary*) Naples-Fuorigrotta, Campania (*www.galassia.org*). Fuorigrotta, an eastern suburb of the city, hosts southern Italy's largest book fair.

Sagra del Mandorlo (*late Jan.–early Feb.*) Agrigento, Sicily. Festival of the Almond Blossom (*www.mandorloinfiore.net*), with folklore and cultural events.

March

Benvenuta Primavera Naples. Theatrical and other events to welcome spring (*primavera*) are held in the city's central squares and gardens.

Easter Celebrations are held in every town and village across southern Italy to mark Pasqua (Easter). Torchlit and other processions, plus religious services, take place on Good Friday. Ceremonies in rural areas are usually the most memorable. Events have a slightly different flavor in the Eastern Orthodox rites observed in the South's Albanian villages (see pp. 162–163).

Nauticsud (*mid-March*) Naples (*www.nauticsud.info*). A vast fair devoted to boats of all kinds.

April

Festa Carciofi *(last 7–9 days of month)* Paestum, Campania. Paestum's artichokes *(carciofi)* are renowned and this festival, when the harvest of the preceding two months is celebrated, is a good example of the many small food festivals dotted across the region.
Linea d'Ombra *(varying weeks in April)* Salerno, Campania *(www.festivalculturegiovani.it)*. This film festival was founded in 1996 and is devoted to movies that look at the passage from youth to adulthood, what writer Joseph Conrad called the crossing of the shadow line, or *linea d'ombra*.
Maggio dei Monumenti *(April, May, & June)* Naples. Numerous concerts and cultural events, plus the opening of historic buildings that are otherwise usually closed.
Settimana per la Cultura *(varying weeks in April)* Naples *(www.beniculturali.it)*. Publicly owned museums are free and open late for a week in this popular cultural initiative.

May

Cavacata *(40 days after Easter, usually last Sun. in May)* Sassari, Sardinia. Sardinia's grandest festival involves thousands of people in traditional island dress parading on horseback, followed by traditional songs and dances.
Festa di San Costanza *(May 16)* Capri, Campania. A procession carries a statue of St. Constance to the sea to celebrate Capri town's patron saint.
Festa di Sant'Efisio *(May 1–4)* Cagliari, Sardinia *(www.festadisantefisio.it)*. Mass processions on foot or horseback, with participants in medieval dress, to commemorate the city's patron saint.
Festa di San Gennaro *(3 times yearly: 1st Sun. in May, Sept. 19, & Dec. 16)* Naples. Celebrations to honor the city's patron saint, including the miraculous liquefaction (or otherwise) of a vial of the saint's blood. See pages 46–47.
Festa di Santa Lucia. *(1st & 2nd Sun.)* Syracuse, Sicily. Feast of St. Lucia celebrations.
Festa di San Nicola *(May 7–9)* Bari, Puglia. Huge celebrations for the city's patron saint, including a parade of boats and a blessing of a statue of the saint at sea.
Festa di San Vito *(May 15)* Positano, Campania. Feast in honor of the town's local saint.
Sfilata del Carretto *(last 3 days of month)* Taormina, Sicily. Traditional painted carts and puppet shows.
Syracuse Festival *(May–June)* Syracuse, Sicily *(www.indafondazione.org)*. Concerts and performances of classical drama and ballet are held at the town's Greek theater.

June

Concerti al Tramonto *(late May or June–Aug.)* Anacapri, Capri, Campania *(www.villasanmichele.eu)*. An annual program of Concerts at Dusk staged in a lovely setting overlooking the sea at the Villa San Michele.
Corpus Domini *(May or early June)* Religious celebrations for this feast day are held across the region, notably in Brindisi (Puglia) and Cefalù (Sicily).
Estate a Napoli *(June–Sept.)* Naples *(www.comune.napoli.it)*. Summer in Naples is a loosely linked series of open-air movies, concerts, and other events at venues across the city.
Festa di Sant'Andrea *(June 27)* Amalfi, Campania. Processions in medieval dress, a blessing of the fishing fleet, and other celebrations, including fireworks, in honor of the town's patron saint.
Festa di Sant'Antonio *(June 13)* Anacapri, Campania. Capri's second town celebrates the feast of its patron, St. Anthony of Padua, with a procession bearing a figure of the saint around the streets.
Festival di Musica *(June–Sept.)* Sorrento, Campania *(www.sorrentoinfo.com or www.friendsofsorrento.co.uk)*. A summer festival of classical music and other concerts in the cloister of San Francesco and other churches and gardens in the town.
Minori Festival *(June–Aug.)* Minori, Campania *(www.jazzonthecoast.it)*. This lovely spot on the Amalfi Coast hosts a summer season of open-air jazz concerts.
Regata Storica *(1st Sun.)* Amalfi, Campania. Italy's four maritime republics (Venice, Pisa, Genoa, and Amalfi) take turns to host this colorful historic pageant. Amalfi will next host in 2013.

July

Festa di Sant'Anna *(July 26)* Ischia, Campania *(www.festadisantanna.it)*. Fireworks and a torchlit procession of hundreds of boats around the Scogli (Rocks) di Sant'Anna to honor the island's patron saint.
Festa di Santa Maria del Carmine *(July 16)* Naples. The climax of this festival comes when the bell tower of the Carmine church features in a staged "burning" and dazzling fireworks display.
Festa di San Panteleone *(July 27)* Ravello, Campania *(www.ravelloinfesta.it)*. Liquefaction of St. Pantelon's blood, plus an extravagant fireworks display.
Festa di Santa Rosalia *(July 12–15)* Palermo, Sicily. An event known locally as "U Fistinu" in honor of one of the city's most important saints. It culminates in a procession to the saint's sanctuary on Monte Pellegrino.
Festival della Valle d'Itria Martina Franca, Puglia *(www.festivaldellavalleditria.it)*. A program of opera and other classical music concerts.

Festival delle Ville Vesuviane
(varying dates in July) Ercolano, Campania *(www.villevesuviane.net)*. A series of concerts staged at historic villas in and around Ercolano (Herculaneum).

Madonna della Bruna
(July 2) Matera, Basilicata. A large religious procession honoring the town's patron saint.

Madonna della Visitazione *(July 2)* Enna, Sicily. A religious festival held in one of the island's nicest central hill towns.

Neapolis Festival Naples *(www.neapolis.it)*. The largest rock festival in southern Italy is staged at Fuorigrotta outside Naples.

Paestum Festival Paestum, Campania *(tel 081 229 5545, www.danzateatro.net)*. A series of musical, drama, and dance performances held in and around Paestum's Greek temples.

Ravello Festival *(July–Sept.)* Ravello, Campania *(www.ravellofestival.com)*. A major program of cultural events in various venues.

Taormina Arte *(July–Sept.)* Taormina, Sicily *(www.taormina-arte.com)*. A prestigious summer-long program of cultural events, including the Taormina international film festival in June or July. Many events are staged in the town's dramatic Greek amphitheater.

August

Ferragosto *(Aug. 21–24)* The processions and fireworks at Positano on the Amalfi Coast are typical of the events held across the South to celebrate the Feast of the Assumption on August 15, one of the most important days in the Catholic religious calendar. Positano's event celebrates the miraculous intervention of the Madonna to save the town during a Saracen attack.

Festa di San Bartolommeo Lipari, Sicily. A festival with offshore fireworks devoted to

one of the patron saints of the Aeolian islands.

Festa di San Nicola Pellegrino *(Aug. 6–8)* Trani, Puglia. A festival held on the waterfront in honor of Trani's patron saint.

September

Antiques fair Caserta, Campania. The last two weeks of the month see a large antiques fair held on the grounds of the Reggia (palace) at Caserta in Campania.

Festa di San Gennaro *(Sept. 19)* Naples. The most important of the three festivals involving Naples's patron saint. The main event (the liquefaction of the saint's blood) takes place in and around the Duomo. See pages 46–47.

Festival di Musica d'Estate *(late Aug.–Sept.)* Positano, Campania. This long-running summer festival of classical music was founded in the 1960s. It is devoted mainly to chamber recitals but also features jazz and other music. You can sign up for classes from leading musicians.

Ischia Jazz Weekend *(usually 2nd weekend)* Ischia, Campania *(www.ischiajazzfestival.com)*. A weekend of jazz concerts from leading local and international performers.

Madonna delle Lacrime *(Aug. 29–Sept. 3)* Syracuse, Sicily. A religious festival and procession.

Palio al Mare *(1st Sun.)* Syracuse, Sicily. Races at sea and a procession of boats.

Palio dei Normanni *(Aug. 13–14)* Piazza Armerina, Sicily. A major festival with a jousting contest between the quarters of the town.

Santa Maria della Libera *(1st Sun. closest to Sept. 12)* Capri, Campania. A religious festival marked by a procession from the church of San Constanza in Marina Grande to Capri town. Also includes a market, fireworks, and cultural events.

October

Festa dell'Uva Many small towns and villages celebrate the October wine harvest *(vendemmia)* with a Festa dell'Uva, or grape festival, during which wine and local foods feature large.

Festival Internazionale del Cinema *(dates vary)* Salerno, Campania *(www.festivaldelcinema.it)*. A wide-ranging international film festival.

November

All Saints' Day *(Nov. 1–2)* This day (known as the Festa dei Morti,or Festival of the Dead) is celebrated across Italy, but especially in the South, and Sicily in particular. It is traditionally the day that Italians visit family graves.

December

Bagpipes The tradition whereby Calabrian *zampognari* (bagpipers) came down from the mountains to play traditional tunes around the region's towns in December is enjoying a revival. The players claim that the Virgin Mary was soothed during her labor by similar instruments.

Christmas *(Dec. 24)*. Special Masses and other religious services take place across the South in the buildup to Christmas, but especially on Christmas Eve

Presepi Ornate and often precious Christmas crèches *(presepi)* are features of churches across Italy in the lead-up to Christmas, but especially in Naples. Many towns have special fairs selling crèche figures and other items.

Santa Lucia *(Dec. 13)* Syracuse, Sicily. Santa Lucia is buried in Venice, but she is widely venerated in Syracuse, where her saint's day is marked by a procession and other festivities.

INDEX

ILLUSTRATIONS CREDITS

All photos by Tino Soriano, unless otherwise
noted below:
11, Stefano Amantini/Atlantide Phototravel/COR-
BIS; 12, Andrey Afanitsky/Dreamstime.com; 25,
andesign101/Shutterstock; 28-29, Stefano Bianchetti/
CORBIS; 31, Alinari Archives/CORBIS; 33, U.S. Army/
Getty Images; 39, Valeria73/Shutterstock; 41, Franco
Origlia/Getty Images; 84, Alfio Ferlito/Shutter-
stock; 86, Maxim Tupikov/Shutterstock; 93, Peter
Grasmanis/ShutterPoint Photography; 97, gallimaufry/
Shutterstock; 145, Valeria73/Shutterstock; 155, Piotr
G/Shutterstock; 166, Massimo Valicchia/Dreamstime.
com; 174, Inacio Pires/Shutterstock; 189, Slim Aarons/
Getty Images.

National Geographic
TRAVELER
Naples &
Southern Italy

Published by the National Geographic Society
John M. Fahey, Jr., *President and Chief Executive Officer*
Gilbert M. Grosvenor, *Chairman of the Board*
Tim T. Kelly, *President, Global Media Group*
John Q. Griffin, *Executive Vice President; President, Publishing*
Nina D. Hoffman, *Executive Vice President; President, Book Publishing Group*

Prepared by the Book Division
Barbara Brownell Grogan, *Vice President and Editor in Chief*
Marianne R. Koszorus, *Director of Design*
Barbara Noe, *Senior Editor*
Carl Mehler, *Director of Maps*
R. Gary Colbert, *Production Director*
Jennifer A. Thornton, *Managing Editor*
Meredith C. Wilcox, *Administrative Director, Illustrations*

Staff for 2011 Edition
Patricia Daniels, *Project Editor*
Kay Kobor Hankins, *Art Director*
Linda Makarov, *Designer*
Lise Sajewski, *Copy Editor*
Al Morrow, *Design Assistant*
Silvia Benvenuto, *Indexer*
Michael McNey and Mapping Specialists, *Map Production*
Caroline Hickey, Susan Straight, *Contributors*

Manufacturing and Quality Management
Christopher A. Liedel, *Chief Financial Officer*
Phillip L. Schlosser, *Vice President*
Chris Brown, *Technical Director*
Nicole Elliott, *Manager*
Rachel Faulise, *Manager*
Robert L. Barr, *Manager*

Cutaway illustrations drawn by Maltings Partnership, Derby, England

National Geographic Traveler: Naples & Southern Italy (Second Edition)
ISBN: 978-1-4262-0710-5
1st. ed. ISBN 978-1-4262-0040-3

Printed in China
10/TS/1

The National Geographic Society is one of the world's largest nonprofit scientific and educational organizations. Founded in 1888 to "increase and diffuse geographic knowledge," the Society works to inspire people to care about the planet. It reaches more than 325 million people worldwide each month through its official journal, *National Geographic*, and other magazines; National Geographic Channel; television documentaries; music; radio; films; books; DVDs; maps; exhibitions; school publishing programs; interactive media; and merchandise. National Geographic has funded more than 9,000 scientific research, conservation and exploration projects and supports an education program combating geographic illiteracy. For more information, visit nationalgeographic.com.

For more information, please call 1-800-NGS LINE (647-5463) or write to the following address:

National Geographic Society
1145 17th Street N.W.
Washington, D.C. 20036-4688 U.S.A.

Visit us online at www.nationalgeographic.com

For information about special discounts for bulk purchases, please contact National Geographic Books Special Sales: ngspecsales@ngs.org

For rights or permissions inquiries, please contact National Geographic Books Subsidiary Rights: ngbookrights@ngs.org

The information in this book has been carefully checked and to the best of our knowledge is accurate. However, details are subject to change, and the National Geographic Society cannot be responsible for such changes, or for errors or omissions. Assessments of sites, hotels, and restaurants are based on the author's subjective opinions, which do not necessarily reflect the publisher's opinion.

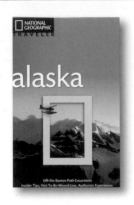

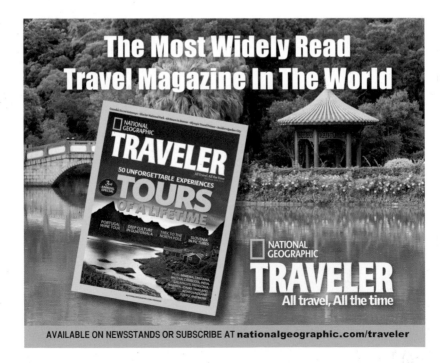